Unbelievers

Unbelievers

An Emotional History of Doubt

Alec Ryrie

The Belknap Press of Harvard University Press

Cambridge, Massachusetts

2019

Copyright © 2019 by Alec Ryrie
Printed in the United States of America

First published in Great Britain by William Collins,
an imprint of HarperCollins*Publishers,* London, 2019

Typeset in Adobe Garamond Pro by
Palimpsest Book Production Ltd, Falkirk, Stirlingshire

First Harvard University Press edition, 2019

CIP data for this book is available from the Library of Congress

978-0-674-24182-4

for Victoria, my believer

Most of us, I suspect . . . make an instinctive decision, then build up an infrastructure of reasoning to justify it. And call the result common sense.

Julian Barnes, The Sense of an Ending

Contents

Introduction

Two friends, Christian and Hopeful, are travelling in search of Heaven. On the road, they meet a man named Atheist. When they tell him about their quest, he erupts into 'a very great Laughter': 'I laugh to see what ignorant persons you are, to take upon you so tedious a Journey . . . There is no such place as you Dream of.'[1]

In John Bunyan's fable, the travellers stop their ears to these siren words and continue on their way. But as Bunyan knew all too well, Atheist's defiance was in fact dangerously compelling. The thought he gave voice to was already haunting the historically Christian cultures of Europe and North America when he wrote *The Pilgrim's Progress* in the 1670s, and has done so ever since. Perhaps you disagree with Atheist, but you are certainly familiar with the point he was making. Or perhaps you think he spoke the plain and self-evident truth.

This book is about one of the most momentous changes in modern history: the appearance in the once-Christian West of post-religious societies.[2] This is not a total transformation (at least, not yet). Europe and especially North America still have a great many believers, who still have a powerful public voice, and Western culture is steeped in Christianity's cultural residue. But in every Western society a rapidly rising share of the population, and especially of young people, claims to have no religion. Even in the assertively pious United States, in 2007 this was true of an unprecedented 16 per cent of adults. By 2014 that share had risen to 23 per cent (that is, around 55 million people), including well over a

1

third of those born since 1980.[3] In many of the regional, educational and political subcultures that make up the modern United States, open and unapologetic unbelief is now the norm: something that has never been true before the current generation. In Europe, the share of adults who profess no religion now ranges from a sixth (in Italy and Ireland), to around a quarter (Britain, France, Germany), to well over 40 per cent (Norway, Sweden, the Netherlands). Other studies put the figures even higher. A 2015 survey had 43 per cent of British adults claiming no religion, a figure rising to 70 per cent of those under 24.[4] And on both sides of the Atlantic, many of those who do still claim a Christian identity do so only nominally or residually, their daily lives largely undisturbed by their professed religion.

'Why,' the philosopher Charles Taylor asks, 'was it virtually impossible not to believe in God in, say, 1500 in our Western society, while in 2000 many of us find this not only easy, but even inescapable?'[5] Many of those who (like Taylor himself) continue to believe are conscious of swimming against a cultural tide. Over a century ago, Friedrich Nietzsche notoriously claimed that 'God is dead . . . and we have killed him'. In large and growing parts of Western society, that shocking claim has turned into a self-evident truth.

As a historian, my question is: so, who killed him, when, and how? The usual answer is: philosophers, scientists and intellectuals; during the Enlightenment and scientific revolution of the eighteenth and nineteenth centuries; and by means of a frontal assault. In the 1660s, so the story goes, Baruch Spinoza first showed that a world without God could be philosophically coherent. In the eighteenth century there was a double assault: polemicists such as Voltaire and Thomas Paine openly attacked the Church's moral authority, and philosophers as varied as David Hume, Immanuel Kant and Jean-Jacques Rousseau constructed systems which, whether or not we classify them as strictly atheist, left Christianity far behind. God became, as Pierre-Simon Laplace supposedly told Napoleon in 1802, a redundant hypothesis. Nineteenth-century philosophers such as Ludwig Feuerbach and Arthur Schopenhauer found the case against religion to be almost self-evident. By the time Charles Darwin provided an explanation for the origins of life without reference to God in 1859, the work was virtually completed. All that the wider culture has done since then is catch up.[6]

I wrote this book because I am not satisfied with that stereotypical account. The timescale, the suspects and the nature of the murder are all wrong. Telling the story a different way not only changes our sense of history; it casts our current moment of pell-mell secularisation in a different light.

To take the simplest problem first: the death-by-philosophy narrative is a poor fit with the actual chronology of Western secularisation. Were the religious revivals of the later eighteenth and nineteenth centuries, or the apparent Christian resurgence across the West in the 1950s, simply religion's death throes? Was the sudden collapse of the West's religious cultures in the 1960s merely the shattering of a husk after centuries of patient hollowing-out?[7] Even if you can explain away this chronological mismatch, the conventional starting point is plainly wrong. If atheism only became a live possibility in the 1660s, how could Bunyan, who was nobody's intellectual elitist, depict such an assertive and recognisable 'Atheist' in the 1670s? How could it be said in the 1620s that there were fifty thousand atheists in Paris, or in the 1590s that 'there is no Sect now in *England* so scattered as Atheism'? How could a preacher in Florence in 1305 warn that the question 'how can it be that God exists?' was being 'put by madmen every day'?[8]

These early testimonies to unbelief are often dismissed on the grounds that they lacked philosophical sophistication. If you are only interested in the history of 'atheism' as a system of ideas, then that is the end of the matter, and this book is not for you. What interests me is that unbelief clearly existed in *practice* (in some form, at some level) before it existed in *theory*. In which case, we have not only been looking at the wrong centuries, but profiling the wrong suspects. Intellectuals and philosophers may think they make the weather, but they are more often driven by it. People who read and write books, like you and me, have a persistent tendency to overestimate the power of ideas. Some of us may occasionally change our beliefs and our lives as the result of a chain of conscious reasoning, but not very often or very honestly. Our own age has forcibly reminded us that intellectual elites often struggle to bring their societies with them. Their default role is to tag along, explaining with perfect hindsight why things inevitably turned out as they did.

The conventional story has it that philosophers attacked religion and people therefore stopped believing. But what if people stopped believing and then found they needed arguments to justify their unbelief? 'The heart has its reasons of which reason knows nothing,' cautioned Blaise Pascal, the seventeenth century's shrewdest wrestler with doubt.[9] Apart from a heroic or cold-hearted few, most of us make our lives' great choices – beliefs, values, identities, purposes – intuitively, with our whole selves, embedded as we are in our social and historical contexts, usually unable to articulate why we have done it, often not even aware we have done it. If we have the inclination, we might then assemble rationalisations for our choices: rationalisations which may be true, but in a meagre, *post hoc* way.[10]

My point, simply, is that it is not only religious belief which is chosen for such instinctive, inarticulate, intuitive reasons. So is unbelief. In which case, the crucial juncture in the history of atheism is the period *before* the philosophers made it intellectually respectable: when the raw dough began to bubble with unexplained energy, making it urgent that intellectuals discover ways to bake, slice and package it. It is no great surprise that Enlightenment thinkers *could* develop atheistic philosophies. Anyone who needs a philosophy badly enough will find one, and as we will see, arguments against

God and against Christianity's core doctrines were nothing new in the mid-seventeenth century. The question is not, where did these criticisms come from, but, why did some people start to find them compelling?[11] To answer that question, we do not need an intellectual or philosophical history of atheism: we need an emotional history.

I do not mean to imply that the intellect and emotions are opposites, or that emotion is irrational. The notion that 'head' and 'heart' are opposites is a seventeenth-century canard that we are still struggling to shrug off. My gripe is with what one outstanding recent historian calls the 'intellectualist fallacy': 'a tendency to privilege the clean logic of ideas above the raw fuel of human experience among the forces of historical change'.[12] The term 'emotion' here does not refer only to spontaneous or involuntary passions. Indeed, it includes (but is not exhausted by) the conscious intellect. We may not be able to govern our emotions fully, but we curate and manage them, and we learn them from the culture around us as well as discovering them within ourselves. It is in this sense that they can be said to have a history.[13]

Pursuing that history gives this book an hourglass shape. We begin in the broad acres of Europe's medieval 'age of faith', before closing in on the so-called 'early modern' period of the sixteenth and seventeenth centuries, and, in particular, on the Protestant world during the Reformation. We then concentrate even more tightly on what I see as the subject's crux: the early and mid-seventeenth century in Protestant north-western Europe. Only in the final chapter do we broaden out again, to see, after that crisis, how unbelief broke cover and emerged into the open in philosophical dress. Beneath that dress, I argue, its emotional shape has remained remarkably consistent down to the present.

The book tells two interwoven emotional stories of unbelief: stories of *anger* and of *anxiety*. Anger is the more obvious of the two: grudges nurtured against an all-embracing Christian society, against the Church in particular and often also against the God who oversaw it all. The unbelief of anxiety was a quite different experience: the unsettling, reluctant inability to keep a firm grip on doctrines that people were convinced, with their conscious minds, were true. On their own, neither of these perennial emotions threatened Christendom. If anything, they were part of the moral equilibrium and self-renewal of a thriving Christian society. What made them dangerous was the Protestant Reformation, which deliberately turned angry unbelief into a weapon of mass theological destruction, and in the process stirred up anxious unbelief like never before. The result was a strange convergence of the two emotional streams. Anger became increasingly righteous in tone: 'atheists' were universally assumed to be monsters of depravity, but angry unbelief turned into a moral revolt and began to find its own, distinct ethics. Meanwhile, as anxious unbelievers found that everything they tried to grapple with turned to mist and shadows, some of them despaired of finding doctrinal certainties and fastened their grip onto ethical certainties instead. So the angry and the anxious found themselves allying against traditional Christianity, opposing it not principally on intellectual grounds but on moral ones.

The emotional history of Western atheism, then, is not a story of an external assault on Christianity. It is a story of Christians and post-Christians attacking from within, and doing so from the moral high ground. When some of them reached the point of wanting to abandon or abolish God, it was not because of their intellectual rationalisations, but because their ethics and even their theology demanded it. As the sociologist Peter Berger has observed, 'historically speaking, Christianity has been its own gravedigger'.[14] This is not chiefly because it generates intellectual critiques of itself. Rather, it generates moral critiques of itself: an operation so successful that, in parts of the Western world, the patient now seems in real danger of death. Whether the story will end that way, or whether Christianity will find that what does not kill it makes it stronger, remains to be seen. My point is simply that the history of unbelief follows a dynamic established in the sixteenth and seventeenth centuries. This dynamic is not separate from the history of belief. It is part of it.

Or so this book will argue. For now, listen to that battle-hardened pastor John Bunyan, who filled his book not with straw men and caricatures, but with acute warnings of the real temptations that awaited his readers. His 'Atheist', with his mocking insults, seems at first to represent angry unbelief at its crudest, but there is more to him than that. He goes on to tell the travellers that, twenty years ago, he himself heard tell of the city of God and set out on a pilgrimage to find it. Only bitter experience convinced him the search was fruitless. His tragedy is not his unbelief, but his faith. 'Had I not, when at home, believed, I had not come thus far to seek.' If there was a Heaven, he warns the younger travellers, he would have found it. 'I have gone to seek it further than you.' So now he is headed wearily home, 'and will seek to refresh myself with the things that I then cast away, for hopes of that, which I now see, is not'.[15] His unbelief is a direct result of the anxious searching that once defined his faith. It has left him with a moral imperative: to save believers from themselves.

So far I have been tossing around words like 'atheist' and 'unbeliever' as if their meanings are obvious and equivalent, which they are not. Before we go any further it is as well to be clear what we are talking about.

Nowadays 'atheism' simply means the claim that there is no God. The word has included this 'hard' or philosophical sense from its beginnings, but only as part of a much wider range of meaning, which we might do well to recover. The Greek word ἄθεος (*atheos*) means, literally, without God or gods. It was a term of abuse, applied in ancient times to people like Socrates, condemned for his supposed rejection or neglect of socially established religious norms. Early

Christians, who would not acknowledge the Graeco-Roman gods, were sometimes also called ἄθεοι, a charge they indignantly denied. But the word *atheos* was scarcely ever used in Latin in ancient times. When the Greek word was translated into Latin, *impius*, 'impious', was usually felt to be the nearest synonym. The word ἄθεοι occurs only once in the Bible, where it was translated into Latin as *sine Deo*, 'without God'. Only with the rediscovery of Greek in the Christian West during the Renaissance did the word come into widespread use – transliterated into Latin as *atheos* in the early sixteenth century, and then very quickly spreading into European vernaculars: Italian *ateo*, German *Atheist*, French *athée*.[16] It arrived late in English, via French, in 1553.[17] Its range of meaning was still much wider than 'hard' atheism. In the 1540s the English scholar John Cheke wrote a Latin treatise in which he lambasted

> those who . . . live as if God were altogether without care of them; and who neither consider with themselves, nor care whether there be a God or no, or whether he has any Administration or Foresight of human Affairs . . . The Scriptures mark them out under several Titles, but it is most agreeable to our present purpose to call them ἄθεοι.[18]

We might question whether such people are atheists or if the nineteenth-century term 'agnostic' would fit better, but the point is that Cheke was not talking about metaphysics at all. His targets were, as we might say, the godless, regardless of what beliefs they formally professed. This was the standard usage until the eighteenth century and even beyond. As well as 'contemplative' or 'speculative' atheists – philosophical deniers of God – there were 'practical' atheists, who claim to believe but live as though they do not. As the seventeenth-century essayist Thomas Fuller put it, the 'practical' atheist is not someone who 'thinks there is no God', but someone who 'thinks not there is a God'.[19]

All this made *atheist* a usefully elastic term of abuse. It was like the word *fascist* in modern, everyday use: a word with a broad but not limitless range of meanings, whose use typically marks the moment when an argument descends into name-calling.[20] Sometimes *atheist* was plainly stretched too far – preachers who claimed that all sinners were atheists, or that disputing one specific Christian doctrine was tantamount to atheism, were playing polemical games rather than advancing serious definitions.[21] Even so, this broad sense of the word is more useful than the narrow modern one, for it takes us away from the abstractions of metaphysical definitions into the everyday reality of how religious cultures thrive, decay or dissolve.

My subject in this book, then, extends beyond 'contemplative' atheism into the penumbras of doubt and unbelief. As a point of metaphysics, whether or not you believe there is a deity is interesting. But in itself it has no more consequences than whether or not you believe there are other universes parallel to our own. As John Gray puts it, someone with 'no use for the idea of God . . . [is] in truth an atheist', whatever such a person claims to believe or disbelieve.[22] 'Practical atheist' remains a sensible term for those whose formal belief in God has no tangible effect on their lives – who observe no religious practices, adhere to no specifically religious ethics, and participate in no avowedly religious community. Our subject is not only those who abandon religious beliefs and change their lives as a result, but also those who abandon religious living and whose residual religious beliefs consequently wither.

In other words, I make no apology for using words – 'atheist', 'sceptic', 'unbeliever' – which describe what people are *not*. Our subject is a disappearance: the evaporation of a once very widespread religious culture. Those curmudgeonly terms are inadequate to describe what, if anything, has taken its place, but that will have to wait until we have a clearer idea of how the disappearance happened. The mystery we are addressing is how believers became

9

unbelievers: and if the word *unbelief* sounds like it still has *belief* at its core, well, I think it does.

Before we embark for the Middle Ages, some readers may have suspicions about the book's scope, and about its agenda.

The book's scope is unashamedly Eurocentric and Christian-centric, with a couple of small but important supporting roles played by European Judaism. Within that frame, it focuses disproportionately on the Protestant world and in particular on England, which is almost the exclusive focus of a couple of crucial chapters. This partly reflects my own historical specialism, but is also because, for reasons that I hope will become clear, I think the Protestant and English material is distinctively important as well as rich.

If this all feels parochial, that is because the phenomenon we are considering – Western secularism – is a parochial one. It is an offshoot of European Christendom, and in particular (so I will argue) of the Protestant world. In global terms, it is a counter-current, even an aberration. The dominant religious story of the past two centuries is surely the spread of Christianity and of Islam around the globe, a race in which those two hares have so far outpaced the secular tortoise that it takes a considerable act of faith to believe it might one day catch up. It is true that Western secularism has spread across the planet along with various other Western cultural exports, but there are relatively few countries beyond the North Atlantic region where it has really put down roots: Uruguay, perhaps, or the 'Anglosphere' outposts of Australia and New Zealand. There are certainly many other modern countries, such as Turkey, India or China, where the 'secular' is a potent social or political force, but these 'secularisms' are not at all Western in flavour. And in most of the world, including many of those countries, 'religion' in its many forms is going from strength to strength. The once-widespread assumption that Euro-American secularisation represented the probable future of humanity as a whole now looks much more like an expression of cultural imperialism than a level-headed forecast. So I am in no sense claiming to write a history of a universal or global phenomenon, but of a specific and local one – important in its own context, to be sure, especially for those of us who live in its homelands, but one that neither foreshadows any kind of global destiny nor is inscribed indelibly into Western culture itself.

As to my agenda: I am a historian of religion, and am myself a believer (and, in the interests of full disclosure, a licensed lay minister in the Church of England). When such a person starts writing about unbelief, it is fair to suspect a hatchet job. I hope that is not what I have done.

Of course, no one can be objective on this subject. We were born into this world and we're going to die here; we all have a stake in this and are forced to make our wager. My own position is that I am a believer with a soft spot for atheism. I abandoned my youthful atheism for reasons that seem to me sufficient and necessary, but I still respect it. Like many of the characters in my story, I find an honest atheism much more honourable and powerful than the religion of many of my fellow believers. I hope readers will find that I have treated unbelievers with due respect – if not always with kid gloves. This is one reason why, throughout the book, I write about what 'you' or 'we' might have experienced as a medieval or early modern believer or unbeliever, rather than using the easy, distancing impassivity of pronouns like 'one' or 'they'. I think it is worth the imaginative effort of trying to put ourselves in their place.

In writing an emotional history of atheism, I am not arguing that atheism is irrational. I am arguing that human beings are irrational; or rather, that we are not calculating machines, and that our 'choices' about what we believe or disbelieve are made intuitively, with our whole selves, not with impersonal logic.[23]

Happily, since I am convinced that arguments as such have precious little bearing on either belief or unbelief, there is no danger of a book such as this converting anyone to or from anything. Nor, of course, is that its aim. My hope is instead that believers and atheists alike might understand better how unbelief has gone from feeling intuitively impossible to feeling, to many people, intuitively obvious; and how, during the long and fractious marriage between faith and doubt, both partners have shaped each other more than they might like to admit. 'If you want to understand atheism and religion,' says the steely atheist John Gray, 'you must forget the popular notion that they are opposites.'[24] My purpose is merely to remind both parties how long their fates have been intertwined and how much they owe to one another, not least so they might be willing to talk and to listen to one another again.

So to atheist readers, my message is: please appreciate that unbelief is, like almost everything else human beings do, very often intuitive, non-rational and the product of historically specific circumstances. If that were not so, it would be fragile indeed. And to believers, my message is: please understand that atheism and doubt are serious. They have real emotional power and moral force, and they have flourished and are flourishing for very good reasons. The fact that those reasons are often deeply rooted in religion itself makes them all the more powerful, and means that the chasms separating us are narrower than we like to imagine.

It only remains to add that, in what follows, all translations are my own unless otherwise indicated; and that in quotations, spelling, punctuation and occasionally usage have been modernised for comprehensibility.

1

An Age of Suspicion

'The bastard! He doesn't exist!'

Samuel Beckett, *Endgame*

Impostors, Drunkards and Flat-Earthers

Frederick II, Holy Roman Emperor, King of Sicily, Germany, Italy and Jerusalem, was perhaps the most powerful ruler of the Middle Ages. According to Pope Gregory IX, he was also an unbeliever. In 1239 the pope accused Frederick of calling Moses, Jesus Christ and Muhammad 'charlatans' and 'deceivers' who had fooled the entire world, of scoffing at the notion 'that a virgin could give birth to the God who created nature', and of maintaining that 'one should accept as truth only that which is proved by force of reason'. The pope and the emperor were bitter and long-standing enemies, and these charges were certainly exaggerated, but it is true that Frederick had a voraciously curious mind. He had been asking his favourite scholars some alarming questions. Where is God? Where are Heaven, Hell and Purgatory? What is beyond Heaven? What is the soul? Is it immortal? If so, why do the dead never return?[1]

Rumour had it that one of those scholars, Pietro della Vigna, had not only suggested to Frederick that Moses, Christ and Muhammad were frauds, but had written a book arguing the case: *Of the Three Impostors*. There is in fact no evidence that this book ever existed. Yet it became notorious purely on the basis of that wickedly alluring title. For nearly five centuries dreadful tales of it were whispered. Della Vigna's name was eventually forgotten, but his imaginary book was not. Almost every unnerving or scandalous figure of the next few centuries was at some point credited with having written *Of the Three Impostors* – Giovanni Boccaccio, Niccolò Machiavelli, Miguel Servetus, Giordano Bruno and many more. Scholars, eccentrics and troublemakers hunted for copies. A scandalous Swedish princess offered a bounty for it. It was easy enough to meet someone who had met someone who had once seen the book, but not to get any closer. Finally, in the early eighteenth century, enterprising French atheists actually wrote a book to go with the fearsome title. Inevitably, the result was an anticlimax.[2]

If we want to understand unbelief in the Middle Ages, the supposed Age of Faith, *Of the Three Impostors* is a good place to start. Like the book, medieval unbelief existed in the imagination rather than in any fully articulated form. It was a rumour, not a manifesto; an inarticulate suspicion, not a philosophical programme. Its vagueness was what made it powerful.

It is sometimes said that atheism in pre-modern times was simply impossible. This claim, supposedly made by the great French literary historian Lucien Febvre, is now routinely dismissed by historians of atheism. But Febvre's point was subtler than that. He was well aware that medieval and sixteenth-century Europeans frequently attacked religion, sometimes in scabrous terms, and that they readily accused one another of unbelief. His point was simply that, like *Of the Three Impostors*, these attacks and accusations had no substance. They were simply imaginings of what atheism might be. As such, Febvre concluded with magnificently Gallic disdain, unbelief of this kind 'did not matter, historically speaking . . . It hardly deserves to be discussed, any more than the sneers of the drunkard in the tavern who guffaws when he is told the earth is moving, under him and with him, at such a speed that it cannot even be felt'.[3]

It is an intriguing comparison. Before we leave the tavern in search of some more genteel atheists, we should let the drunkard have his say.

How do we, in the early twenty-first century, know that Febvre's drunkard is wrong and that the earth is indeed moving? Very few of us have the astronomical skill to determine the question for ourselves. We believe it because learned authority tells us it is true; because it is an important part of a wider web of knowledge we have about the world around us; and because we have seen very persuasive pictures explaining it. And yet, like Febvre's drunkard, we sometimes struggle to hold on to the fact. We say that the sun 'rises' even though we know it does no such thing. We treat the ground beneath our feet as if it were stationary. It *feels* stationary. For most practical purposes, it might as well be.

To wonder nowadays whether the earth really is moving, and whether five centuries' worth of accumulated astronomy is a hoax, you do not need to be a drunkard or a fool. You need to be independent-minded and self-confident. You need to be suspicious: ready to believe you are being lied to. And it helps if you are not very well educated. If you are woven too tightly into our civilisation's web of knowledge, you will not be able to kick against it. To see this at work, I recommend visiting the websites of modern flat-earther organisations – which, in their stubborn refusal to be hoodwinked by the intellectual consensus of their age, are the closest thing our own world has to medieval atheists.[4] Of course, whether you are a modern flat-earther or a medieval atheist, the lack of deep engagement with the dominant intellectual systems of your age which makes your doubts possible also blunts their power. You may have some slogans and some hunches, but you will be unable to refute astronomers who come at you with their orbits and laws of motion, or theologians wielding essences and ontologies. You can only reply with the perennial mulish wisdom of the sceptic who is told to admire the stitching on the emperor's clothes: I just don't see it.

Independent-minded, suspicious and uneducated people were in plentiful supply in medieval Europe. It is no coincidence that the original story of the emperor's new clothes dates back to fourteenth-century Spain. Raw and inarticulate as this scepticism was, it should not be ignored. It set the tone both for the more dangerous unbelief that was to follow, and for the way Christian society would respond.

The Fool's Heart

Medieval Europeans did not have the word 'atheism', but they understood the idea well enough. When the founder of medieval theology, Anselm of Canterbury, wrote his famous 'ontological' proof that there is a God in the 1070s, it was a devotional exercise in using reason to praise God, not a serious attempt to persuade actual sceptics. Still, he imagined and tried to reply to the counter-arguments which a sceptic would make. The scholarly method he was pioneering required him to do it. Medieval theologians built up their schemes of knowledge by systematically examining all possible objections to them. The greatest of those theologians, Thomas Aquinas, whose proofs of God were less dreamlike than Anselm's, did not merely conjure up an opponent as a debating foil. Imagining what an atheist's arguments might be, he affirmed that it is perfectly possible to think that there is no God.[5] But there is little sign of these scarecrows coming to life and turning into real doubters.

Anselm called his imagined sceptic 'the fool'. This was not a gratuitous insult. It was a deliberate allusion to a rather different stereotype of unbelief. Twice in the book of Psalms we read, 'The fool says in his heart, "There is no God"'. This biblical 'fool' is not a simpleton, but a villain who refuses to believe so that he can do vile deeds, untroubled by fears of divine justice.[6] That is obviously a grossly unfair caricature. But to judge by the cases of people accused of unbelief before medieval church courts, it was at least partly correct.

In 1273 a merchant named Durandus de Rufficiaco de Olmeira was hauled before officials of the bishop of Rodez, in southern France. He confessed to telling a friend that profit was better than virtue. When the friend teased him, saying that he did not care for his soul, he replied, 'Do you think there is any soul in the body other than the blood?' As a young man, he said, he used to cross himself piously, but it never did him any good, nor had his fortune suffered when he stopped. He also admitted to having scorned the miracle of transubstantiation, in which the sacramental bread is transformed into Christ's body. 'Even if the body of Christ were large as a mountain, it would long ago have been eaten up by priests.' Likewise, in 1299, Uguzzone dei Tattalisina, a notoriously tight-fisted moneylender from Bologna, was accused of dismissing the Bible as a mere fiction. He allegedly told Mass-goers that they might as well venerate their dinner as the consecrated bread; claimed that the True Cross, Christendom's most venerated relic, was just a piece of a bench; and said that 'there is no other world than this'. Another Mass-mocking moneylender from the same city was more explicit in denying that there was any afterlife or resurrection. When challenged on the point, he retorted, 'When did you see the dead return to us?'[7]

The courts do not seem to have found these cases of unbelief especially surprising. These men were grasping, stone-hearted money-grubbers, so it made theological sense that they should have no faith. When Nicholas, the abbot of Pasignano, was accused before the Italian Inquisition in 1351 of various acts of fraud and extortion, including threats to castrate anyone who dared testify against him, it was positively a relief to discover that he also believed that it was better to be rich than to be in holy orders, or that he treated the liturgy with contempt.[8] It hardly mattered whether these people lived wicked lives because they had abandoned their faith, or had abandoned their faith in order to live wicked lives. Either way, angry and contemptuous unbelievers of this kind did not threaten the religious world around them. They reinforced it.

The same was true of an even angrier species of 'unbelief': blasphemy. In 1526 a servant boy in Toledo was hauled before the Spanish Inquisition after multiple witnesses reported him for saying 'I deny God and Our Fucking Lady, the whore of the cuckolded arsehole'. Unusually inventive, but not unique. Blasphemy was by far the most common offence brought before the Inquisition: typically words uttered during a quarrel, in a tavern or at a gaming table. Crying out 'I deny God and the bastard of his lineage', as one Juan de la Calle did during a bad losing streak, might get you into trouble, but it was not a serious atheist's manifesto. Thomas Aquinas argued that such blasphemies were sinful, but not heretical: mere insults to God, arising from a momentary, almost involuntary eruption of rage. And what more potent way to insult God than to deny him altogether? Like another common medieval oath – cursing your own parents – this was about shock and macho posturing. It was playing Russian roulette with your own soul, to show that, since you were plainly not afraid of God, you were not afraid of anything. Another Spaniard, Juan Gutierrez, was accused in 1516 of saying 'God is nothing'. In the cold light of day before the tribunal, he admitted the charge, but maintained plaintively that he had of course not meant it. He had simply been 'fired up by anger and passion and dismay'. He had, he said, lashed out at God much as he might have said to a neighbour in a quarrel, 'Go on, you're nothing!' Most inquisitors were content to accept this kind of excuse. Even when blasphemy was too serious to go unpunished, the penalties – the pillory, cutting off the ears – were typically designed to humiliate. These people were not seriously arguing that there is no God. They were just showing off.[9]

Blasphemers insulted God but did not forget him. If they were angry with him, that was simply a recognition of his power. If you believe in an omnipotent God, everything is his fault. The irony, as pious commentators observed, was how constantly God's name was on blasphemers' lips. But this did not make their defiance trivial. Blasphemy had the effect of scent-marking places – alehouses, gambling dens, brothels, barracks, ships – where different rules applied, and where a degree of demonstrative impiety was expected or even rewarded. In the centuries to come, these irreligious spaces would serve as reservoirs of angry, scornful or contemptuous unbelief, from which it could seep out into the wider culture. It is no coincidence that these were all thoroughly male-dominated spaces. Blasphemy was, the lawyers agreed, a gender-specific crime. Women, it was said, blasphemed less than and differently from men. They typically complained to God of their suffering, challenged his justice or cursed their own births.[10]

Even if you did not mean it when you defied God, your words had consequences. If God did not strike you down for your wickedness, you might reach for the dread words more readily next time – or go further, since blasphemy depends on shock value and is therefore liable to runaway inflation. You might find yourself asking in your heart: *is* there really a God? Even to try out the feel of the words on your tongue was to peer over the edge of a cliff. Perhaps you were only trying to scare yourself, or others, and had no intention of actually leaping off. But you had looked, you had imagined, and felt a thrill that was more than fear. If the time ever came to jump – or if the cliff ever began to crumble beneath you – you would not be entirely unready.

Losing your temper with God might feel good, but it did not achieve very much. A more practical and dangerous target for anger was his self-appointed representatives on earth. The case of Isambardus de Sancto Antonio, in thirteenth-century southern France, ought never to have come to anything. All that had happened was that, when a preacher introduced his sermon by promising to 'say a few words about God', Isambardus said audibly, 'the fewer the better'. If he had apologised to the court, nothing more would have happened. But he refused, and instead launched into a series of tart remarks about how priests invented ceremonies to extort money from the people. Likewise the Montauban peasant who claimed in 1276 that he would not confess his sins to a priest even if he had sex with every woman in the village. He was no more making a theological argument than he was eyeing up his neighbours; he was simply railing against one of the most widely resented pinch points of priestly control over lay people. Another Spaniard was accused before the Inquisition in the late fifteenth century for saying, 'I swear to God that this hell and paradise is nothing more than a way of frightening us, like people saying to children "the bogeyman will get you"'. This is resentment at being manipulated, not speculation about the fate of the dead.[11]

I do not mean that these incidents were trivial: quite the reverse. Amateur theological speculation was a minority activity in the Middle Ages, but resentment of priests was a sport for all. Historians disagree over how widespread 'anticlericalism' was in medieval Europe, but everyday life certainly offered plenty of potential points of friction between priests and common people: from the gathering of tithes, fees and offerings, to the imposition of tedious moral and ritual constraints. Any priest who found himself at odds with an awkward parishioner might naturally fall back on his authority as God's representative, forcing the parishioner either to give way, or to enlarge his quarrel to include God. A dispute over a few pence or an illicit pat of butter in Lent could very quickly escalate into something much more serious.

In practice, one issue above all tended to trigger these escalations: the medieval clergy's most visible and most outrageous claim to spiritual authority. In the Mass, every priest presided at a daily miracle, in which bread and wine were wholly but undetectably transformed into the literal substance of Christ's body and blood. The reason the Western Church formally defined this doctrine of transubstantiation in 1215 was that dissident groups were questioning it. Thereafter the sacrament of unity became a shibboleth, dividing those who could and could not embrace this hard teaching. Transubstantiation made sense in Aristotelian philosophical terms, but it was always counterintuitive, and only became more so as philosophy moved on during the later Middle Ages. Hence the procession of medieval miracle stories in which unbelievers suddenly saw the ritual at the altar as it 'truly' was: a broken human body, a blood-filled chalice. In the stories, these visions were typically judgements on unbelief rather than rewards for faith. In the earliest and best known of them, Pope Gregory the Great prayed for the gory truth to be shown to a woman who laughed at the thought that bread she herself had baked could be Christ's body. Invariably, these doubters begged for the dreadful vision to be hidden from them again.

The Church, in other words, did not downplay the difficulty of believing in the sacrament. It revelled in it. The reason Christ's body looked, felt and tasted like bread, according to the encyclopaedic medieval theologian Peter Lombard, was 'so that faith may obtain its merit'. Believing was meant to be hard. Stories of bloody visions did not settle doubts so much as tease hearers with a certainty they could not have, rubbing their noses in the incongruous and glorious truth that their incredulous hearts were commanded to embrace.[12] Denials of this miracle were not unthinkable: they were necessary. Every Doubting Thomas story needs a sceptic.

Doubting transubstantiation was hardly exclusive to atheists. It was a point on which Jews, Muslims and Christian dissidents of various kinds could all agree. The Inquisition's chief purpose was to hunt for heretics, not unbelievers. Yet their dragnets did not discriminate. Some of their catch were not members of any organised or coherent heretical group, but seemed to represent distinctive, sceptical traditions – or simply to be speaking for themselves. When the bishop of Worcester interrogated a heresy suspect named Thomas Semer in 1448, for example, he was looking for so-called Lollards, members of an English sect who disparaged priests' status and traditional ceremonies. It quickly became clear, however, that Semer was something different. He not only denied transubstantiation, as the Lollards did, but dismissed the Mass entirely as an empty ritual. He rejected the Bible – which Lollards venerated – as a cynical tool of social control: 'a set of prescriptions for human behaviour of human devising to keep the peace'. He claimed that Jesus Christ was simply the natural son of Mary and Joseph. At a second inter-rogation, Semer claimed that paganism was better than Christianity, and that everyday life proved that the devil was stronger than God. Unlike most Lollards, he persisted in his denials until he was executed by burning.[13] What we cannot know is to what extent this kind of scepticism was an ever-present feature of medieval religion's sea floor, only stirred up by trawling inquisi-tors; and to what extent it specifically flourished in those corners of the ocean which were filled with heretical variety and therefore attracted the inquisitors' attention.

Another of Semer's shocking denials provides an important clue: he rejected any notion of the soul, of Heaven or of Hell. Wherever we find serious unbelief in medieval or early modern Europe, we find this 'mortalist' claim – that dead means dead, end of story. Mortalism is entirely compatible with belief in a God, but it was more than just an attack on a specific Christian (and Jewish, and Muslim)[14] doctrine. Medieval and early modern Christianity was intensely focused on salvation, the last judgement and the state of the dead. Strip that out, and while you might still have a rather abstract God, you have precious little religion. In theory, mortalism is not atheism. In practice, it might as well be.

So we find, for example, Jacopo Fiammenghi, an elderly Italian monk whose decades of debauchery, fraud and intimidation finally caught up with him in 1299. Witnesses accused him of saying that 'there was not another world, neither heaven nor hell, but only this world'. When asked about his soul, *anima*, he replied, 'a peach has an *anima*' – the same word meant the fruit's stone. An Englishman named Thomas Tailour confessed in 1491 to believing 'that when a man or woman dieth in body, then [he] also dieth in soul; for as the light of a candle is put out . . . so the soul is quenched by the death of the body'.[15] A slightly later preacher's anecdote picked up the same vivid image. In this story, a believer and an 'atheist' fall to arguing over the nature of the soul:

> The Atheist said: I will show you what it is. So he caused a candle to be lighted and brought to the table; he blew it out, and said: your soul is no more than the flame of that candle . . . It is blown out, and so shall it be with your soul when you die.

Medieval churchmen certainly believed that mortalism was enough of a problem to need regular denunciation.[16]

So we have anger with God, hatred for priests, rejection of transubstantiation, scepticism about life after death. What does it all add up to? Medieval inquisitors, who liked their heresies neatly classified, had a ready label to hand: Epicureanism. The ancient philosopher Epicurus, whose name is now associated with pleasure-seeking, was notorious in the Middle Ages both for his mortalism and for his strictly naturalistic account of the universe. If the gods existed in this worldview, they were little more than a curiosity. Dante put heretics in the sixth circle of Hell, but he named only one actual sect: the Epicureans, 'who with the body make the spirit die', and who are therefore condemned to lie for ever in opened tombs, unwillingly immortal. (Emperor Frederick II was among them.) Dante singled the Epicureans out, one near-contemporary reader claimed, because they are 'a sect which seems to have more followers than others'.[17]

In fact there is no evidence that this was a 'sect' with 'followers' at all. Frederick II, Jacopo Fiammenghi and Thomas Tailour did not all belong to some hidden, counter-cultural tradition. Most of the unbelieving voices we can recover sound as if they were isolated individuals working matters out for themselves, using everyday analogies. To take a slippery example: we do not need to believe the wild accusations of heresy flung at Pope Boniface VIII by his enemies in 1303 to recognise the kind of picture that was being painted. The pope supposedly mocked any notion of resurrection in bluntly rationalistic terms, telling believers to go and look at a graveyard: 'When is your grandmother coming back to tell us about the other world?' Were all the bones of the dead seriously going to be gathered for the general resurrection? Pointing to the bird on his dinner plate, he allegedly told his companion, 'you have no more soul than this capon'.[18] Whether dreamed up by the pope himself or by an imaginative accuser, none of these claims suggest intellectual influences. Some insights – that the world is flat, that dead is dead, that bread is bread – simply thrust themselves onto the mind with or without a tradition behind them.[19] Medieval Europeans respected inherited authority, but they could also think for themselves. The conundrum that our lives feel as if they mean something, while the world looks as if it means nothing, confronted them as it confronts us all. Like us all, they found their own solutions as best they could.

The plainest sign of this is that, together with unbelievers and garden-variety heretics, inquisitors regularly dredged up self-taught individuals who spanned the range from idiosyncratic through eccentric to insane. The Italian who argued in 1275 that our bodies cannot be made by God, since death would not otherwise extinguish our senses, claimed to have deduced this and other weird doctrines 'from his own cogitations'.[20] English bishops hunting Lollards came across individuals whose claims – that Heaven is below the earth, that the Virgin Mary belonged to the Holy Trinity while Christ did not, that Christ had had eighteen apostles – do not reflect any known theological system. A later generation of churchmen enjoyed shocking one another with tales of the man who 'thought Christ was the Sun, that shineth in the firmament; and the Holy Ghost was the Moon', or the one who believed his soul was 'a great bone in his body, and . . . after he was dead, . . . if he had done well, he should be put into a pleasant green meadow'.[21] These people are witnesses to an eternal truth: you don't need to know what you're talking about in order to have an opinion.

By now we have strayed into a different mood. Mortalism and wilder speculations were not usually fired by anger, but by anxiety, that meeting point of curiosity and fear. What happens to us after we die is a subject worth being anxious about. In the late 1160s, King Amalric of Jerusalem – a corpulent, studious prince who was no friend of the Church's privileges – fell ill. He summoned William, the archbishop of Tyre, to ask a question that William thought 'hardly admitted of discussion': 'whether . . . there was any way of proving by reliable and authoritative evidence that there was a future resurrection?' The shocked archbishop insisted that Christ's teaching was all the evidence needed, but Amalric asked 'whether this can be proved to one who doubts these things and does not accept the doctrine of Christ and believe in a future resurrection'. William claimed to have settled the royal conscience with only a few words. Perhaps: but the episode suggests that doubt could surface literally anywhere in medieval Christendom, especially when a brush with illness or danger made fine words about immortality sound flimsy.[22]

King Amalric's scepticism may have pained his archbishop, but it did not deeply alarm him. Anxieties of this kind – shallow-rooted, always springing up afresh – were a perennial feature of medieval Christendom, but not a serious threat to it. Perhaps they were mere weeds, a tolerable and inescapable problem that could never be permanently eradicated but could be managed. Perhaps they were even a necessary part of the ecosystem, helping the true faith to stay limber. There was no reason to suspect that these medieval doubters were the start of anything. A few weeds were not about to uproot the tree of faith. But when fresh doubts did begin to sprout, they did not do so in virgin soil in which no seed of unbelief had ever been sown.

Physicians, 'Naturians' and 'Nulla Fidians'

If the bishop at King Amalric's sickbed tried to preserve him in the faith, the same may not have been true of his physicians. To summon medical help was to enter a notoriously sceptical world, a nest of paganism at the heart of Christendom.

Medieval and early modern medicine owed virtually nothing to Christianity. It drew partly on Islamic and, especially, Jewish sources: whether ailing Christians might put themselves in the hands of Jewish doctors was a long-standing dilemma, in which niceties of conscience were usually overwhelmed by practical urgency. Beneath it all, however, Europe's medical tradition looked to Galen, the great Greek physician of the second century, 'the most heathenish of all writers', who did not believe in an immortal soul and whose towering authority Christianity struggled either to undermine or to co-opt.[23]

Even apart from this dangerous inheritance, physicians' vocation was in inevitable tension with Christianity. They were in the business of changing fate, not submitting to it. They were interested in natural causes of illness, which could be treated, not supernatural ones, against which they were powerless. And they had a vested interest in persuading patients that their methods were more effective than any priest's rituals. In the twelfth century, it was already said that physicians tended to place 'undue emphasis upon nature, in . . . opposition to faith'. In the thirteenth century 'damned and false men' were arguing that the Bible 'speaks falsely' by describing epilepsy as demonic possession.[24] The fourteenth-century Italian physician Peter of Abano claimed that supposed resurrections were merely natural resuscitations of people who were not in fact dead, and indeed that 'there is an infirmity which can keep a man insensible for three days and nights, so that he appears dead'. Perhaps Christ had merely passed out and then recovered? Peter died before these remarks could catch up with him, but he was posthumously burned for heresy just in case he was right.[25] In 1497 another physician was tried in Bologna on charges of dismissing Christ's miracles as natural phenomena. 'It's simply not possible', a Venetian physician supposedly said in 1575 of the miracles worked by his professional rivals in the Church: 'it's all an invention of the priests to get more money'.[26] Unbelief, admitted the seventeenth-century English doctor Sir Thomas Browne, was 'the general scandal of my profession'.[27]

How widespread this sort of thing really was is impossible to say. What is clear is that, running right through the medieval and early modern periods and beyond, there was a well-established stereotype: the sceptical, amoral and self-serving physician, a colleague to the deceitful, amoral and self-serving lawyer and the hypocritical, amoral and self-serving priest. It is already there in Chaucer, whose physician's studies were 'but little on the Bible'. A seventeenth-century proverb had it that 'where there are three physicians, there are two atheists'.[28] Stereotypes of this kind may be unfair or ill-founded, but they take on a life of their own. Sometimes people who grow weary of labouring under hostile assumptions decide they may as well be hanged for a sheep as a lamb.

Medics' supposed atheism was of a specific kind. They were described as 'naturians', often 'mere' or 'sole' naturians. 'The disease incident to your profession', one preacher told physicians, is 'even to be half Atheists, and that by ascribing so much to natural and second causes, and too little to God'. What made it worse was that their patients might be tempted into similar unbelief, placing their hopes for recovery in a doctor's skill rather than God's mercy.[29] The more expert the physician, the more likely that his expertise would blind him to the larger truth, and that he would, as the great physician-philosopher Robert Burton warned, 'attribute all to natural causes'.[30]

In the 1560s, the English physician William Bullein penned a vivid fictional portrait of this kind of unbelief. Antonius, a wealthy merchant, consults Medicus, his physician, frankly admitting that he would spend his entire fortune to save his life, and recalling that in his 'last great Fever' he had paid Medicus handsomely. Already we are some way from the Christian ideal, in which the sick submit to God's will and devote themselves to prayer and charity. But Medicus, knowing on which side his bread is buttered, praises Antonius' attitude, and supports it by quoting an obscure biblical verse: 'Honour the Physician, with the honour that is due unto him.'[31] Antonius, amused, points out that Medicus has left out the rest of the verse, which attributes all true healing to God. Lest he seem like a Bible-basher, he hastily adds that he only recognises the verse because he recently chanced to hear it being read when he and his bailiffs were in a church, lying in wait to ambush a pair of bankrupts. Medicus is unabashed at being caught out. 'I care not, for I meddle with no Scripture matters, but to serve my turn.' And he points out that, if either of them were to take heed of preachers quoting awkward Bible verses, they could hardly ply their trades as they do. Antonius happily agrees: the Bible is full of ridiculous principles that would bring all normal human society to a standstill, such as 'the Ten Commandments, etcetera'. If we are really going to be damned for everyday profanity and hating our enemies, 'then I warrant you, Hell is well furnished'.[32]

So far this is mere impiety, but now matters take a new turn. 'I think that we two are of one religion,' Medicus says, conspiratorially.

Antonius is nonplussed: 'I know not mine own religion', so how can it be the same as someone else's? Medicus now asks him to check that no one else can overhear them: secrets are about to be spoken. When he is certain that they are alone, he says to Antonius: 'Hark in your ear sir, I am neither Catholic, Papist, Protestant, nor Anabaptist.' Antonius asks, 'What do you honour? The sun, the moon, or the stars?' None of them, says Medicus. 'To be plain, I am a *Nulla fidian*': a person of no faith. (The newly coined English word *atheist* was not yet in widespread use.) 'There are many of our sect', he adds. And then comes the truly remarkable feature of this exchange. Having heard what ought to be the most shocking religious confession imaginable, Antonius is almost disappointed. He had apparently been hoping for something more novel. 'Oh. One who says in his heart there is no God. Well, we differ very little in this point.' He takes his prescription and leaves Medicus to his next patient.[33]

This was satirical fiction, the work of an author who was himself an ardent believer, and ought not to be taken too literally. Still, this much is plain. Physicians were the heirs to medieval Europe's most robustly secular intellectual tradition. And while they might accept God's role in human health and sickness, they could do nothing about it and so inevitably tended to ignore it. Whatever their own beliefs, their vocation led them to neglect God, and to do so at a moment when a patient might otherwise be rediscovering the urgency of faith.

So the physician's consulting room can join the alehouse and gaming table on our list of secularised spaces. Since learned medicine was a tiny world, the preserve of a handful of university-educated doctors and those wealthy enough to be able to afford their services, this is perhaps not very important. Moreover, for all medieval and early modern medicine's self-importance, it was very often useless and frequently worse, which did not increase its moral authority. Even the staunchest atheist might have been wiser to trust in God's mercy than to submit to a medieval physician.

Nevertheless, medical secularism could be corrosive, for even in the Middle Ages medicine always held the potential for innovation and scepticism. Patients had an irritating tendency to be more interested in whether a treatment worked than in whether it had good scholarly credentials. When the medical establishment despised experimenters as 'empirics' and froze them out of the academy, this merely spurred them on. It is no coincidence that the most notorious Christian dissident of the sixteenth century, Miguel Servetus, who denied the doctrines of the Trinity and of original sin, was also a physician who pioneered theories of the circulation of blood. In the following century, Sir Thomas Browne peered over the edge of unbelief with a coolly critical eye, and used his professional skills to ask searching questions of his religion. The method for determining virginity provided in the book of Deuteronomy, 'I find . . . is very fallible'. He suggested that the supposed miracle by which Moses defended the Israelites from snakebite was 'but an Egyptian trick'; that the fire Elijah had called down from Heaven could be explained chemically; that the destruction of Sodom and Gomorrah was due to 'Asphaltic and Bituminous' materials in the water rather than to the people's sin. This kind of thinking was by no means a slippery slope to atheism – Browne's case proves that, as we will see – but nor was it a path to simple faith.[34]

In the late 1650s, a Parisian priest named Paul Beurrier visited an aged physician in his parish, whose name he gave only as Basin. This man had travelled widely in Europe, in Turkey and in the East Indies, and had studied with Protestants, Jews, Muslims and Indian Brahmins. In the end, he concluded that 'all religions were only dreams, and political institutions used by rulers to use the deception of religion and the fear of Divinity to procure their subjects' submission'. He returned to Paris, 'determined to live and to die in philosophy'. Beurrier, the kind of priest who enjoys a challenge, visited Basin several times, and Basin eventually laid out for him what he called 'my philosopher's religion'. He accepted the existence of a distant, impersonal God who 'did not involve himself in our affairs, as being beneath him', but he insisted: 'First, that the Christian religion is the greatest of all fables; second, that the Bible is the oldest of all fictions; third, that the greatest of all deceivers and impostors is Jesus Christ.'

Basin's profession was no incidental part of his identity. Early in their acquaintance, Beurrier remarked platitudinously that Basin surely wished to live and die a good Christian. Basin indignantly denied it: 'I am a physician and philosopher. I have no other religion than to be a philosopher, and wish to die a philosopher, as I have lived.'

Basin is not the only shockingly frank character in Beurrier's memoirs, and the story seems to have lost nothing in the telling.[35] But with its suggestion that *Christian* and *physician* were incompatible alternatives, it implies that the medical world was one of those reservoirs in which unbelief lay dormant throughout the Middle Ages – until stirred into life by what Basin called 'philosophy'. That brings us out of this medical byway into the cultural upheaval that defined the modern age.

From Ancient to Modern

Medieval Europe was Christian to its bones; but it also venerated the ancient world, which had only latterly embraced Christianity, and some of whose greatest minds had rejected religion of any kind. Medieval theology's central scholarly project was to reconcile the Christian and Graeco-Roman intellectual legacies. In its own terms, this project was impressively successful, but no sooner was the battle won in the thirteenth century than an unexpected new front opened up. The brash new movement that arose in the city-states of northern Italy was not trying to cause religious trouble. This 'Renaissance', as we now call it, was a cultural and a political project. A series of scrappy, turbulent and remarkably wealthy miniature republics were trying to stabilise themselves and to protect their independence from one another, and from the twin threats of the papacy to the south and the Holy Roman Empire to the north.

In an era when hereditary monarchy was the norm, republican city-states were a novelty, but there was an obvious precedent: the pagan republics of ancient Greece and Rome. Italians who studied those examples quickly found that their political lifeblood had been oratory, rhetoric and the art of persuasion. So what we call the Renaissance began as an attempt to recover the eloquence of the age of Cicero, to scale once again the heights of Latin as it had been used in the classical era, in order to rebuild Rome's glories in Florence, Pisa and Siena.

These pioneers of the Renaissance venerated the ancient world at least as much as any other medieval scholars, but they used that veneration in a new way. Instead of humbly seeing themselves as heirs of an unbroken tradition, charged with preserving, transmitting and (perhaps, cautiously) interpreting it, they came to suspect that during the long ages separating themselves from the ancients, corruptions had crept in. The everyday Latin of the medieval Church and university seemed barbarous and uncouth next to the elegance of the ancient rhetors. At the start, this modest philological observation seemed innocent of religious implications. Yet they had started using the ancient, pagan past as a yardstick with which to measure the more recent, Christian past.

These scholars described their field as *studia humanitatis*: the study of human authorities, as opposed to divinity. From this they are nowadays often called 'humanists'. The word is misleading – they were, as we would now say, students of the humanities, rather than 'humanists' in the modern, atheistic sense – but the implications are not entirely wrong. It is partly that Christianity could not be completely insulated from the new critical methods these scholars were developing. The Bible is an ancient text, and Renaissance scholarship began to raise awkward questions about whether it had been translated and interpreted correctly; whether its text, as generally accepted, was accurate; even whether a correct translation or an accurate text would ever be possible.

For the moment, this was not much more than a whisper of unease, although it would build into an insistent din over the centuries ahead.[36] A more immediate threat came directly from the attempt to bring classical values into the late medieval world, a project which unmistakably gave Renaissance humanism a certain secular flavour. The challenge this posed to Christian orthodoxy was latent, slow-burning and eminently avoidable. But it was there.

In 1417, the Florentine scholar and manuscript hunter Gianfrancesco Poggio Bracciolini discovered the lost text of Lucretius' *Of the Nature of Things*. This epic poem from the first century BCE is the best surviving summary of Epicurean philosophy, but that was not why fifteenth-century Italians copied and re-copied it so avidly. It was rather that, in an age hungry for the best Latin style, Lucretius was hard to beat. Like modern film critics watching *The Birth of a Nation* or *The Triumph of the Will*, Lucretius' Renaissance readers admired him despite his ideas, not because of them. He was so eloquent that even the authors of anti-atheist tracts could not resist quoting his aphorisms.[37] And so Epicureanism, which for centuries had been an imagined poison, began to seep into Europe's groundwater for real.

In 1431 Lorenzo Valla, a pioneer of biblical criticism and a bitter rival of Poggio, wrote *On Pleasure*, a dialogue between a Stoic, an Epicurean and a Christian. Naturally the Christian had the last word, but the Epicurean had by far the most lines and, readers generally agree, the greatest share of the author's sympathies.[38] By the end of the century, some Italians were no longer simply playing with Epicureanism. In 1482 the brilliant, unorthodox theologian and magician Marsilio Ficino claimed that sufferers from melancholy, whose bodily humours were 'cold, dry, and black' and whose spirits were therefore 'doubtful and mistrusting', were drawn to Lucretius and to unbelief. Ficino's suggested regime to alleviate this malady has more than a whiff of self-medication.[39] In 1517 the city of Florence banned the reading of Lucretius in schools, worried by the unhealthy interest he was generating.

Lucretius was only one face of a larger problem. Even the Renaissance humanists' most revered political mentor, Cicero, had written a treatise, *Of the Nature of the Gods*, that almost persuaded a young French student into what he called 'atheism'. When an English poet in the 1570s wrote a dialogue between a believer and an atheist, he lifted his atheist's arguments wholesale from Cicero.[40] Equally dangerous ideas could be found in Pliny the Elder's *Natural History*, one of medieval Europe's best-known classical works and one of the first to find print publication, in 1469. Pliny – now better known for having been killed by his own reckless curiosity during the eruption of Vesuvius at Pompeii – was a Stoic, not an Epicurean, but he too professed a wearied ignorance about whether there were any gods, and mocked the notion 'that the sovereign power and deity, whatsoever it is, should have regard of mankind'. He dismissed any notions of life beyond death or of a soul as 'fantastical, foolish, and childish', called the idea of divine omnipotence ridiculous, and directed his readers' attention instead to 'the power of Nature', saying, 'it is she, and nothing else, which we call God'. His book was read with particular attention by physicians.[41]

Still, we should not overestimate the impact of these ideas. It was not news to late medieval Europeans that most ancient writers were not Christians. When Lucretius, Cicero and Pliny dismissed pagan religion, good Christians were happy to agree, simply regretting that those virtuous men had not had the opportunity to take the final step of faith in Christ. When the daring Mantuan philosopher Pietro Pomponazzi argued in 1516 that Pliny and Aristotle had been mortalists, he provoked furious controversy and accusations of heresy – but there is no good reason to doubt his insistence that, regardless of what Aristotle might have thought, he himself believed the Church's doctrine.[42] The actual idea of mortalism was blandly familiar, not disturbingly novel. The same is true of anti-providentialism: the argument that the world is governed simply by nature (Pliny) or by chance (Lucretius), so that God becomes an abstract curiosity, unable to answer prayers or work miracles. This is, the literary critic Stephen Greenblatt has argued, the idea which gave birth to the Renaissance and to the modern world. It is true enough that amid the chaotic opportunities of fifteenth-century Italy, anti-providentialism had a certain appeal.[43] But it was hardly new. The French builder accused in 1273 of saying he would only trust God and the Virgin Mary if he received bankable guarantees from them, and of insisting that his career was founded on hard work, not God's favour, had not been reading the ancients.[44] The notion that God does not hear prayers and either does not or cannot act is quite capable of suggesting itself to people who are unfamiliar with Lucretius. Anyone who has ever had a heartfelt or desperate prayer rebuffed can hardly avoid the thought. If all Europeans before the Renaissance had truly believed in divine providence, the words that sprang instinctively to gamblers' lips would have been prayers, not blasphemies.

One particular medieval notion, however, does seem to have been given new force by the Renaissance: the festering suspicion, not that religion is an error, but that it is a trick. The Vatican Library contains a manuscript copy of Lucretius' poem made, apparently in 1497, by a young Florentine scholar whose name would soon become a synonym for atheism: Niccolò Machiavelli. Unlike most Renaissance readers, Machiavelli's comments on Lucretius pass swiftly over literary, historical and ethical matters, concentrating instead on his materialism and especially his doctrine of chance.[45]

Machiavelli was no Epicurean. In his mature career he showed no discernible interest in doctrine or metaphysics at all. A friend said of him that he 'finds it difficult to believe the things that should be believed'. When he was appointed to choose a Lenten preacher for Florence in 1521, another friend found the idea laughable, saying that if Machiavelli turned pious it would be proof of senility. Neither of the two surviving versions of Machiavelli's will made any provision for his soul, and he deleted the word *soul* from a draft preface to one of his books.[46] His interests were strictly in politics and practical ethics. What made his treatment of religion so shocking was not a new idea, but a new way of applying a very old one.

Machiavelli's 1517 *Discourses on Livy*, a splendidly Renaissance distillation of the political lessons of ancient Rome for his own times, includes a substantial section on religion and politics. This begins innocently enough, with the commonplace observation that religion is 'the instrument necessary above all others for the main-tenance of a civilized state', and that a wise ruler ought always to uphold religion and encourage piety. Most medieval Christians would have agreed, believing this to be one of the God-given bene-fits of true religion. Lucretius, by contrast, had deplored how politicians used religion to manipulate the people's fears. Machiavelli agreed with Lucretius' analysis, but with one crucial difference: he thought manipulation was a good thing. He praised an early Roman king for faking divine authority for his laws: how else would they ever have been accepted? 'The times were so impregnated with a religious spirit and the men with whom he had to deal so stupid' – two facts that he plainly believed went together. He recommended that governments should encourage religion 'even though they be convinced that it is quite fallacious'. He added a breathtakingly cynical story about a Roman general preparing for battle who cast auguries to boost morale. Awkwardly, the auguries warned against an attack. So, with the chief priest's connivance, the general lied, telling his men that the results were favourable. When rumours of the true result nevertheless leaked out, the general publicly blamed the hapless priest for spreading subversion, and sent him to the front of the attack. The priest was killed early in the battle, allowing the general to declare that this was divine vengeance for his lies; he proceeded to win his victory.[47] Low cunning like this is as old as war and politics, but no one had ever earnestly described it as praiseworthy before.

By contrast, in Machiavelli's first and most infamous book, *The Prince* (1513), religion is notable chiefly by its absence. In this utterly pragmatic, amoral worldview, popes and bishops are political players like any other. Machiavelli not only dismissed Christian ethics as nonsense for simpletons; he apparently despised Jesus Christ himself. He was not so foolhardy as to say so explicitly, and indeed avoided naming Christ at all. But how else are we to read his praise of Moses, who as an 'armed prophet' had compelled obedience, and who was therefore vastly superior to the (unnamed) 'unarmed prophets . . . who must use persuasion . . . They always come to grief, having achieved nothing'. His statement that 'a prince must have no other object or thought, nor acquire skill in anything, except war' is hardly an endorsement of the Prince of Peace.[48]

Was any of this actually dangerous? Even if we take the cynicism of *The Prince* at face value, Machiavelli was not openly trying to subvert Christianity. By his own theory, in fact, rulers ought to encourage it. Perhaps the contradiction lay in writing any of this down, rather than whispering it in a ruler's ear – but then, Machiavelli was a less successful politician in practice than in theory. The point remains: arguing that a political or intellectual elite should be above religion is not, in itself, a threat to religion. At most it creates another secularised space. Alongside the alehouse, the gaming table and the consulting room, we now have the council chamber. But as long as the theory underpinning the council chamber's religious cynicism requires the rest of the population to be trained in religious enthusiasm, that theory's impact will be self-limiting. Ruling elites who secretly disdain the ideology they formally proclaim tend not to endure very long, not least because they usually insist that their wives, children and servants adhere sincerely to that ideology. So, in the end, if they avoid collapsing into internecine quarrels, they are replaced by true believers.

Unless their cynicism leaks out into the wider populace. Machiavelli wrote that Italy in his own time had 'lost all devotion and all religion' and become 'irreligious and perverse'. He described this as a 'debt' Italians owed to the Renaissance papacy, whose open corruption had destroyed their faith. He meant it ironically, but it is hard not to hear a note of appreciation. If the purpose of religion was to build a strong state, then – as Machiavelli saw it – Christianity was not a very good religion. Ideally it ought to be replaced with something more muscular and (to be plain) more manly.[49] In this Machiavelli belongs to a strand of anti-Christian thought stretching back to the Emperor Julian and forward to Edward Gibbon and Friedrich Nietzsche: a strand which despises Christianity for its otherworldliness, its cherishing of weakness and its tendency to pacifism.

In the intellectual history of atheism, this strand of thought is decisively important. In the social, political and emotional history of unbelief, it is peripheral. Far from renouncing Christianity's distinctive ethic of mercy, most modern atheism has redoubled it. Even Nietzsche was far more governed by Christian-style ethics than he liked to admit.[50] The only serious attempt to put this strand of anti-Christian thought into practice is twentieth-century fascism, which ended by pulling the house down on itself and everyone around. Machiavelli's unbelief was genuinely shocking, but – for that very reason – it was a dead end: a position that was prevented by its own inner logic from building any kind of mass following. So does it matter to our story at all?

Perhaps only for this reason: Machiavelli gave new voice to an old, corrosive thought, and so gave new fuel to the unbelief of anger. He was (naturally) eventually credited with having written

Of the Three Impostors, and it is almost true. *The Prince* is
book, but it is also an imaginary one, indeed a much-imagined
whispered about in fascinated horror more than it was read.
power of Machiavelli's writing even now is not that it tell
anything new, but that it tells us what we have always suspec
bluntly and without qualm or apology. The hunch that religion
a political trick played by the powerful was as old as politics its
But now that hunch had a name. The play *The Jew of Malta*, writt
in 1589–90 by the English dramatist Christopher Marlowe, opei
with a prologue to the audience by a speaker who identifies himse
as 'Machiavel', and explains:

> Albeit the world think Machevill is dead,
> Yet was his soul but flown beyond the Alps . . .
> Though some speak openly against my books,
> Yet will they read me . . .
> I count Religion but a childish Toy,
> And hold there is no sin but Ignorance.

Marlowe himself was accused of claiming that 'the first beginning
of Religion was only to keep men in awe'.[51] Machiavelli's contribution was to say out loud what others had long whispered,
breathing new confidence into the long-standing suspicion that
religion was all a giant trick. When the sixteenth century's religious
crises broke, this began to matter.

In the meantime, some of those who were enthralled by the
Renaissance's ancient novelties acquired a reputation for unbelief,
sometimes justified, often not. Perhaps Étienne Dolet really did
deny the immortality of the soul – the charge for which he was
burned to death in Paris in 1546. What we know for certain is that
his view of the question was almost wholly pagan. The true immortal,
he wrote in 1538, is one to whom 'for all future time life after
death has been gained by his reputation . . . renowned either by

military glory or by literary reputation'. This was the immortality he himself sought, adding:

> What indeed has death been able to accomplish as yet against Themistocles, Epaminondas, Alexander the Great, Hannibal, Caesar, Pompey, the Scipios, Demosthenes, Isocrates, Lysias, Homer, Pindar, Aristophanes, Cicero, Sallust, Plautus, Terence, Virgil, Ovid?

This was the company for which Dolet longed, not dreary Christian saints. He was so immersed in classicism that he had lost his moorings in his own century. It was like the Italian friar who told inquisitors in 1550 that there was no soul and that Christ was merely human, adding that he put more faith in Ovid than in the Bible. (As if to confirm his affinity with all things Graeco-Roman, he added that 'he would rather worship a pretty little boy in the flesh than God'.)[52] At the very least, the Renaissance ensured that anyone searching for unbelief knew where to look. In the mid-seventeenth century, an unknown French scholar put together a hefty compilation of extracts from ancient and Renaissance writers which argue that there is no God and no soul, and that religion is a political device. This document appears to have been a wholly private project: unpublished and, as far as we know, unread until its modern rediscovery.[53] Its contents might once have been disconcerting. By the mid-seventeenth century, they were banal.

This compilation's most insidious claim was that the truly wise had always known that religion was a lie. This condescending conspiracy theory was perhaps the Renaissance's most important, direct contribution to unbelief. When the radical Italian theologian Lelio Sozzini wrote in 1549 that 'most of my friends are so well educated they can scarcely believe God exists', he was joking, but the joke depends on the stereotype of the learned unbeliever who

is too sophisticated for faith.[54] North of the Alps, the association between Italians and atheism became proverbial. 'Italy', wrote the Englishman Richard Harvey in 1590, 'hath been noted to breed up infinite Atheists.' If his own countrymen were tempted by doubt, they were liable to be called Italianate.[55] The pungently nationalistic English scholar Roger Ascham admitted that he had only been to Italy once, for nine days, but it was enough to convince him that the 'special point that is to be learned in *Italy*' was 'first, to think ill of all true Religion, and at last to think nothing of God himself'. The very word *atheist*, Ascham lamented, was unknown in England 'until some Englishman took pains to fetch that devilish opinion out of Italy'.[56]

For all the nationalistic tub-thumping, there is no mistaking the undercurrent of concern. The old unbelief of anger had acquired a new mood of cosmopolitan, satirical scorn. The rumoured covens of mocking atheists gathering in sixteenth-century cities, calling themselves 'the damned crew', are probably as imaginary as *Of the Three Impostors*, but like that phantom book, they matter. Believers began to hear knowing laughter at the back of their minds, 'turning things that are serious into mockery'.[57] Faith felt simple; doubt, sophisticated. In the 1580s, Jacques du Perron, a French royal servant and future cardinal, presented an argument for the existence of God to King Henry III's court, as a formal exercise and an entertainment. Basking in his audience's applause, he was foolish enough to add that, if they wanted, he could present the opposite case as well. The king, who already had quite enough problems with religious extremists, was furious, but there is no reason to think that du Perron was a secret atheist. He explained, backpedalling frantically, that he was merely hoping 'to demonstrate his wit' – and nothing was wittier than a knowing flirtation with atheism.[58] That flirtation did not, in itself, significantly threaten Europe's long marriage to the old faith. Only if the marriage itself ran into trouble might it become dangerous.

The cynicism and mockery of Renaissance humanists did not mark the start of a high road to modern atheism, any more than the anger of medieval blasphemers or the professional disdain of learned physicians. Self-limiting and by definition marginal, these atheisms were irritants, in equilibrium with the faith rather than destabilising it. If the Renaissance contained a serious threat to Christendom, it was of a subtler kind.

Machiavelli's open fascination with Lucretius' doctrine of chance was very unusual. Most Renaissance scholars treated Lucretius the way medieval theologians had treated Aristotle: they took what they could use and left the rest. The historian Ada Palmer has recently examined all fifty-two extant fifteenth-century manuscripts of Lucretius' poem. Machiavelli's is quite unlike any of the others. The sections of the poem which deny the immortality of the soul and assert that the world is governed by chance were sedulously ignored by most fifteenth-century commentators. More than 90 per cent of the notes Palmer has found comment either on Lucretius' style and language, or on incidental historical information in the poem. Most of the rest focus on Lucretius' moral philosophy or medical opinions. Aside from Machiavelli's, only five of the manuscripts pay more than the most passing attention to Lucretius' dangerous ideas, one of them only briefly, the other four in order firmly to mark them as errors.[59] Most Renaissance readers believed, or wanted to believe, that Epicureanism could be house-trained.

It did not quite work. Renaissance scholars were keen to learn from the ancients' exemplary lives as well as their exemplary Latin (indeed, they were convinced the two were connected). Surely – so the argument went – Christians should be spurred to new heights of righteousness by the shameful thought that these mere pagans had outstripped them in virtue? It was an innocent rhetorical ploy, its double edge quite unintended. Christianity was, in this view, simply the consummation of all that was best about ancient philosophy. The greatest of the Renaissance's house-trainers, the Dutch scholar Desiderius Erasmus, included in his *Colloquies* a self-styled Epicurean who claimed that 'there are no people more Epicurean than godly Christians': for Epicureans held that the purpose of human life is the pursuit of happiness, and as everyone knows, true happiness is to be found in virtue. It was an over-tidy view of Epicureanism – Lucretius' work has rather more sex in it than Erasmus' – but also a singular view of Christianity. Erasmus united Renaissance philosophy with his homeland's tradition of practical devotion, and a dash of German mysticism, to conclude that the heart of Christianity was its ethics. Christian theology conventionally emphasises that human sin is pervasive and that sinners must be saved by God's grace. Erasmus, who was suspicious of too much theology, wanted his readers to strive not to be sinners at all. Christians had traditionally thrown themselves on Jesus Christ's mercy, as their Saviour. Now they were being urged to imitate him, as their exemplar.[60]

So far, this was no more than a shift of emphasis. Erasmus remained a faithful, if provocative, Catholic Christian. But the implications were unsettling. If Christianity was supremely about ethics, and if ancient pagans had been outstandingly virtuous, did that mean unbelievers could achieve true godliness? Christ might be the ideal example, but did that mean he was necessarily essential? Could reason and the God-given natural law implanted in every human soul not bring us to the same destination? In which case, should Christians concentrate less on the devotional and sacramental life of the Church and more on cultivating the kinds of virtues which pagans and Christians might share? Erasmus and his colleagues were in no sense trying to ask such provocative questions. They were trying to purify Christianity, not undermine it. That is what, in the centuries to come, would make their approach so dangerous.

2

The Reformation and the Battle for Credulity

"'I dare say you haven't had much practice,' said the Queen. "When I was your age, I always did it for half an hour a day. Why, sometimes I've believed as many as six impossible things before breakfast.'"

Lewis Carroll, *Through the Looking Glass*

'The impossible often has a kind of integrity to it which the merely improbable lacks.'

Douglas Adams, *The Long Dark Tea-Time of the Soul*

There is a well-established view that the credit, or blame, for modern unbelief lies with the Protestant Reformation, a view most recently laid out in Brad Gregory's 2012 book *The Unintended Reformation*. The argument goes something like this. Martin Luther's defiance of the pope from 1517 onwards ended up shattering Western Christendom into rival parties, each of which regarded the others' errors as intolerable. As they dug their trenches and pounded each other with polemical and then with literal artillery, they tore up the religious landscape that they were fighting over until it could no longer be recognised. With all sides condemning each other's false beliefs, it was hard to prevent civilians caught in the crossfire from reaching the conclusion none of the combatants wanted: what if they are all wrong? As battles subsided into exhausted ceasefires, armed truces and frozen conflicts, ordinary people and their governments began systematically to evade those conflicts and the terrible destruction they could cause by confining 'religion' to a private sphere and creating a new 'secular' public space. People who could not agree about religion could at least work around it, and discovered that they did not particularly miss it. And so religion was confined to quarters, like a once-formidable relative sent to a nursing home: spoken of with respect, paid a ritual visit occasionally, its debts honoured, but not allowed out in public where it might cause distress or embarrassment. In truth – though it would be crass to say so out loud – it was simply kept ticking over until it died a natural death.[1]

It is a powerful story with a lot of truth in it. But the world it explains is not quite the world we have. It does not explain why European Christianity endured for so many centuries after the Reformation; nor why, in our own times, a religiously fractured society like the United States is so much less secular than relatively homogeneous ones like Norway or France. Above all, it mistakes the part that unbelief played in the Reformation itself. Unbelievers did not merely play supporting roles, as battlefield medics or architects of postwar reconstruction. Unbelief was a part of the action from the beginning, and its role in the conflict was decisive. It was not a by-product of the Reformation conflicts. It was a weapon in them.

Calvin and the Epicures

In 1542 John Calvin, the French Protestant leader in exile in Geneva, received an unwelcome letter from a friend in Paris. The French capital, Antoine Fumée warned Calvin, was being overrun by 'Epicureans', whose doctrines were spreading like a cancer.

Fumée's description of these wild-living unbelievers is suspiciously vague. There are no names, dates or places. It is not clear how much of this is eyewitness testimony and how much rumour. He did claim to have spoken to some such people, describing their 'charming words' and how they 'sedulously avoid trouble'. Their typical opening gambit was to 'annul faith in the New Testament', suggesting that Plato's works were wiser and more learned than the Gospels, even though no one considered him to be God. As conversation progressed, their attacks on the Bible would become progressively more barbed. A particular butt for their 'impudence', apparently, was the Song of Songs: the Old Testament book of love poetry which Jews and Christians have always taken as an allegory of God's love for humanity, but which for these scoffers was shamelessly indecent, a mockery of the notion of Holy Scripture. The fact that their own lives were far more debauched did not trouble them.[2]

Perhaps this was just another rumour of sophisticated Renaissance atheists. Some of these Epicureans' supposed talking points were lifted almost verbatim from Machiavelli.[3] But the reason this was unnerving to Calvin was that they also seemed to be familiar with Protestant doctrine. As Europe's religious divisions widened, people were starting to fall through the cracks.

Calvin did not respond immediately, but a few years later he was confronted with a case he could not ignore. On 27 June 1547, an anonymous death threat was left in the pulpit of Calvin's church in Geneva. In a city seething with religio-political tensions, this was a serious matter. An informant traced the threat to one Jacques Gruet, an impoverished former cathedral canon and serial trouble-maker from a once-grand Genevan family. Gruet's house was searched. Among his papers was a tract in his own hand in which, as Calvin summarised it, 'the whole of Scripture is laughed at, Christ aspersed, the immortality of the soul called a dream and a fable, and finally the whole matter of religion torn in pieces'.

Gruet denied holding any of these views, but eventually, under torture, he confessed to having left the note threatening Calvin – and also to having corresponded with Étienne Dolet, who had been executed for mortalism in Paris the previous year. Gruet was executed for sedition, blasphemy and atheism on 26 July. Any disquiet about this summary process was silenced two years later, when a much longer book in Gruet's hand was discovered hidden in the rafters of his old house, 'full of . . . detestable blasphemies against the power, honor and essence of God'. On Calvin's advice, the book was solemnly and publicly burned.[4]

Much of the content of Gruet's documents – so far as we can reconstruct them – was simply the medieval unbelief of anger brought to boiling point. 'God is nothing . . . Men are like beasts.' The soul, or any afterlife, are 'things invented by the fancy of men': 'I believe that when man is dead there is no hope of life.' Jesus Christ was not God's son, but 'a fool who wanted to claim glory for himself', and who deserved his fate. Gruet ridiculed divine providence: 'it is absurd: do not you see that all prosper, Turks as much as Christians? . . . Everything that has been written about the power of God is falsehood, fantasy and dream'. All religion was a human fabrication.

But there is a new note to the rage that seethes through these texts. Much of it settled on Calvin himself, one of whose books Gruet had filled with furious annotations. An (undelivered) letter to Calvin praised him with vitriolic irony as 'greater than God', and urged him to 'reject the doctrine of Christ and say . . . that you have found by the Scriptures that it is not he who was the Messiah, but yourself. Then you will have an immortal name, as you desire.'

Gruet was not the only person to be alienated by Calvin's fierce self-belief, but his grudge against the reformer gave his religious criticism a new focus. Like Fumée's Epicureans, Gruet's most consistent target was the Protestants' most prized asset: the Bible.

He ridiculed the Creation story: how could anyone know, 'since there was nobody there at the time?' The authors of the New Testament were 'marauders, scoundrels, apostates'. The Bible as a whole contained 'nothing but lies' and taught 'false and mad doctrine . . . All the Scripture is false and wicked and . . . there is less sense than in Aesop's fables'.[5]

In 1550, the year after Gruet's book was discovered, Calvin at last did as Fumée had asked eight years before, and wrote a book, *Concerning Scandals*, denouncing the rising tide of godlessness. He had a simple explanation of when and why this surge had started. It was all because of the Protestant Reformation: 'Whereas thirty years ago religion was flourishing everywhere, and we were all in agreement about the common and customary worship of God, without any controversy, now ungodliness and contempt for God are breaking out on all sides.'

An awkward admission for a Protestant leader to make; but Calvin could explain it. Before the Reformation the devil had kept Christendom in darkness, 'benumbed' in conscience. The dawn of the true gospel had merely exposed the unbelief that had always been there. Calvin was forced to concede, however, that these unbelievers were not simply Catholics revealed in their true colours. They were people who had 'sampled the gospel', even if it were only 'a contemptuous nibble'. Protestantism had taught them to 'make witty mockery of the absurdities of the papists', which in itself was a good thing, but they then proceeded to 'pour out the poison of their ungodliness in all directions, so that they fill the world with atheism'. In particular, Calvin believed, they had drunk too deeply from one intoxicating Protestant doctrine: gospel freedom, the heady claim that Christians ought to be liberated from the laws and regulations of formal piety. 'A great many people', Calvin feared, were using that principle to 'emancipate themselves from obeying God himself'.[6]

You could hardly find a less neutral witness. Yet Calvin had one of the sharpest minds of his age, and we do not need to share his theology to accept his observation. The Reformation had done more than simply create a fog of religious confusion in which unbelief could move relatively freely. It was actively leading Christians away from faith.

Between Superstition and Impiety

The Protestant Reformers saw their movement as – among other things – a crusade against 'superstition'. That immensely useful word was applied to any false or misconceived religious practice: religion which was 'zealous without knowledge, and too solicitous about that which is not necessary'. Since classical times, superstition has had an opposite: impiety, or atheism.[7] So this was the unwelcome choice set before Christians in the Reformation age. If your balance on the knife edge of true religion wavered, and you were forced to fall either to superstition or impiety, which way would you go? Your answer to that question more or less determined whether you chose Catholicism or Protestantism. Catholics might loathe superstition: Thomas More's *Utopia* included a diatribe against it. Yet More was, as his friend Erasmus said, so 'addicted' to piety that he would in the end rather be superstitious than impious.[8] Better to eat the religious diet put in front of you, however questionable, than to turn up your nose and risk starvation. By contrast, Protestants preferred to be 'famished' rather than 'devour the pestiferous dung of papistry'. The old religion was so rotten with superstitious error that they would risk a measure of unbelief in order to be rid of it. As one Catholic put it, not unfairly: 'a Catholic may commonly become sooner Superstitious, than a Protestant; And a Protestant sooner become an Atheist, than a Catholic'.[9]

Naturally Protestants denied it, insisting they were steering a narrow course midway between the opposing dangers. But the undertow consistently pulled them in one direction, and occasionally they admitted it. Francis Bacon – a tricksy, saturnine Protestant, certainly no religious zealot, but no atheist either – argued in 1612 that atheism was better than superstition. 'It were better to have no Opinion of *God* at all; than such an Opinion, as is unworthy of him.' He justified this with a lawyer's technicality – that ignorance is better than slander – but also with a disconcerting claim: the historical record, he reckoned, showed that atheism was less likely to lead to public calamities than superstition.[10] Plenty of Protestants who would wince at such frankness nevertheless agreed. Better to brave the dangerous wilderness of unbelief than to return to Rome's dungeon of superstition. That was how Henry More, a subtle English Protestant theologian of the mid-seventeenth century, explained the growth of atheism in his own times. In the Reformation, he argued, God had graciously permitted 'a more large release from Superstition . . . a freer perusal of matters of Religion, than in former Ages'. The devil, however, had spotted an opportunity 'to carry men captive out of one dark prison into another, out of *Superstition* into *Atheism* itself'. The smashing of the 'external frame of godliness', which had kept medieval Europeans in 'blind obedience', meant that many of them now simply gave in to their unrestrained sinfulness: 'Being emboldened by the tottering and falling of what they took for Religion before, they will gladly . . . conclude that there is as well no God as no Religion.'[11] More saw opposing this kind of atheism as his life's work. There was, however, one solution he would never consider: to rebuild the prison.

As Catholics pointed out, this was not some incidental side effect of the Protestant Reformation. It was integral to it. The Protestants mounted frontal assaults on long-accepted Christian doctrines: transubstantiation, the authority of the pope, the value of relics. They did not merely argue that Catholic doctrine was incorrect, but mercilessly mocked anyone gullible enough to believe the ridiculous lies with which priests feathered their nests. So when, for example, a Catholic missionary was exposed as defending forged miracles on the grounds that 'godly credulity doth much good, for the furthering of the Catholic cause', it played directly into the Protestants' narrative.[12] The problem was that to mock 'godly credulity' was to play with fire. Protestants were still Christians. Indeed, they preached the supreme value of faith. They derided credulity, but had no wish to foster incredulity.

This problem – how do you reject some beliefs while still embracing others? – is an old one for Christians. Traditionally the solution involves carefully chosen acts of defiant credulity: avowing your belief in the unbelievable specifically because it is unbelievable, because that is how you show that your faith has transcended reason. *Orthodoxy* means submitting yourself – including your faithless, sceptical mind – to the teaching of the Church; *heresy* literally means 'choice', the choice to follow your own wayward thoughts. To be orthodox, then, was to defy those thoughts and obey instead. Among mystics, it was a pious discipline; the third-century theologian Tertullian famously claimed to believe in Christ's incarnation 'because it is absurd'. Among religious polemicists, this can degenerate into a kind of pious eating contest, in which the contestant who can swallow the most implausible claim wins. The result is that religious opponents may find themselves arguing simultaneously both that their beliefs are reasonable, true and self-evident, and also that those beliefs are mysteries which surpass reason and are inaccessible except through faith. For in Christian terms, that is itself one of the most powerful logical proofs that a doctrine is true.

It is important to be clear that this approach is not anti-rational. If it looks so to us, that is because – and this will be a crucial element of our entire story – we understand *reason* differently from our forebears. Since the eighteenth century, we have thought of reason as a method: the application of logic to solving problems, a steady, prosaic and scientific process. To medieval and early modern minds, reason was not a method but a power of perception: almost a sixth sense. For example: how do you know that 1 + 1 = 2? Modern philosophy has struggled mightily with that question, but the pre-modern view is that the question is unanswerable. You simply know intuitively that it is so, and the (God-given) faculty of intuition which provides that knowledge is called *reason*. If you possess that faculty, then 1 + 1 = 2 is self-evidently true. If your reason is defective, or absent, you will not be able to see it; in which case, there is no persuading you. Blaise Pascal, the seventeenth-century mathematician and mystic who sat at the fulcrum of these two views of reason, distinguished between the 'mathematical' and the 'intuitive' mind. There are uncontested truths, he argued, which the mathematical mind cannot prove, such as 'knowledge of first principles, like space, time, motion, number'.[13] To accept such truths is an act of reason, but not a process of logical deduction. It is much more like a leap of faith.

In which case, the most important thing reason has to teach us is that reason itself is fallible. Since reason is a power to perceive truths that lie outside us, there is in fact nothing more rational than to submit your reason humbly to those authorities that are set above it. The word for that is *faith*. To defy those authorities in the name of reason is to do violence to reason itself. So if there is any apparent conflict between our frail and fallible rationality and the certainties of the true faith, it stands to reason that reason should give way. In its own way, this principle still holds. Many of us, in the modern world, might struggle to refute a flat-earther armed with jargon and ingenious technicalities. But we trust that there are astronomers who can, and are content to submit our reason to their authority.

The Protestant Reformation, by using reason as a battering ram against the papacy, destabilised this entire structure. Catholics quickly became convinced that their enemies were decaying 'from faithful believing, to carnal reasoning'.[14] And so, as well as fighting fire with fire, and defending their doctrines as logical and rational,

Catholics emphasised that the Protestants were guilty of something much worse than honest mistakes about theology. They were revealing themselves to be incredulous – and therefore, in Christian terms, self-evidently wrong. At the heart of the Reformation struggles was a battle for credulity.

The chief arena of this battle was that perennial lightning rod for scepticism, the doctrine of transubstantiation. Protestants were bitterly split among themselves over what to make of the sacrament of the Eucharist. Martin Luther continued to insist that Christ's body was physically present in the bread and wine, while Calvinist and Reformed Protestants talked of a spiritual or even merely a symbolic presence. But they were united in rejecting transubstantiation, and many of their arguments against it boiled down to claiming that it was impossible, ridiculous, or an offence against reason. To call something impossible, however, was to say that God could not do it – which sounded blasphemous. Catholics worked hard to turn this into a dispute over whether God had the power to perform the miracle of transubstantiation. It was strikingly rare for Protestants to give what might seem the obvious rejoinder: that God could do it but there was no reason to believe he actually did.[15]

In the mid-1540s, as Calvin was waking up to the threat of Protestant-accented scepticism, a group of English Catholics laid out a defence of transubstantiation, asserting not only that it was reasonable but also that it transcended rationality and credibility, 'surmounting incomparably all wit and reason of man . . . The more that [a doubter] by reason, ransacketh and searcheth for reason, in those things that passeth reason . . . into the further doubt he falleth'.[16] These Catholics did not disapprove of reason, but of *carnal* reason: doubting, disbelieving, self-based and so self-limiting. Richard Smith, the Regius Professor of Divinity at Oxford, argued that in the doctrine of the Mass, there be many things that appear strange . . . unto carnal reason . . . Unless we believe we shall not understand . . . Unless we be humble and low in our own sight, and think ourselves unworthy, and unable to know or to be made privy to such high mysteries and secret things, the said mysteries and secret things shall be hid from us.[17]

The most formidable of these writers, Bishop Stephen Gardiner, argued that even to ask how the miracle of transubstantiation was performed was 'a token of incredulity'. He pointedly praised the apostles who, when Christ spoke about his body being eaten, had 'needed no further explanation to understand it, but faith to believe it'. Like many others, Gardiner contrasted those apostles with another set of biblical characters: the Capernaites, who, when Christ claimed to be the bread of life, asked incredulously how this man could give them his flesh to eat.[18] The Capernaites became a favourite symbol for carnality: a lumpish species of error distinguished by its failure to lift its eyes above the human and the mundane.

What made this charge so effective was that it was so nearly true. Protestant attacks on the Mass really did have a whiff of incredulity about them. They tended to meet Catholic theology's philosophical precision not with counter-arguments, but with derision. How can Christ's body be in so many places at once? With all those Masses celebrated daily, surely Christ's body must be the size of a mountain? – as if those thoughts had never occurred to Thomas Aquinas. They used scoffing hypothetical cases: if a mouse happens to eat a consecrated Host, does it receive Christ? If someone is seasick after receiving the sacrament, does he vomit his Saviour half-digested onto the deck?[19] According to one Protestant, Catholics are 'not ashamed to swear, that . . . they eat [Christ] up raw, and swallow down into their guts every member and parcel of him: and last of all, that they convey him into the place where they bestow the residue of all that which they haue devoured'.[20] That is not an argument; it is a gag reflex. And it proved his opponents' point.

The shrewd, deeply sceptical but equally deeply Catholic French essayist Michel de Montaigne believed that the Protestants' reckless scorn had started a fire that swept quickly out of control among the common people:

> Once you have put into their hands the foolhardiness of despising and criticizing opinions . . . and once you have thrown into the balance of doubt and uncertainty any articles of their religion, they soon cast all the rest of their beliefs into similar uncertainty. They had no more authority for them, no more foundation, than for those you have just undermined . . . They then take it upon themselves to accept nothing on which they have not pronounced their own approval, subjecting it to their individual assent.[21]

Before long, rueful Protestants were agreeing. The devil, it was said, whispered in believers' ears: 'You thought that this and that was a *truth,* but you see now it comes to be *debated,* it proves but a *shadow,* and so are other things you believe, if once they were *sifted* and debated.' In one imagined debate between an atheist and a Protestant, the atheist mocked the Protestant for appealing to long-standing tradition. 'The Church of *Rome* being ancienter . . . why then are you not of it, if you will go for long received opinions?'[22]

Nor was it all just rumours. Noël Journet was a soldier-turned-schoolmaster who converted to Protestantism in the late 1570s, only to be expelled from the French Protestant church for circulating handwritten tracts which ridiculed the Bible's supposed contradictions as 'fables . . . dreams and lies'. He proposed to replace Christianity with a 'strange religion of which one never speaks'. This, Catholic pamphleteers warned after Journet was put to death, was where Protestantism led. Geoffroy Vallée, another Frenchman executed for being somewhere between religiously eccentric and insane, also claimed that most doubters had first 'passed through Protestantism'.[23] The same trajectory was visible in attacks on Protestant orthodoxy in England in the next century. Right-thinking Protestants were outraged when radical dissidents claimed there was no such place as Hell. The radicals replied that Catholics had said the same when Purgatory had been questioned a century before. And while orthodox Protestants might have distinguished sharply between burning popish service-books (good) and burning Bibles (bad), it is no surprise that zealots in the heat of the moment might not have known when to stop. Likewise, when you were used to deriding transubstantiation as idolatry, it did not sound too outlandish to say that 'the *flesh of Christ*, and *Letter of Scripture*, were the two great Idols of Antichrist'. Protestants had worked long and hard to train their people to beware of the devil masquerading as an angel of light. They could hardly claim innocence when the same principle was turned back on them.[24] The Reformation's lesson, it seems, was summed up in a newly coined proverb: 'He that deceives me once, it's his fault, but if twice, it's my fault.'[25]

For all these reasons, Catholics naturally concluded that unbelief was a peculiarly Protestant problem. Protestants were quick to disabuse them. The shrewd and unorthodox Protestant polemicist William Chillingworth, who had spent a brief and unhappy stint as a convert to Catholicism, blamed the rise of unbelief squarely on the Catholics. What else could they expect when they imposed tyrannical discipline, forged miracles, promulgated 'weak and silly Ceremonies and ridiculous observances', and demanded that Christians accept doctrines – such as transubstantiation – which are 'in human reason impossible'? The inevitable result was 'secret contempt and scorn . . . and consequently Atheism and impiety'. Suppress reason too harshly, and it will eventually revolt.[26]

Even if we dismiss that as a partisan case, the battle for credulity was an arms race. Catholics and Protestants were forced to parry one another blow for blow. So Protestants were almost as quick as

Catholics were to deploy accusations of incredulity, insisting piously that God wanted 'not a curious head, but a credulous and plaine heart', and lambasting Catholics' supposed use of 'blind and foolish' reason as 'the sole judge and norm of faith'.[27] Some even tried to turn the tables on transubstantiation, claiming that the doctrine was so lumpish and carnal that it amounted to atheism.[28] On his deathbed in 1551, John Redman, a giant of theology at Cambridge University whose long-standing Catholicism was now crumbling into doubt, wrestled openly with this subject: in his case, with more anxiety than anger. When asked to affirm his faith in transubstantiation, he replied that the doctrine as usually formulated 'was too gross, and could not well be excused from the opinion of the Capernaites', who had thought that the sacrament was a form of cannibalism. His Catholic friends, anxious to prove his orthodoxy, rephrased the question more delicately. Did he agree that Christ's body was received in the mouth?

> He paused and did hold his peace a little space, and shortly after he spoke, saying: 'I will not say so; I cannot tell; it is a hard question. But, surely,' saith he, 'we receive Christ in our soul by faith. When you speak of it other ways, it soundeth grossly, and savoureth of the Capernaites.'[29]

From a Catholic perspective, his faith was seeping away. From a Protestant one, he was at last seeing beyond crude, faithless literalism to the deeper, spiritual reality. It was the distinction, as George Herbert put it, between looking *at* glass or looking *through* it. Herbert, perhaps orthodox Protestantism's finest poet, was uncharacteristically blunt on the question of transubstantiation. Christ, he wrote, came 'to abolish Sin, not Wheat / . . . Flesh . . . cannot turn to soul. / Bodies and Minds are different Spheres'.[30] That *cannot* is the heart of the matter. To Catholic ears it is incredulity, binding God's omnipotence in the weak chains of human reason. To Protestants it is an insistence that the Catholic doctrine fundamentally misunderstands Christ's sacrifice and drags him down to the filth of humanity.

Protestants were just as ready as Catholics to claim that it was in fact *their* doctrine which transcended reason and could only be approached through faith. A bestselling early seventeenth-century book of sermons laid out the Calvinist doctrine of Christ's spiritual presence in the sacrament, adding: 'Unbelief cannot see how this should be effected: and therefore ignorant unbelieving Papists have invented a carnal manner of eating and drinking the body and blood of Christ.' Another bestselling handbook of sacramental devotion began with a diatribe against over-rationalisation that could have been lifted directly from a Catholic writer, insisting that to enquire into the manner of Christ's spiritual presence is to be 'overwitted in seeking or doubting', leads into 'a labyrinth of doubts', and fosters incredulity and (of course) the error of the Capernaites.[31]

This was more than just knockabout fun. The accusation of incredulity was an invaluable way of explaining why your arguments had failed to persuade the other side. It was not because they were idiots who could not follow a line of reasoning. It was because they were fools, who were saying in their hearts that there is no God – even if they did not realise the fact. Your dispute was therefore not fundamentally about doctrine or interpretation. It was about your opponents' carnal inability to see the ravishing spiritual vision which was before your own eyes. Defined that way, you could lay claim to an effortless superiority while simultaneously closing down any possibility of further argument. And so the pursuit of ever more authentic faith generated constant accusations of unbelief.

If Protestants diagnosed Catholics as incredulous, Catholics were quick to mock Protestant credulity when they had the chance. In one case, the fire consuming a Protestant martyr smoked a pair of pigeons out of their nest, so that they flew over the stake. The dying man saw them and cried out that the Holy Spirit had descended as a dove. His Catholic denouncers were quick to ask: 'What blasphemy is this, such opinionative fools to believe or credit such fancies?' It is part of true faith to know when not to believe.[32]

Such Catholic attacks focused on one issue above all. Protestants took their stand on the Bible, which naturally raised the question of how they knew that the Bible was in fact the inspired Word of God. Protestants were surprisingly reluctant to address this issue directly. This is not because their convictions on the subject were shaky, but because their position depended ultimately, not on arguments, but on faith: an intuitive recognition of God's Word which, like reason itself, was in the end incommunicable.[33] To claim that you accept the Bible because the Holy Spirit tells you to is to accuse anyone who disagrees with you of not receiving that divine message, and so of unbelief. Catholics were quick to return the compliment.

In the hands of Catholic polemicists like the French Jesuit François Veron, the argument was brutally effective. So, the Holy Spirit teaches you that the Bible is the word of God? Does this inner conviction extend equally to all sixty-six books of the Old and New Testament? To every chapter and verse of them? And to nothing else? Does the Spirit then guide your understanding of it? If so, why do so many other readers interpret it differently? If not, how can it be that the Spirit authorises Scripture but leaves it opaque? And what about the textual glitches and variations between different manuscripts of the Bible? Which is the inspired version? How can you be sure? Has the Spirit told you that too? The purpose of this Catholic argument was of course not to dismiss the Bible, but to prove that the Bible's authority ultimately derived from the Church, and therefore that all Christians ought to submit themselves to that Church rather than to their own judgement or sense of inner inspiration. But it was much easier to demolish Protestants' claims about the Bible than to establish Catholic ones in their place. Protestants were not wrong to worry that this supposedly pro-Catholic argument in fact tended to 'the overthrow of all Religion'.[34]

All's fair in religious polemic, and we should not take outraged accusations of unbelief too seriously. But this much is true: the Reformation era's battle for credulity was a high-wire act. To attack your opponents' doctrines as nonsensical and an affront to reason, while defending your own as incomprehensible and transcending reason, was a heady, exhilarating and dangerous rhetorical achievement. All sides in the Reformation debates were encouraging both credulity and a corrosive scepticism, teaching believers simultaneously to doubt and to loathe doubting. Scepticism was now not the opposite of faith, but a necessary component of it.

'Doubt Wisely': From Innocence to Experience

Catholics and Protestants wrote about one another as if they were different species. The reality was much more frightening. They were the same people, and they were liable to convert from one to the other. Every Protestant of the first generation had been raised a Catholic. Battle lines hardened thereafter, but conversions in all directions continued. The Reformation offered believers a religious choice. Most did not want such a thing and stuck to the faith in which they had been raised, but even that was a choice. For Christians who had grown up knowing that *choosing* is what heretics do, to be forced to choose was itself profoundly disturbing.

In 1565, the Protestant preacher Pierre Viret described some alarming people he had met in southern France. 'Since the abuses of false religion were demonstrated to them, they judge both the true and the false in the same way and despise them both as if all was merely the dreams and reveries of the human mind.' These people, who called themselves 'deists' – the earliest known use of that word – had a clear hierarchy of truth. Catholics, they said, were blind; Protestants, one-eyed; and they themselves were 'deniaisez'. The word has a double meaning. As well as 'enlightened' or 'educated', it can mean 'deflowered' or 'sexually experienced'.[35] These people were serial converts, whose 'education' in unbelief consisted of the multiple religions through which they had passed. Their enlightenment had cost them their religious virginity, and they could not go back even if they wanted to. Viret's account is a picture of the Reformation as a journey from innocence to experience. It implies that the battle for credulity was ultimately fought, not only angrily, between competing religious parties, but anxiously, within individuals. Three contrasting examples – one French, two English – can show us how that battle could play out.

Our first character was almost the first person to look the emerging crisis of credulity dead in the eye: the wry, teasing nobleman Michel de Montaigne, who wrote his *Essays* in genteel retirement while his beloved France was stretched on the rack of religious civil war. Nothing riled him more than the 'crowd of everyday chroniclers and interpreters of God's purposes' who recklessly conscripted God to their own cause without even properly understanding it. Self-styled Catholics and Protestants rushed to soak the land in one another's blood, but 'how many men are there who can proudly claim to have mastered in detail the reasons and fundamental positions of both sides?' Most religion, he feared, was actually habit, ignorance and prejudice.[36]

Sentiments like these have given Montaigne a persistent reputation for atheism, despite his outward profession of Catholicism. Pascal, another Catholic who wrestled with doubt at close quarters, revered Montaigne's style and could not stop himself from quoting him, but sharply criticised his 'completely pagan views'.[37] It is true that the *Essays* are – for the most part – astonishingly secular. Montaigne cites the Bible occasionally, but much less than Lucretius or other ancient pagans. God rates an occasional passing mention, but so too do Fate and 'mother-like' Nature, and all of them are treated as metaphorical abstractions. The essay 'To Philosophise is to Learn How to Die' does say, in passing, that 'death is the origin of another life', but its main thrust is that we ought to take comfort in death's absolute finality. 'Do you not know', he imagines Nature saying to those who fear death, 'that in real death there will be no second You, living to lament your death and standing by your corpse. "You" will not desire the life which now you so much lament . . . Death does not concern you, dead or alive; alive, because you are: dead, because you are no more.'[38] Lucretius would have applauded.

Montaigne was in truth no atheist, and it takes some very selective quotation to make him seem so, but neither was his Catholicism simple and straightforward. He admitted that as a young man he had been drawn to Protestantism, lured by 'an ambition to share in the hazards and hardships attendant upon that fresh young enterprise'. Many years later, some friends were convinced that he was still a Protestant 'deep down inside'. He indignantly denied it, but he admitted that he found some Catholic practices 'rather odd or rather empty'. He made fun of his fellow believers, finding it ridiculous, for example, that Catholic armies treated victory as vindication from God but refused to see defeat as vindication for their enemies. In a famous essay on the cannibals of the New World, he argued that only parochial prejudice convinced Europeans that they were civilised and indigenous Americans were barbarians. Torturing and burning heretics is not obviously nobler than cooking and eating people. And, he added, astonishingly, 'there is more barbarity in eating a man alive than in eating him dead'. Since eating living people was not commonplace in sixteenth-century France, Montaigne can only have been referring to one thing: the Mass, in which Catholics believe they are consuming the literal human body of their living Saviour. It is the kind of remark that normally came from enraged Protestants. A Catholic who could say that was, to put it mildly, capable of impressive imaginative detachment from his own beliefs.[39]

This has left historians to conclude that Montaigne was 'at best . . . probably mildly religious', as if his faith was a habit he had never quite bothered to break.[40] But there is something more interesting going on here. The driving force of Montaigne's thought was philosophical scepticism: the argument, exemplified by the ancient Greek philosopher Sextus Empiricus, that no certain knowledge of any kind at all is possible. Montaigne, like many others who rediscovered these arguments in the Renaissance age, was deeply affected by them. For Montaigne, it became a rule 'not to believe too rashly: not to disbelieve too easily', and above all not to rely on 'that fine brain of yours'. 'There is a plague on Man,' he warned: 'his opinion that he knows something.' One of Montaigne's best-known lines – 'When I play with my cat, how do I know that she is not passing time with me rather than I with her?' – is more than just an animal lover's whimsy. He dwelt on how animal we humans are, and traced our worst faults to our deluded conviction that we are capable of transcending that status and attaining true knowledge or wisdom. Instead we should remember that 'upon the highest throne in the world, we are seated, still, upon our arses'. If we search for certainty on any subject, he warned, we will at length discover that 'it is impossible to find two opinions which are exactly alike, not only in different men but in the same men at different times'. No truth is ever definitively established. For example, he chose a lively current dispute: does the sun circle the earth, or vice versa? It is not only that there were cogent arguments on both sides. But 'for all we know, in a thousand years' time another opinion will overthrow them both'.[41]

Such corrosive scepticism looks pretty atheistic, and there is no doubt that philosophical scepticism could stir up deeply troubling religious anxieties. We do not know why the French courtier-scholar Bonaventure des Périers took his own life in 1544, but we do know he had drunk deeply from the sceptics. One student who discovered Sextus Empiricus in Cambridge in the early seventeenth century remembered being so 'disquieted' that he even wondered if the entire visible world 'were any more than a mere Phantasm or

Imagination', and spent some time caught in 'these troublesome Labyrinths'.[42]

But while scepticism was dizzying, most of those who sampled it ultimately recovered their balance. A doctrine which makes God and the material world equally unknowable is in the end neither very practical nor very dangerous. Short of suicide or madness, we have no choice but to find a way of dealing with the material world that our senses report to us. If that kind of uncertainty can be managed, then religious uncertainty can be too. As Pascal put it, when we are awake, 'we know that we are not dreaming'. We cannot prove the fact, but that merely demonstrates 'the weakness of our reason, and not the uncertainty of all knowledge'. He argued that perfect scepticism is both impossible in practice ('nature backs up helpless reason and stops it going so wildly astray') and a logical contradiction ('it is not certain that everything is uncertain').[43]

Indeed, with a little nimble footwork, scepticism could be finessed into an argument *for* Catholic orthodoxy. Montaigne himself showed the way. Once you have accepted that your own reason 'always hobbles, limps and walks askew', that it is 'a two-handled pot: you can grab it from the right or the left', you are forced to look beyond it:

> As I do not have the capacity for making a choice myself, I accept Another's choice and remain where God put me. Otherwise I would not know how to save myself from endlessly rolling. And thus, by God's grace, without worry or a troubled conscience, I have kept myself whole, within the ancient beliefs of our religion, through all the sects and schisms that our century has produced.[44]

You may or may not find a particular doctrine credible. But your opinion has no bearing on whether it is actually true. 'It is madness to judge the true and the false from our own capacities.' Instead, we need to look outside ourselves entirely, and for Montaigne that meant looking to 'the holy teachings of the Church Catholic, Apostolic and Roman, in which I die and in which I was born'. Nor could he embrace those teachings with reservations or doubts. 'We must either totally submit to the authority of our ecclesiastical polity or else totally release ourselves from it.' The very fact that he was so beset with doubts showed why he must submit his own feeble reason to the eternal certainties of the Catholic faith once revealed to the apostles and maintained faithfully in France for over a thousand years:

> Our religion did not come to us through reasoned arguments or from our own intelligence: it came to us from outside authority, by commandments. That being so, weakness of judgement helps us more than strength; blindness, more than clarity of vision.[45]

So scepticism is not the bedrock of atheism. It is the solvent of all our pretensions to knowledge, and therefore the necessary beginning of any true faith.

This gambit, which came to be called *fideism*, was weaponised against Protestantism by Montaigne's successors. The method was to weigh the utter emptiness of what humans can know against the fullness of what God has revealed. If all human certainties crumble to dust, what alternative is there but to cling to the rock of the Church?[46] The argument could prove devastatingly effective. But it did not answer doubts; it simply bypassed them. And as our second character shows, it was a game which Protestants could play too.

William Chillingworth should have been an uncomplicated man: born in Protestant England, raised as a scholar in Oxford, godson to a future archbishop of Canterbury. As a student in the 1620s, he proved an exceptionally skilled debater. Unfortunately, he was an intense young man given to 'sleeping too little, and thinking too much', and took his academic games to heart. He 'much delighted in Sextus Empiricus', and scepticism soaked into his bones. From the realisation that there are two sides to every question, he eventually 'contracted such an irresolution and habit of doubting, that by degrees he grew confident of nothing, and a sceptic, at least, in the greatest mysteries of faith'. In 1629, these mounting anxieties erupted into a crisis. He converted to Catholicism, and enrolled in a seminary for English Catholic exiles in France. It was a bold decision, whose most likely consequence would be lifelong exile. He did it, he later recalled, in a desperate search for certainty. Catholic arguments had made him doubt that there was any sure and reliable truth to be found in Protestantism, and so he sought it in the bosom of the church of Rome. It was a textbook example of how Catholic fideism was supposed to bring Protestants to their knees.[47]

Within months, however, Chillingworth was back in England, having found that the supposedly solid rock of the church of Rome was, for him, no firmer underfoot than the mire of Protestantism. The reality of seventeenth-century Catholicism – its insistence on suppressing rather than discussing scruples and awkward questions, and its exuberantly baroque piety which gave no quarter to austere Protestant sensibilities – was shockingly different from the idealised universal Church which the fideists described. But Chillingworth did not slot back happily into Protestantism. For as much as five years, he was 'doubting between communions'. His godfather William Laud, by then bishop of London, conferred patiently with him, but by 1632 he still believed that Chillingworth was in need of 'conversion'. Chillingworth's own plan to resolve his crisis, characteristically, was to write a book thrashing it out. He apparently swore an oath before Laud to withdraw from communion with *either* church for two years. He claimed that this was so that the planned book would appear impartial, but he was plainly also buying time for his own indecision. This was still his situation in 1634, when Lady Falkland,

Catholic matriarch of a religiously mixed family, hired Chillingworth to be a tutor to her daughters. She believed that he was still a Catholic and would bolster the younger women in that faith. Instead, Chillingworth encouraged them to explore their doubts. He told them that Catholicism was 'founded on lies', and explained that his conversion had been because of 'the unsoundness of Protestant religion . . . and not the truth of the Catholic'. He mused to them that 'if a third way were opened, the Catholics would have no less to do to defend themselves than the Protestants'. Unsurprisingly, the scandalised Lady Falkland threw him out.[48]

In 1635, Chillingworth finally conformed to his godfather's church once again. By the time the long-awaited book was published in 1638, it had evolved into an anti-Catholic polemic, titled *The Religion of Protestants a Safe Way to Salvation*. But the 'Protestantism' he was defending was distinctly odd. He had told the Falkland girls that his imagined third alternative to Catholicism and Protestantism, which he called simply 'Christian', would fit better in the Protestant than the Catholic Church – not because Protestantism's doctrines were truer, but simply because it was 'not . . . so strait-laced'. That seems to have been the spirit in which he eventually conformed. His book firmly rejected the Catholic fideists' claim to find infallible authority in the Church, but despite the book's most famous line – 'The BIBLE, I say, The BIBLE only is the Religion of Protestants!' – he was not simply setting another infallible authority in the Church's place. Instead, he had concluded that the infallibility which the hard men of both faiths claimed to offer was an illusion, and was trying to deal with the fact.[49]

The book's argument falls into two dangerously unbalanced halves. His attack on the Catholic fideists' claim that their Church was infallible and immune to scepticism is devastatingly effective. But he was much less successful in building up his own side of the case than at demolishing his opponents'. How can we be certain that the Bible is God's Word? He could only answer this question by redefining *certainty*, in line with the latest Dutch rationalist philosophy. We cannot, he admitted, be certain of the Bible's authority in the same way we can be certain of a mathematical theorem or even of an established scientific fact. Since we are asking historical questions about a specific book, certainty of that kind simply is not possible. So we can be 'certain enough, morally certain, as certain as the nature of the thing will bear'. This 'moral certainty' is the certainty with which juries send criminals to be hanged; or, in another much-cited example, the certainty with which you know who your own parents are. It is not absolute certainty, but certainty beyond a reasonable doubt.[50]

In one extraordinary passage in the book's preface, Chillingworth tells his Catholic opponents that if their arguments, 'weighed in an even balance . . . would have turned the scale, and have made your Religion more credible then the contrary; certainly I should . . . with both mine arms and all my heart most readily have embraced it'.[51] There is a juddering, grinding gear change in the middle of that sentence. At the start he is talking about the most finely balanced of reasoned judgements, made according to the balance of probabilities, which can be tipped by a hair: one of the two religious alternatives might emerge looking fractionally more likely than the other. But having made such a carefully weighed judgement, he then promises to embrace whichever conclusion he reaches with 'all my heart'. Give him 51 per cent confidence that you are correct, and he will give you 100 per cent commitment.

It is plain enough why he ended up in this bizarre position. He wanted to give 100 per cent commitment, because that is what Christians do. But he no longer believed that much more than 51 per cent certainty could be had. He had been playing theological beggar-my-neighbour, ensuring that everyone else's religious arguments were left looking as fragile as his own, and was making the miserable best of what was left. It is no surprise that when Chillingworth died only six years later, at the age of forty-one, the minister who attended him in his last sickness was appalled. Having failed to persuade the dying Chillingworth into a more conventional Protestantism, he presided at the funeral, and buried a copy of Chillingworth's book with him, saying, 'Get thee gone then, thou cursed book . . . that thou mayest rot with thy author, and see corruption.'[52]

By then England's reading public had been introduced by our third character to another unnerving model of how to be a Protestant in a world of religious uncertainty: less agonised than Chillingworth, subtler, and much more charming. Sir Thomas Browne's *Religio Medici*, an instant bestseller on its publication in 1642, was a sly meditation on Christianity from a physician's perspective. Browne, whom we met briefly in the previous chapter, was by now a more or less orthodox Protestant, but he had taken an unorthodox route. He began by admitting that 'the general scandal of my profession, the natural course of my studies, [and] the indifferency of my behaviour, and discourse in matters of Religion' would make it reasonable to guess he had no religion. And yet 'I dare, without usurpation, assume the honourable style of a Christian'. It was hardly the conventional bold declaration of willingness to live and die in the true faith. That lack of convention was very deliberate. Browne was not, he wanted his readers to know, one of Montaigne's unthinking partisans. His religion was not a matter of habit: he had actively chosen it. 'The rules of my Religion' were drawn, not from any particular church, but from 'the dictates of my own reason'. If this was not unsettling enough, he added that reason had once led him to doubt the immortality of the soul and the existence of Hell. He had now left these errors behind him, but he continued to believe that Christian orthodoxy was beset with 'sturdy doubts, and boisterous objections'. Some of the Bible's stories 'exceed the fables of Poets'. How, he asked, did Noah fit all the world's animals, plus six weeks' fodder, into a 300-cubit ark? After the Flood, how did the animals come to be dispersed across the world so quickly, not least to the Americas? It is difficult, he says, to answer such questions without 'the refuge of a miracle': his distaste for supernatural explanations is palpable.[53] This does not sound much like a defence of the true faith.

But Browne was no atheist. He was a post-atheist: a believer who had returned to faith after a dalliance with unbelief, and had been changed by the experience. Browne's readers could be reassured by the fact that he had ended up a more-or-less orthodox Christian, but he had picked up some disturbing notions on the way. The reason he listed all these objections was not to refute them, but to celebrate how hard they made true faith. 'Methinks there be not impossibilities enough in Religion for an active faith . . . I love to lose myself in a mystery.' To believe something because you are convinced of it by reason 'is not faith, but persuasion'. He eventually conquered his doubts, not with reasoned arguments, but 'on my knees', in prayer. He came to be convinced that true faith is 'to believe a thing not only above, but contrary to reason, and against the arguments of our proper senses'. This is neither ridiculous nor even anti-rational. A faith which claimed to be transcendent but was in fact entirely comprehensible by human reason would be self-evidently false. Instead, Browne had arrived at a fully Protestant version of fideism, which made the impossibility of reasoned certainty into a virtue. He even had the nerve to cite Tertullian's dangerous principle: 'it is certain because it is impossible'.[54]

The brutal religious conflicts of the Reformation era did not in fact reduce Christendom's faith to rubble. Courageous, independent-minded individuals like Montaigne, Chillingworth and Browne were not driven into atheism, for all that they were intensely aware that simple, unreflective acceptance of universal truths was no longer possible. People like them who wanted to hold on to their faith could find serious, honest, intellectually rigorous and emotionally satisfying ways to do so. There was

Montaigne's surrender to uncertainty: accept that once you have doubted everything, including your own doubts, there is nothing left but to embrace the ancient faith. There is Chillingworth's armed truce with uncertainty: recognise that absolute truth is beyond our grasp, and resolve to make the best of the shaky and partial truths which our shaky and partial minds can grasp. Or there is Browne's joyful embrace of uncertainty: believe all the more strongly precisely because faith is out of the reach of human reason.

The poet John Donne, a convert to Protestantism who never left his cradle Catholicism entirely behind him, observed that his age's religious dilemmas did not have simple answers. Should you, for example, 'adore, or scorn' an image such as a crucifix, or indeed – a potent word – 'protest' at it? Those answers 'may all be bad'. His advice in such a predicament was to

> . . . Doubt wisely; in strange way
> To stand inquiring right, is not to stray;
> To sleep, or run wrong, is. On a huge hill,
> Cragged and steep, Truth stands, and he that will
> Reach her, about must and about must go,
> And what the hill's suddenness resists, win so.[55]

Montaigne, Chillingworth and Browne had done it. Instead of being consumed by their anxieties, they had doubted wisely, picked their way gingerly up the cragged and steep path, and found their way, if not to the summit, at least to secure and level ground. But not every believer in post-Reformation Europe was such a skilled mountaineer. Anyone who tried to follow them quickly discovered that the climb demanded nimble footwork and a cool head. It is perfectly possible to keep your balance when out on a precipice, trying to seize hold of scepticism and bend it to your own purposes while the battle for credulity swirls around you – so long as you don't look down.

For such mountaineers, there is no going back. You may survive doubt and anxiety, but you will be changed by them. Witness the apparent absence of Christianity from most of Montaigne's writings. This is not a sign that he was a closet atheist, as is sometimes suggested. It is explained in his remarkable essay 'On Prayer', in which he tells us almost in passing that he prayed the Lord's Prayer many times each day and that he 'continually' crossed himself. But in the same essay he deplored habits such as singing the Psalms around the household, so that 'the Sacred Book of the holy mysteries of our faith [is] dragged about through hall or kitchen', or routinely reading the Bible – 'it is not a story to be told but a story to be reverenced, feared, adored'. Perhaps these claims, like his argument that most people are too ready to thoughtlessly invoke the name of God without amending their lives, were mendacious attempts at self-defence, although it is not at all clear why he deserves such suspicion. But the essay goes further than that, explaining why his own writings are so conspicuously devoid of religious references. Theology, he argues, is a high mystery and ought to be honoured as such. Mere 'humanists' (that ambiguous word again) such as himself should not aspire to theology, and theologians should not stoop to the level of humanists:

> The language of men has its own less elevated forms and must not make use of the dignity, majesty and authority of the language of God. [When] I myself . . . say . . . fortune, destiny, accident, good luck, bad luck, the gods and similar phrases . . . I am offering my own human thoughts as human thoughts . . . matters of opinion not matters of faith.

He avoids God-talk, he says, not because he despises it but because he reveres it. We ought not to be too quick to prayer, he suggests, since we cannot often put our hearts into a prayerful attitude. He even wonders if 'a decree forbidding anyone to write about religion', priests excepted, would be just and prudent – 'as perhaps would one requiring me too to hold my peace on the subject'.[56] Which he thereafter proceeds to do.

He was not alone. If Montaigne stayed above the fray of France's religious wars, his contemporary Jean Bodin did not. Bodin studied in Calvinist Geneva and married a Protestant, swore loyalty to Catholic orthodoxy when teaching law in Paris, was imprisoned for suspected heresy, served as an ambassador to Protestant England, narrowly escaped being murdered by Catholic rioters in Paris, served both the Catholic and Protestant sides in the terrible wars of the 1590s, and at his death in 1596 sought, and was granted, Catholic burial. What faith he was able to hold on to amid this confusion remains unclear: he once observed that wishing to return to a religion you have abandoned was like a eunuch aspiring to be whole again. That line is from a book he wrote in the 1580s but dared not publish. *The Colloquium of the Seven* is a dialogue whose seven characters represent the three major Christian confessions, plus a Jew, a Muslim, a Platonist and a philosophical sceptic. It is a strange, meandering, slippery book, much of it focused on Bodin's peculiar scientific and demonological interests. It is unclear which, if any, of the characters speak for Bodin himself – it is often argued that he is most sympathetic to the Jew. If the book as a whole teaches a lesson, it is that pluralism, toleration and civilised debate are better than hatred and warfare. But occasionally the characters unite to agree on a point. 'Is it proper for a good man to discuss religions?' the Catholic asks. 'It is better to be silent altogether than to speak rashly about the holiest matters', replies the Platonist. 'Conversation about religion has always seemed dangerous to me', adds the Jew: 'it is a serious offence to speak about God in any way other than with dignity'. The sceptic agrees it is wrong to disturb old pieties with a vain attempt to search for truth. Only the Lutheran cautiously ventures that educated men might be allowed to discuss religion, in private. It appears that Bodin, whose own piety was unorthodox but who certainly loathed atheism, believed that discretion was sometimes the better part of faith.[57]

Half a century later and on the cusp of another religious civil war, Sir Thomas Browne agreed. Although he advanced his own religious views, he also warned against staking out too bold a position. 'Every man is not a proper Champion for Truth.' You may be sure you are on God's side, but in debate as in battle, victory does not always go to those who deserve it. This, he said, is why he dealt with his own doubts as he did: 'I do forget them, or at least defer them, till my better settled judgement . . . be able to resolve them.' Rather than striking out on his own in search of the truth, 'I love to keep the road.'[58]

Do we believe these convenient explanations for apparent godlessness – that these men's lack of ostentatious piety arose more from scrupulous reverence than from blank indifference? For myself I do, since they were not compelled to make any of these claims: but the matter is certainly open to question. When Montaigne justified his argument against frequent prayer by citing a classical pagan, Xenophon, maybe he was exemplifying his principles, or maybe he was discreetly signalling that it was all an act. None of us can ever know; nor does it really matter, for the practical result is the same either way. Take these sceptics and post-sceptics entirely at their word, and accept that as a matter of conscience they were withdrawing their faith reverently from the brutal public turmoil of their age, and building it a cloister where it could enjoy a peaceful and honoured separation from the rest of their lives. The effect was still that God was newly absent from the everyday world. Contemporaries had a word for that absence, however piously it was intended: 'atheism'.

3

The Atheist's Comedy

Faustus: Come, I think hell's a fable.
Mephistopheles: Ay, think so still, till experience change thy mind.

Christopher Marlowe, Doctor Faustus

By the early seventeenth century, it was generally agreed, Europe was drowning under a rising tide of atheism. The French Protestant statesman Philippe du Plessis-Mornay wrote *Of the Truth of the Christian Religion* (1581) – the first major book devoted explicitly to attacking atheism – because he felt there was an unprecedented crisis. 'In this wretched time,' he lamented, 'ungodliness . . . hath been so bold as to step into the pulpit, and to belch out blasphemies against God.' The readers who bought at least thirty-seven editions of his book in six languages evidently agreed.[1] An English scholar in 1599 lugubriously invited his readers to 'consider how Atheism doth daily prevail among men, yea, far more than it did amongst either the superstitious papists, or the idolatrous heathen . . . Nowadays, few do make any account of religion or of the worship of God'. The author of England's first homegrown anti-atheist tract explained, with disarming directness, that he had chosen to write against atheism simply because 'there are many Atheists'. One of his successors lamented living amid 'this generation that deny God'.[2] By the mid-seventeenth century, a level-headed commentator could write:

The state of the controversy then is this: which of the parties is in the wisest way? The Atheist thinks that the Religious is a fool; the Religious, that he is a fool that saith in his heart there is no God; the Atheist, that the souls of men are mortal, as the souls of beasts; the Religious, that the Atheist is a beast to say so, etc.[3]

Never mind the arguments on either side; listen to the weary familiarity with which he describes an apparently equal division into two well-established factions.

We should not, however, take this surge of fear at face value. It is true that the seeds of atheism had already been present in the soil of medieval Europe, and that the Reformation then cultivated them. But Christian preaching lends itself to anguished denunciations of sin, to laments about the unprecedented evils of the speaker's own times, and to contrasts between the godless majority and the small remnant of the holy. Many of the same preachers who were worked up about the spread of atheism were equally exercised by the spread of witchcraft. Rhetorical devices and excitable outbreaks of moral panic are not the same as sober reporting.[4]

What these panickers offer us is a set of caricatures and stereotypes: the imagined atheists who haunted post-Reformation Europe. These caricatures are worth our attention, and not simply because they are readily accessible, while real unbelievers were of necessity more discreet. The very fact that these invented atheists were imaginary means they can tell us not only about the real doubters on whom they were modelled, but also about the fears and preconceptions of the culture which imagined them. And that will matter when we look beneath the caricatures to see how they reflected, shaped and – in important ways – completely missed the truth.

Incest, Thunder and Wishful Thinking

Some descriptions of 'atheism' do not ask to be taken seriously. In 1647, there was an outbreak of plague in Ayr, in south-western Scotland. The local minister organised a very Presbyterian response: a six-day festival of repentance. Each of the town's trade societies met to prepare public confessions of their sins, hoping to turn aside God's wrath, vying with one another to make the most fulsome declarations. On 15 September, it was the turn of the town's merchants. Most of the sins they came up with were pretty routine: Sabbath-breaking, idleness, sharp dealing. But they added a new one that none of the other guilds had thought of. Some of the merchants 'acknowledged their atheism, that for a long time they lived and knew not whether there was a God or no, esteeming two pennies of gain more than the seeking of God's word'.

There is considerably less to this than meets the eye. To say that they 'knew not' whether there was a God plainly means, not that they consciously entertained serious doubts on the subject, but that they did not care; or rather, that they sometimes did not attend to God very closely. They were more interested in profit than in sermons – which is not terribly surprising for merchants. This was not an earnest confession: it was a stroke of genius. In the competitive arena of public self-flagellation, the merchants had found a way to give their bland sins a dramatic edge. The next group of penitents, the sailors, took the hint. As the first order of business in their confession, 'they acknowledged atheism, unbelief and that plague of hardness of the heart among all of them to abound'.[5]

Atheism was here a hyperbolic code word for worldliness and run-of-the-mill sinfulness. This was how preachers used it: to try to shock their congregations, sunk in lax observance and petty wickedness, into recognising their true spiritual peril. If people truly believed there was a God, one preacher asked in 1643, 'were it possible for them to live as they live, and to do what they do?' A sinner who claims to believe is, according to the poet and preacher John Donne, 'an Atheist everywhere, but in his Catechisme'. Stretch this only a little, and you have the argument that 'he that never prays in secret', or anyone who does not frequently think of the Last Judgement, or anyone who relies on practical effort rather than prayer, or anyone who 'place[s] his affections upon anything in the world more than upon God', or even anyone who is unwilling to risk death for the sake of faith, 'is a very Atheist'. One preacher even extended this to anyone who knowingly commits any kind of sin. 'O man, thou that thinkest God sees not thy works, thou art an Atheist.' This is all good clean rhetorical fun, but it stretches the term *atheist* so far that it loses its elastic entirely.[6]

Still, in their exaggerated way, these preachers were onto something. Belief or unbelief is more than a matter of formal credal profession. Montaigne made this point mercilessly:

> Some people make the world believe that they hold beliefs they do not hold. A great number make themselves believe it, having no idea what 'believing' really means . . . If we believed in God . . . and knew him just as we believe historical events or one of our companions, then we would love him above all things . . . The best among us does not fear to offend him as much as offending neighbour, kinsman, master.[7]

In part this is a theological point. True faith is not something that can be achieved by an effort of the will. It is a gift, which God either bestows or withholds. As historians are now recognising, the early modern age endured a crisis of belief as well as of unbelief. Christians of all kinds were being asked, and were asking themselves, whether their 'beliefs' were wavering opinions, lazy assumptions, heartfelt convictions or true faith founded on rock.[8] Set against that daunting standard, the only conclusion must be that a great many people do not truly believe what they believe they believe. It could even be hard to believe that you yourself believe what you believe you believe. And by the time you are worrying about that, you are already caught inside a self-referential hall of mirrors, from which the only obvious escape is to dismiss the whole thing as ridiculous – which is the archetypal response of the unbeliever. In other words, if you have too high or idealistic a definition of *belief*, you turn everyone, including yourself, into an unbeliever.

The preachers' expansive definition of atheism also made sense on a more pragmatic level. The basic logic is perfectly sound. If people act in ways that flagrantly violate the beliefs they profess, presumably those beliefs are not very deeply held. Hence the core 'fact' which everyone 'knew' about atheists in the early modern period: that they were moral monsters, creatures of utter depravity enslaved to their lusts, who had either abandoned their faith in order to wallow in sin, or had become so sunk in sin that they had lost hold of their faith. We should not necessarily believe this grotesquely self-serving caricature. But we should follow its scent.

In 1611, the English playwright Cyril Tourneur published *The Atheist's Tragedy*. The printed version's title page claims that it had 'often been acted' in 'divers places', but in fact we have no direct evidence that it was ever staged anywhere in the world until the 1990s. And for good reason. It is not one of the jewels of the age of Shakespeare. The plot mostly rollicks along merrily enough, helped by a slew of engagingly filthy jokes. But the wheels come off in Act IV, as virtually the play's entire cast converge independently on the same churchyard on the same night, mostly intent on murder, seduction or both, and spend a lengthy scene missing each other, bumping into each other and passing around the same increasingly implausible disguise. If you make it through this with a straight face, the play's concluding trial scene awaits you. After a convoluted set of claims and counter-claims, the play's hero decides, for no very good reason, to submit to being beheaded. D'Amville, the eponymous and villainous atheist, takes it on himself to act as executioner. However, the printed stage direction tells us that 'as he raises up the Axe, [he] strikes out his own brains'. He dies, but not before delivering an improving little speech of repentance in which he confesses to his various crimes and admits that 'there is a power above . . . that hath overthrown the pride of all my projects'. Some stage tragedies of the era delivered a bleak and harrowing realism; not this one.[9]

What it did deliver, in D'Amville (the name means 'evil-spirited'), was a distillation of the age's stereotypes about atheism. The play begins with D'Amville and his henchman discussing the nature of humanity. They swiftly decide that we are no different from animals and that death is the end for us. In which case, D'Amville concludes 'that pleasure only flows / Upon the stream of riches', and rejects any notion of morality. 'Let all men lose, so I increase my gain / I have no feeling of another's pain.' The rest of the play's action is driven by his fiendish plots to kill his brother and his nephew and seize their inheritance, and to seduce or rape the virtuous and beautiful Castabella. His designs on Castabella are especially villainous since he has already forced her to marry his own loath-some son. Therefore, when he propositions her, she protests that that would be incest. He replies: 'Incest? Tush, these distances affinity observes are articles of bondage cast upon our freedoms by our own subjections. Nature allows a gen'ral liberty of generation to all creatures else.' Humans ought to be able to copulate as freely as any animal.[10]

Incest would become a hallmark of the imaginary seventeenth-century atheist, and not by accident. According to early modern ethicists, we only know incest is wrong by God's commandment, not by nature or reason. By that logic atheists will naturally be drawn to incest, and the incestuous will naturally be drawn to atheism. But there was more to this than logic. Since early modern Europeans, like most human societies, loathed incest for reasons that they struggled to articulate, associating atheism with incest was more than a logical deduction; it was a powerfully effective scare tactic.[11] And so the incestuous atheist became a stock figure. A bestselling ballad first published around 1600 tells the shocking story of how one Jasper Coningham of Aberdeen tries to seduce his sister. When she warns him that Hell's 'quenchless flames of fire' are prepared for anyone who commits such a dreadful sin, he replies that both Heaven and Hell are 'devised fables / to keep poor fools in fear':

> . . . These things are nothing so:
> No God nor devil is biding, no Heaven nor Hell I know.
> All things are wrought by Nature, the earth, the air, and sky:
> There is no joy nor sorrow after that man doth die.
> Therefore let me have pleasure, while here I do remain:
> I fear not God's displeasure, nor Hell's tormenting pain.

No sooner has he spoken than he is struck down by fire from Heaven.[12]

By contrast, in John Ford's play *'Tis Pity She's a Whore* (1628), a brother and sister willingly give way to their incestuous lusts. In the final scene, as they face their imminent deaths, he declares that he no more believes in Heaven and Hell than he believes that water can burn. She protests, but he insists that it is 'a dream, a dream'.[13] If you found these literary inventions too fanciful, there was a classical exemplar: the emperor Caligula, 'a notable scorner and condemner of God', whose incest and other notorious crimes followed his atheism like the stench following a corpse.[14]

What made Caligula's story particularly juicy was another detail: despite all his blasphemous bluster, he was so terrified of thunder that he hid under his bed during storms. Thunder was as much a part of the cliché of atheism as was incest. It was proverbial in early modern times that thunder and lightning were a 'notorious and terrible' judgement from God. In a generally hushed world, thunder was the loudest noise most people ever heard, unless they were unlucky enough to be close to a cannon. 'Who heareth the thunder, that thinks not of God?' – it was a proverbial question that needed no answer. The pious huddled together during storms, 'full of terror', sublimating their fears with their prayers as they admitted to God that the thunder was 'but as a taste and touch of thy power'.[15] Even the impious could be shocked into temporary righteousness. 'Doth not every thunderclap constrain you to tremble at the blast of his voice?' one writer asked the godless. He added a cautionary tale of three soldiers out in a thunderstorm, which 'commonly . . . maketh the greatest Atheists to tremble'. One of them was foolhardy enough to fall to blaspheming, and was promptly killed by a falling tree.[16]

That was how stereotypical atheists dealt with thunderstorms: with brittle and usually short-lived bravado. Inevitably there is a thunderstorm scene in *The Atheist's Tragedy*, in which D'Amville tells his terrified sidekick that it is all 'a mere effect of nature'. In Sir Philip Sidney's *New Arcadia*, a wicked queen tries to corrupt her pious niece by claiming that all religion is merely 'foolish fear'. In ancient times, she explains, 'when they heard it thunder, not knowing the natural cause, they thought there was some angry body above that spake so loud'. In a more lowbrow dialogue published in 1608, the despicable Atheos is so panicked by thunder that, like Caligula, he dives under his bed. Then a tremulous voice issues from beneath the covers to explain it all away. It is merely, he explains, that the 'viscous vapours' in a cloud are condensed into a small solid stone, which is then violently expelled from the cloud like a cannonball. His claim that this is all merely natural is rather undermined when, as soon as he finishes speaking, another thunderclap strikes him dead.[17]

From these and a few other, equally ridiculous examples we can assemble the identikit early modern atheist. He is almost always male: women's unbelief certainly existed in reality, as we shall see, but not in the popular imagination. He is a figure of some wealth and social standing: ''tis nothing but plenty and abundance that maketh men Atheists'. He is educated, at least to some degree: 'a little or superficial taste of *Philosophy*, may perchance incline the Mind of Man to *Atheism*'. He is in good health, perhaps a 'young fool given over to . . . pleasure'. This is partly because his atheism is flimsy, a matter of bluster rather than conviction: he doubts his own doubts. 'Many would be *Atheists* if they could,' warned one preacher, 'but a secret whisper haunts and pursues them.'[18] 'Atheism,' Francis Bacon maintained, 'is rather in the *Lip*, than in the *Heart* of Man . . . Atheists will ever be talking of that their Opinion, as if they fainted in it, within themselves, and would be glad to be strengthened, by the Consent of others.'[19]

The atheist's 'armoury of arguments' against God are in truth an effort 'to fight against his own conscience'.[20] John Donne asked the atheist: if there is truly no God, who do you swear by, who do you cry out to in danger, who do you 'tremble at, and sweat under, at midnight'? Some preachers told atheists, with macabre relish, that one day they would discover for themselves that there truly was a Hell. Donne thought he could wrap the question up more quickly. Atheists might blaspheme boldly with their witty friends, but he asked them to wait 'but six hours . . . till midnight. Wake then; and then, dark and alone . . . remember that I asked thee now, Is there a God? and if thou darest, say No'.[21] In fact, Donne had no idea what atheists did alone in the dark. He simply took it for granted that no one could be truly convinced that there was no God, and therefore that atheists' consciences must gnaw at them like worms.

Most of these stereotypical 'atheists', however, had surprisingly little to say about whether or not there is a God. Their anti-religious positions were more immediate and pragmatic. Richard Hooker, the founding father of Anglican theology, picked out two doctrines which atheists denied 'above all': 'the authority of Scripture . . . and the soul's immortality'.[22] It is a pairing that will become familiar.

Pre-Reformation sceptics had choked on the miracle of transubstantiation, but in the post-Reformation world their stumbling block was the Bible. Our stereotypical atheists delight in posing 'unnecessary questions out of the Bible': do the dates in the book of Genesis add up? Where did Lazarus' soul go during the four days when he was dead? Sometimes these questions were pure mischief, the work of malicious prospectors panning the text for 'absurdities'. Sometimes they began as games, as quibblers played with unbelief to seem sophisticated. Either way, the result was the same. 'They who will not feed on the plain meat of his Word, [are] choked with the bones thereof.' It is hard to treat Scripture as a joke and still to believe it. This kind of sceptic, we read, began by tugging at textual niggles, then asked more fundamental questions about the text, then wondered if Scripture was the Word of God at all, 'till by degrees he came to be a very atheist, and to question whether there were a God or no'.[23]

But as D'Amville, Jasper Coningham and the medieval unbelievers we met in Chapter 1 show, the more fundamental issue was mortalism. Our stereotypical atheist maintained there was no Heaven or Hell; that the human soul was 'not eternal, but like a dog's soul'; or indeed that there was no such thing as a soul at all. These were metaphysical questions, but they were rarely addressed in those terms. A few of our imagined atheists attempted philosophical arguments against immortality, or simply 'puffe[d] out a little warm breath in scorn and derision, saying, there goeth my soul'. But their supposed denials were generally more pragmatic. Immortality and the prospect of God's judgement were, Hooker believed, the 'principal spurs and motives unto all virtue'. If your real reason for rejecting Christianity is that you want to shrug off Christian (or any) morals, then mortalism is the doctrine you need. And this, above all, was what respectable early modern people believed about the atheists who were infesting their society. Reason alone could never (it was axiomatic) lead honest souls to doubt immortality. But if you are enslaved by your lusts, you may become 'ambitious to be like the beasts that perish . . . well content to be annihilated'.[24] If you have despaired of Heaven, you will then be eager to dismiss Hell and damnation as 'trifles and mere old wives' tales', 'bugbears' used to frighten children. And the less certain you are that this is true, the more brazenly you will assert it to your comrades, and the more anxiously you will repeat it to yourself.[25]

So, in contemporary eyes, post-Reformation atheism was not really a doctrinal error. It was a form of wishful thinking. Men and (very occasionally) women whose lives were sufficiently easy and prosperous that they did not feel the need for God in this world, and who wanted to reject any constraints on their behaviour, preferred to imagine that there was no eternal judgement to fear, no inspired Scripture to obey and, ideally, no God to lay bare the secrets of their foolish hearts. And so the distinction between speculative and practical atheists – those who claim there is no God, and those who live as if they believed that – broke down. 'Men become first Atheists in their life and conversation,' argued one preacher, and 'wallow in their sins and sensuality'. But because they cannot avoid occasional thoughts of God, 'they become Atheists in their desire and affection, wishing that there were not a God to be avenged upon them for their wickedness; and in [the] end the Lord giveth them up to Atheism in their judgement and opinion'.[26]

It was proverbial that 'never was man that said, There was no God, but he wished it first'. Atheists 'could wish there were no God, or devil, as thieves would have no judge nor jailor'. And as one moralist pointed out, accurately enough: 'what we would have to be, we are apt to believe'.[27]

This leap from wish to conviction was natural, but it was also wilful, and therefore culpable. Unbelievers, one French anti-atheist claimed, had 'gouged out their own eyes expressly in order not to see God'. An English preacher argued that they had 'voluntarily, violently, extinguished to themselves' the light of divine revelation and natural reason alike, in order that 'they might prodigally act the works of darkness'.[28] Atheism was therefore an ethical rather than a philosophical stance. As such it did not threaten the moral economy of Christendom. Instead it reinforced it, by lining unbelief up with intolerable antisocial depravity. It was a most convenient conclusion. It meant that unbelief did not need to be listened to: merely condemned.

Shaking Off the Yoke

Should we believe a word of this? The atheist of preachers' and balladeers' imagination was a caricature. But as with most caricatures, we can catch glimpses of living people beneath them, and some at least of those glimpses will seem familiar.

England in 1592 was already facing a daunting series of foreign and domestic dangers when a new scandal erupted: rumours of a nest of atheists close to the heart of the state. The courtier-explorer Sir Walter Raleigh was accused of presiding over a 'school of atheism', luring young gentlemen into gatherings at which 'the Old and New Testament are jested at' and God himself mocked. The tang of atheism hung around Raleigh for the rest of his life. When he was convicted of treason in 1603, the judge urged him to renounce his 'blasphemous opinions', in particular his supposed denial of immortality, 'for if you think thus, you shall find there is eternity in hell fire'. Raleigh never admitted holding such beliefs, but he certainly owned, and may have translated, an extract from Sextus Empiricus' philosophy which was later published under the title *The Sceptick*. Even on the scaffold in 1618 he felt the need to insist, 'Never Atheist I, as is reported.' The reputation of the rest of his supposed 'school of night' was even more alarming.[29] A whole coven of them were allegedly plotting 'to draw her majesty's subiects to be Atheists . . . [and] after her majesty's decease to make a king among them-

selves and live according to their own laws'. One of th
they would soon convert so many English people that atl
outnumber Christians.[30] The scandal eventually provok
event: a full-scale legal inquiry, authorised by the cou
Commission, into atheism in and around Raleigh's esta
an unprecedented opportunity to see how the atheist
fear and rumour looked when dragged out into the cc
day.

The commissioners knew what they were looking for.
tions drawn up for witnesses asked about anyone who h
or spoken against . . . the being of any God . . . or wha
God is'; about denials of the world's creation, of God's p
of immortality, of Heaven and Hell, or of 'the truth of (
Word revealed to us in the Scriptures'. Over two days o
ings in March 1594 they heard from at least sixteen witi
as the testimony mounted, the allegations dissolved in
and contradiction. Plenty of witnesses agreed that 'Sir Walt
and his retinue are generally suspected of Atheism', but ge
rumours to hard evidence proved frustratingly difficult. A
minister reported that a parishioner had told him:

> There is a company about this town that say that Hell i
> other but poverty, and penury in this world; and Hea
> none other but to be rich, and enjoy pleasures; and tl
> die like beasts, and when we are gone there is no more re
> brance of us.

But when the man himself was hauled in, he claimed to ha
about these views from his brother, who had in turn on
about them from a preacher who was denouncing them. C
there was some excitement about Thomas Allen, the lieut
Portland Castle, whose atheism was 'generally reported by
everybody'. There were second-hand reports that he den

immortality of the soul, or that he had torn pages out of his Bible to dry tobacco on; but nothing direct. The most substantial allegation was that one of Allen's servants had insulted Moses and spoken 'in derogation of God and the scriptures'. It turned out that once, when drunk, the servant had grumbled about an overlong sermon and had become confused between Moses and King Solomon. The virtuous women whom he had shocked simply 'bade him go home to sleep'. None of this was a threat to Christendom.[31]

The most serious claims concerned a dinner at the house of a local knight, at which Sir Walter Raleigh and his elder brother Carew had allegedly denied the immortality of the soul. But it so happened that the minister they had been arguing with, Ralph Ironside, was now acting as the commission's secretary, and he was able to inform his colleagues that 'the matter was not as the voice of the country reported'. As he explained it, one guest at the dinner had reproached Carew Raleigh for his foul language, and Ironside had sententiously added that the wages of sin is death. Carew retorted that death comes to the good and the bad alike. Ironside replied that of course he meant the death of the soul. 'Soul,' said Carew; 'what is that?' Ironside tried to sidestep the trap, saying that it was more important to save your soul than to define it, but now Sir Walter intervened on his brother's side. He had studied at Oxford with great scholars, he said, but had never found a satisfactory answer to the question, 'what the reasonable soul of man is'. How did it relate to the brain, or to the heart? Ironside, put in the spotlight, tried first an Aristotelian definition, which Sir Walter rejected as 'obscure and intricate', and then a theological definition, which Sir Walter dismissed as a circular argument. Spirits, Ironside said at last, are beyond the reach of reason, like God himself. Sir Walter agreed that the two questions are alike, 'for neither could I learn hitherto what God is'. Ironside, now committed, ventured a definition of God: *ens entium*, one 'having being of himself'. 'Yea, but what is this *ens entium*, saith Sir Walter?' Ironside could only reply 'it is God'. Whereupon Sir Walter,

growing tired of his game, called for grace to be said to end the meal, 'for that . . . is better than this disputation'.[32]

The commission was wrapped up without any prosecutions. They had discovered, not a 'school of atheism', but a clique of loose-tongued young men whose soldiers' taste for danger extended to banter and debate. The Raleigh brothers did not deny the existence of the soul or of God. The questions of how to define those terms were real ones, on which scholars disagreed. But nor were the Raleighs holding a metaphysics seminar across the dining table. They were testing the limits of what they dared to say. And they were making mischief, using a difficult and dangerous question to tease a man who was both their educational and social inferior. They were playing games, and tweaking the noses of the self-important sobersides who disapproved. If there is a unifying note to all of this, it is not rejection of Christian doctrine. It is defiance: of any magistrate, churchman, monarch or God who might presume to tell these lords of the world how to speak and to live.

By 1594, one vital witness was beyond the commissioners' reach. The playwright Christopher Marlowe is now the most famous supposed atheist in Elizabethan England. One informant said that he had 'read the Atheist lecture to Sir Walter Raleigh and others' and was 'able to show more sound reasons for Atheism than any divine in England is able to give to prove divinity'.[33] It is certainly true that Marlowe was a member of Raleigh's circle, but his supposed atheism is a hall of mirrors. There is no hard evidence: only rumours, hints and conspiracies, and the texts of his plays and poems, most of which survive only in copies made after his death in 1593. One thing of which we can be reasonably confident is that Marlowe worked as an English spy during the late 1580s – in other words, that he was a man used to weaving deceits around himself, who had rivals and enemies with the same skills. But even with all those warnings in mind, it is still possible to spot some patterns.

No literary form is better suited to concealing the author's opinions than a play. We never hear the playwright's own voice, only the conflicting words given to the characters. And so Marlowe's choice of 'Machiavel' to introduce *The Jew of Malta* means nothing in itself.[34] Yet it is intriguing how often Marlowe's characters find themselves defying God. At the climax of *Tamburlaine*, the only one of Marlowe's plays published in his lifetime, the nominally Muslim hero orders the Qur'an burned, saying

> Now Mahomet, if thou have any power,
> Come down thyself and work a miracle.
> Thou art not worthy to be worshipped,
> That suffers flames of fire to burn the writ
> Wherein the sum of thy religion rests.

A Christian audience could only applaud. But in a century when so many Catholic images and Protestant Bibles had been burned, and so many men and women of both faiths had been martyred, all without an answering voice from Heaven, those lines might also give them pause. The most notorious of those mass martyrdoms, the St Bartholomew's Day Massacre in Paris in 1572, was the subject of another of Marlowe's plays. Marlowe depicts the villainous duke of Guise not as a papist fanatic but as a Machiavellian schemer who cynically exploits religion in the pursuit of wealth and power. 'Religion!' Guise says early in the play:

> Fie, I am ashamed, how ever that I seem,
> To think a word of such a simple sound,
> Of so great matter should be made the ground.[35]

A far more determined revolt against religion is the central theme of Marlowe's best-known play, *Doctor Faustus*, the dreadful cautionary tale of the scholar who sells his soul to the devil. Marlowe's Faustus is not a self-portrait, but he is, at least, a compelling depiction of a particular kind of unbeliever. In the opening scene, Faustus picks out contradictions in the Bible to argue that Christianity is ridiculous, and calls theology the 'basest' of all disciplines, 'unpleasant, harsh, contemptible, and vile'. Prayer and repentance, which his guardian angel begs him to embrace, are dismissed by the demon Mephistopheles as 'illusions, fruits of lunacy, / That makes men foolish that do trust them most'. And yet Faustus knows – it is the heart of his pact – that he is Hell-bound. He claims not to believe in Hell, but the very first question he asks when he has sealed the pact is whether there is a Hell. His rejection of it is less an opinion about the nature of reality than a defiant refusal to submit to it. Mephistopheles, in a vivid statement of Christian orthodoxy, gestures around himself and explains, 'this is hell, nor am I out of it'. Hell is not a physical location; it is the eternal exclusion from God's presence which is the sum of all torments. Faustus will have none of it. 'Learn thou of Faustus manly fortitude,' he mocks the demon, 'And scorn those joys thou never shalt possess.'[36]

Marlowe was a writer of prodigious invention, but like any author he also drew from life. We can easily imagine that he may have been, let us say, closely acquainted with someone given to contemptuous defiance of God's power, ready to treat religion as a mere tool for befuddling simple minds; someone who was not so much persuaded that there is no God as determined not to submit to one, preferring 'manly fortitude' to mewling piety – even if he could not quite shake off the anxious thought that it might all be true.

If this is all circumstance and supposition, our direct evidence about Marlowe's own supposed unbelief is equally shaky. What we know is that, in a slippery, mischievous tract published in 1592, the scurrilous pamphleteer Robert Greene confessed that he and Marlowe had once said together, '(like the fool in his heart), There is no God'. Greene accused Marlowe of having studied 'pestilent Machiavellian policy'.[37] The further accusations that surfaced in May 1593 are more vivid but no more dependable. Queen Elizabeth

I's council was looking into the Raleigh circle, and Marlowe's name kept coming up. A spy who accused another suspect of spreading blasphemies claimed that the ultimate source of the poison was Marlowe. In the same month, Marlowe's rival and former housemate Thomas Kyd was arrested on suspicion of fomenting violence against immigrant traders in London. When a dangerously heretical document was found among his papers, he claimed it was Marlowe's, and added further damaging claims about Marlowe's beliefs. Marlowe was arrested, and interrogated on 20 May, but released on bail. Then, on or shortly after 27 May, a further, much more detailed and damning denunciation landed: this from Richard Baines, a long-time antagonist of Marlowe's who had accused him of forgery the previous year. Baines' document was certainly taken seriously, to the extent that a copy was made for the queen herself. Its claims were never tested, however. On 30 May, Marlowe was killed in a house in Deptford, just south-east of London. According to the inquest, he fell out with a friend over the bill for their dinner, flew at him with a knife, and in the struggle received a fatal stab wound to the head. The coroner ruled it self-defence. Perhaps so, but there do seem to have been people who were keen to shut Marlowe up, one way or another.[38]

All we can do with the claims Kyd and Baines made about 'Marlowe's monstrous opinions' is take them at face value. They do at least paint a consistent picture. They do not accuse him of openly denying God. The closest we get is the reported statement 'that if there be any God or any good religion, then it is in the papists, because the service of God is performed with more ceremonies'. Even there, the focus is not on that portentous *if*, but on his contempt for the religion of England. 'All Protestants are hypocritical asses . . . If he were put to write a new Religion, he would undertake both a more excellent and admirable method.' But this was not about preferring one form of Christianity to another. He also criticised Christ himself for not having 'instituted the sacrament with more Ceremonial Reverence'. As befits a member of Raleigh's circle, Marlowe suggested Christ should have used tobacco rather than bread and wine. Many of his other reported remarks conform to the atheist stereotype of mocking and picking at the Bible's flaws. The chronology of the Genesis story was wrong. Moses was a 'juggler' who deceived the ancient Hebrews, implanting 'an everlasting superstition' in the hearts of a 'gross and rude people'. Christ's apostles were 'fishermen and base fellows, neither of wit nor worth' – all except St Paul, who had 'wit' but was a coward.[39]

According to the stereotype, we might expect a hint of incest next, but Baines' Marlowe offers a different variation on that theme: claiming 'that Christ was a bastard and his mother dishonest' – *dishonest* meaning unchaste. 'That he was the son of a carpenter, and that if the Jews among whom he was born did crucify him, they best knew him and whence he came.' He 'deserved better to die than Barabbas . . . though Barabbas were both a thief and a murderer'. Why so? In part because the women who accompanied Christ and his disciples 'were whores . . . Christ knew them dishonestly'. Nor was it only the women. The apostle John 'was bedfellow to Christ and leaned always in his bosom . . . he used him as the sinners of Sodom'. That last charge was corroborated by Kyd, who wrote that Marlowe 'would report St John to be our saviour Christ's Alexis – I cover it with reverence and trembling – that is, that Christ did love him with an extraordinary love'.[40] Evidently Kyd could hardly bring himself to write it down.

What kind of atheist would this make Marlowe, if we assume it is true? Not a sceptical rationalist. His reported statements are not even consistent. Christ might have been the son of a carpenter, or the Angel Gabriel might have pimped the Virgin Mary to the Holy Spirit, but both cannot be true. What holds together these outbursts, and the hints of scepticism in the plays, is not a theory but an emotion: fury. A wild, bitter refusal to submit to authority. Amid Baines' string of explosive charges came a now-famous claim: 'that all they that love not Tobacco and Boys were fools'. If you loved tobacco and boys in late Elizabethan England, then it was hard not to defy the Church, the Christ and the God in whose name you were commanded to abstain from them.

According to one wit writing shortly after this scandal, the name of the devil who chiefly inspired atheism was not Doubt, or Lust, but Derision, whose 'profession is Atheism' because he loves above all 'to mock at the simplicity of the just':

> It is meat and drink to him when he is mocking another man: Christ his Saviour is a Carpenter's son: Christians, 'Galileans', in contempt. Nay, such blasphemy uttereth he between the Holy Ghost and the blessed and Immaculate Virgin Mary, as my heart trembleth to think them.[41]

If this was not written with Marlowe's circle in mind, it might as well have been. Marlowe and Raleigh alike were mockers. Or to put it more kindly: they were gadflies, jesting about matters that were too serious for jest, playing with different and contradictory unorthodoxies without committing themselves to any of them, consistent only in their refusal to bow to authority. The difference is one of mood. Marlowe's mockery was furious while Raleigh's was coolly mischievous, and Marlowe was swiftly murdered while Raleigh was beheaded twenty-five years later. They took different routes to the same destination.

Sketchy as all this is, the Raleigh–Marlowe circle gives us an unusually consistent picture of what unbelief could actually mean in this period. And its restless, reckless and insolent 'atheism' has echoes elsewhere. On the rare occasions when early modern courts dealt with allegations of atheism, they often turn out to have been more about defiance of moral authority than about doctrine. One John Mignot was accused in 1589 of claiming 'that there is no God, no devil, no Heaven, no Hell, no life after this life, no judgement'. The case, however, was really about Mignot's grasping, miserly conduct as a landowner. A desperate tenant had begged Mignot to forgive a debt of twelve pence, 'for God's sake'. Mignot replied that he would do it 'neither for God's sake nor for the devil's', and the damning charges were confected from that careless remark. Plainly, however, Mignot was interested neither in God nor the devil, but in money.[42] In a similar case in 1635, one Brian Walker was sentenced to a year in prison, plus a hefty fine, for saying that 'I do not believe there is either God or devil, neither will I believe any thing but what I see.' Once again, this was not really about his metaphysical opinions. Walker was embroiled in a long, bitter dispute with a neighbouring family, fell to cursing them, and uttered the dread words when one of them said to him, 'Do you not fear God?' He was simply in no mood to acknowledge any authority to which his enemies might appeal.[43]

This sort of thing scarcely deserves to be called unbelief. But defiance of this kind could become more settled, especially if directed at the early modern world's most ever-present and intrusive moral authority: the Christian churches. One of the side effects of the Reformation was an arms race between the competing religious parties, as they tried to stymie one another's missionary efforts and to bolster their own moral authority by asserting control over their own populations. The result was that churches of all stripes began trying to regulate the everyday life of ordinary lay people more, and more consistently, than ever before. Naturally, some people bridled at this, and reviled the clergy as officious hypocrites. The clergy, equally naturally, insisted that they were merely messengers, implementing the will of God. So what was a resentful lay person to do, but shake the fist at God, too? Some unbelievers, Pascal thought, had no interest in questions of ultimate meaning. Such a person would merely say that 'he has shaken off the yoke, that he does not believe that there is a God watching over his actions, that he considers himself sole master of his behaviour, and that he proposes to account for it to no one but himself'.[44] Pascal found that attitude appalling, and baffling: perhaps we find it more understandable.

The blame for this kind of atheism was sometimes laid squarely on the clergy themselves. 'It is only ridiculous dull Preachers . . . that have revived this scornful Sect of Atheists,' one Englishman reckoned.[45] One of the more memorable characters in Tourneur's *Atheist's Tragedy* is the preacher, Languebeau Snuff, whose hypocrisy is so gross that D'Amville reckons he only aims 'to divert the world from sin, that he / More easily might engross it to himself'. D'Amville claims that it is through Snuff's behaviour that 'I am confirmed an atheist.'[46]

Churchmen responded to these charges as institutions always do: by pointing out that the flaws of a few messengers have no bearing on the truthfulness of the message. Which is not quite true. It is not simply that corrupt, grasping and tedious clergy were unable to invest their preaching with moral authority. D'Amville's point was that Languebeau Snuff was a practical atheist. He demonstrated by his conduct that he did not believe the gospel he preached. Since he was the religious professional who was supposed to know the truth on these points, what was a lay person to do but learn from his example?

The Good Atheist

For good Christians, the unbelief associated with the Raleigh–Marlowe circle was both appalling and reassuring. It was what unbelief ought to be. This is why the words *libertine* and *atheist* were virtual synonyms throughout the early modern period.[47] Atheists of this kind were monsters, but manageable ones, because whatever other appeal they might have, by definition they had no moral authority. Fumée's description of the libertines of Paris in

1542 included a telling detail: they wanted their wives to remain pious, to keep themselves from being cuckolded.[48] This Machiavellian argument – that religion was a lie which it was necessary for all but a small, self-selected group to embrace – was self-limiting if not actively self-defeating. If you believe that religion and morals are inextricably linked, and that social order depends on almost everyone accepting both, then it makes little difference if you yourself contract out of them. It makes you a kind of parasite on Christian society: an annoyance, not an existential threat.

Unfortunately there is not much direct evidence that real unbelievers frankly abandoned their ethics in this way. The closest we can come is in the widespread observation that unbelievers concealed their unbelief. Since the alternative was to risk execution or at the very least notoriety, this is not very surprising, but there is some modest significance to it. In the Reformation age, plenty of people had excellent reasons to conceal all manner of religious views, but this was usually thought of as shameful or cowardly.[49] Atheists, by contrast, were widely presumed to be completely unconcerned about concealing their unbelief, whether because they were indifferent to notions of shame or cowardice, or simply because they were not trying to share a gospel that was going to save anyone's soul. Occasional cases bear this out, like the mortally wounded Italian soldier-scholar who renounced any belief in God and in immortality on his deathbed in 1558: the time for caution had passed. Similarly, the Parisian priest Paul Beurrier, whom we met in Chapter 1, was summoned in 1661 to minister to a dying lawyer. This man refused to receive the sacrament on account of 'the difficulties which I have with the Christian religion', which he called 'a fable . . . a worldly policy invented to keep the people in subjection and obedience to rulers through the fear of imaginary hellfire . . . When we die, everything is dead for us'. But for all these years, he said, he had conformed outwardly, 'so as not to be remarked upon and for the sake of appearance'.[50] How common this kind of deliberate deception was we cannot know, although it was certainly rarer than orthodoxy's more paranoid defenders feared, and probably rarer than atheism's more assiduous modern chroniclers have hoped.

But was it a sign that atheists had no morals? Another example suggests not. It is true that at a crucial point of his career, this individual rejected all religion and found himself a friendless outcast as a result. And so he thought to himself:

> What can it profit me to spend all my days in this melancholy state, separated from the society of this people? . . . How much better will it be for me to return to their communion, and conform to their ways, in compliance with the Proverb, which directs us at *Rome* to *do as they do at Rome!*

But this was not so much an act of cynical conformity as a moment of weakness which he profoundly regretted. 'I wish I had never entertained such a thought!' His story as a whole teaches a very different lesson.[51] He was born Gabriel Acosta in Portugal in 1585, and was a *converso*: that is, a Catholic descended from Jews who had been forcibly converted, and whose Christianity was therefore permanently suspect in his countrymen's eyes. A *converso*'s ambiguous status made for a precarious life, but sometimes also for wider horizons. Acosta tells us that Catholicism took 'deep root' in him, but that around the age of twenty he began to be troubled by doubts about the immortality of the soul. He set himself to intensive study of the Bible, and eventually concluded that the New Testament contradicted the Old and must be discarded. So he became 'a convert to the law of *Moses*'. This act of apostasy could easily have cost him his life in Portugal, so in 1614, aged twenty-nine, he fled to Amsterdam. There he joined the city's Jewish community, was circumcised and changed his name from Gabriel to Uriel.

But, like other converts we have met, Acosta did not settle

happily into his new orthodoxy. He had learned his Judaism through reading the Hebrew Bible, and quickly discovered that real-life seventeenth-century Judaism was not what he had expected. He fell out with the Amsterdam synagogue. The key issue, again, was immortality, which contemporary Jews affirmed but which Acosta could not discover anywhere in the Hebrew Bible. In 1623 he published a book against the doctrine, and the synagogue denounced him to the authorities as a subverter of all true religion. He was briefly imprisoned and virtually all copies of his book were destroyed.[52]

Acosta's denouncers called him an atheist. It was not yet true – so far he was simply an unorthodox Jew – but as he scrambled to defend his position, 'I began to question with myself, whether the law of *Moses* ought to be accounted the law of God . . . At last I came to be fully of the opinion, that it was nothing but a human invention, like many other systems in the world.'

This was the point when his resolve wobbled and he decided to conform to a religion he no longer believed. But the Jewish community did not trust him, nor could he keep up the pretence for long. His account seethes with bitterness towards their treatment of him. In particular, he rejected the accusation that, by renouncing the faith, he had renounced morality. Not so, he insisted. He based his ethics not on God's commandments, but on 'the law of nature . . . the common rule of action to all men . . . which distinguishes between right and wrong'. When his opponents objected that there was more to religious ethics than this bare natural law, he agreed: that was his point. Religions, he argued, either taught futile ceremonies and self-serving regulations, or else made demands – such as the command to love one's enemies – that went beyond nature, and so were not merely impossible but destructive. This was why 'false religion, invented by weak and wicked men', led believers into tormenting themselves with self-denial, using tales of hellfire 'to frighten weak people out of their senses', torturing or killing out of a terrible zeal to save non-existent immortal souls. Acosta had become convinced that irreligious morality was not only possible, but truer and purer than the religious kind.[53]

Acosta was unique, but his subversive notion of morals without religion was not. It was in part a legacy of the Renaissance's enchantment with the pagan, classical world. If reason, or a divine law written in every human heart, had been enough to make the ancients virtuous, surely it was enough for their modern disciples too? The great Dutch moralist Dirck Volckerstz Coornhert saw himself as standing in succession to Erasmus' ethics-centred vision of Christianity. He deliberately wrote his *Ethics* (1586) without a single citation from Scripture: apparently a friend had challenged him to see if he could do it. He was not trying to reject the Bible; he was trying to bolster it by demonstrating that a truly biblical moral code could be reached simply by the use of reason. He did not mean to imply that it was therefore possible to be truly righteous while rejecting any divine revelation. Nor, when he argued that evil consisted of lack of true knowledge and understanding, did he mean the same as Marlowe's Machiavel did when he said 'there is no sin but Ignorance'. But readers who found such ideas in his works were not imagining them.[54]

In 1606, a provincial English physician named Eleazar Duncan wrote a tract warning against using unlicensed, untrained healers, however impeccable their religion might be. Instead, he urged, a patient should resort only to 'the learned Physician (though he have no religion)'. The point is not merely to observe, again, that medics had a reputation for atheism. Duncan's claim was that even an atheist physician could be trusted to care for his patients. The urge to save others' lives, Duncan insisted, is 'naturally implanted in the heart of man'. Why else, he asked, would anyone ever leap into deep water to rescue others from drowning, or run into a burning building to save the occupants? There was nothing specifically

Christian about the desire to help and serve others. It was an instinct as natural as breathing.[55]

That argument was nakedly self-serving, but there is corroboration from a surprising quarter. Amid the comforting caricatures of Tourneur's *Atheist's Tragedy*, one character strikes a discordant note. Sebastian, the younger son of the villainous D'Amville, is an atheist like his father. He is a self-confessed coward and a serial philanderer. 'The love of a woman,' he says, 'is like a mushroom; it grows in one night and will serve somewhat pleasingly next morning to breakfast, but afterwards waxes fulsome and unwholesome.' And yet, unexpectedly, he is also a man of principle. He opposes a forced marriage being plotted by his father as tantamount to rape, standing firm even when he is cut off without an income. Eventually his father relents, and gives him some money – which he promptly hands over as bail to free a man whom his father has unjustly imprisoned. At the end of the play, when Sebastian at last manages to arrange an assignation with a lustful noblewoman he has been courting, her vengeful husband and his soldiers track them down and set about breaking down the door of their chamber. 'If you love me, save my honour,' she begs Sebastian: and he does. She flees through another door, and to give her time to escape, he stays, barring the way with sword drawn. When the husband bursts in, he demands that Sebastian stand aside, 'or I will make my passage through thy blood'. 'My blood would make it slippery, my lord,' he replies; ''twere better you would take another way.' And he dies with that quip on his lips, killing the cuckolded husband in the process.[56] Neither pious Christian, virtuous pagan nor villainous atheist, Sebastian represents a dangerous possibility: that unbelief might discover ethics of its own.

If the Renaissance stage fostered atheism, as its Puritan critics claimed, this is how it happened. Not by dealing in reassuring stock villains such as D'Amville, nor by directly attacking the question in plays like *Faustus*: but by the accumulation of hints and examples suggesting that atheism was not a uniquely depraved spectacle of horror, but a tolerable everyday phenomenon, to be joked about rather than feared. Preachers had been denouncing commonplace sins as atheism for so long that atheism now seemed commonplace. Tourneur's contemporary Ben Jonson used the word *atheist* half a dozen times in his plays, usually to refer to the profane and the impious. In his co-written play *Eastward Ho!*, a gaoler reels off a list of the different religions he has had in his prison: first various Christian sects, and then, 'Jew, Turk, infidel, atheist, good fellow, etc'. When asked which is the best, he replies, 'They that pay fees best. We never examine their consciences farther.' So an *atheist* is halfway between an *infidel* and a *good fellow*, a man of the world: a figure of fun more than of fear. In Jonson's *The New Inn*, a rake tries to seduce a lady, and she teasingly questions whether there is any such thing as love. Pretending to be shocked, he replies, 'I did not expect / To meet an infidel, much less an atheist.' For Jonson, atheism was a joke. As when Shakespeare's Juliet calls Romeo the 'god of my idolatry', these are lines which would have caused a *frisson* in their audience. But those audiences had come, in part, to witness dramatists playing with fire, and to do so with a thrill rather than a shudder.

As to Shakespeare himself: his personal religion remains hidden from us, and all we can say for certain is that he was not an atheist, at least not in any dogmatic or embittered sense of the word. In his poetry, he could even be conventionally pious.[57] It is striking, however, that nowhere in any of his surviving works did he use the words *atheist*, *unbeliever* or any of their cognates. He did use *infidel*, but only to refer to non-Christian religions. Given how widely used and emotionally charged the word *atheist* was at the time, and the famous breadth of his vocabulary, that silence suggests that he was consciously avoiding the topic, indulging neither in Tourneur's self-righteousness nor in Jonson's fun and games. But if he side-stepped the word, he was nevertheless capable of putting shockingly atheist sentiments in his characters' mouths. Human life, according to Macbeth's famous nihilist creed, is

> a walking shadow, a poor player
> That struts and frets his hour upon the stage
> And then is heard no more. It is a tale
> Told by an idiot, full of sound and fury
> Signifying nothing.

Claudio, in *Measure for Measure*, quails at the prospect of death, begging his sister Isabella to prostitute herself to save his life (a proposal she calls 'a kind of incest'). He says:

> To die, and go we know not where;
> To lie in cold obstruction and to rot;
> This sensible warm motion to become
> A kneaded clod . . .
> . . . 'Tis too horrible!

Starkest of all is the villainous Aaron in *Titus Andronicus*. 'Thou believ'st no god,' his captors say at the play's end. 'What if I do not? as, indeed, I do not,' he replies; 'an idiot holds his bauble for a god.' As he dies, he reviles his enemies, declaring, 'If there be devils, would I were a devil,' and proudly claiming that 'I have done a thousand dreadful things / As willingly as one would kill a fly.' And yet, like Tourneur's Sebastian, the audience knows that this defiantly unrepentant death is a ploy. By submitting to it, Aaron hopes to save the life of his bastard son.[58]

All these stage atheists are villains, and certainly none of them speak for their creator. Yet if Shakespeare's cast of stage characters is well populated with unbelievers, it is strangely empty of devout and pious Christians. Isabella in *Measure for Measure* is a possible exception; I am not persuaded there are any more. This silence is genuinely difficult to explain. Religious controversy was illegal on the Elizabethan stage, but piety was not. Perhaps such characters are tricky to bring to life, but Shakespeare knew his craft, and he lived in a self-consciously devout age which offered plenty of models to draw on. Instead we have the supposedly 'puritan' Malvolio in *Twelfth Night*, whose religion makes him an 'affectioned ass'. As the great literary critic George Santayana put it, if the works of Shakespeare were all that some alien civilisation or future age had of humanity, 'they would hardly understand that man had had a religion'.[59]

It is perhaps relevant that Shakespeare knew his Montaigne. He 'borrowed' a decent chunk of text directly from one of the *Essays* and apparently had an acquaintance with many more.[60] Montaigne would certainly have offered him a sophisticated, rich, whimsical and deeply humane world from which God was strangely absent. Santayana concluded that 'the silence of Shakespeare' on religion had 'something in [it] that is still heathen', which may be going too far.[61] But it is certainly true that Shakespeare's stage could be a startlingly secular space.

The source text behind Shakespeare's *King Lear*, the 1605 *True Chronicle History of King Leir*, tells the story of the elderly king and his three daughters as a morality tale governed by God's providence, and gives it a happy ending. Shakespeare turned it into an exceptionally bleak tragedy set in a world with no sign of God's presence, let alone of his justice. The closest the play comes to a religious vision is blind Gloucester's claim that 'as flies to wanton boys are we to the gods, / They kill us for their sport'.[62] If there was any meaning or morality to be found on this stage – and the question is open – the characters would have to find it for themselves.

So the popular caricature of the atheist was not entirely wrong. There was indeed a vein of unbelief whose emotional register was anger, resentment, mockery and scorn, whose temperature ranged from Jonson's cool amusement through Raleigh's barbed playfulness to Marlowe's fire and fury. But those emotions were lived out in ways that were both better and worse than the preachers feared. Better, because the unbelief of anger seems in fact still to have been inchoate, more a matter of defiant carving out of secular spaces than of direct, earnest denials of core Christian doctrines. But also worse, because it was not, as the caricature insisted, a simple cloak for moral bankruptcy. What makes Marlowe's defiance and even D'Amville's anticlerical contempt compelling is their moral edge. And in their very different ways, Acosta, Coornhert, Eleazar Duncan, Tourneur's Sebastian and Shakespeare's secularised ethical vision suggest that it was not only possible, but even natural for the unbelief of anger to be fired by its own moral code. The Church wanted angry unbelievers to stick to their role as villains. Instead, they were beginning to bid for the moral high ground.

4

The Puritan Atheist

'It's not the despair . . . I can take the despair. It's the hope I can't stand.'

Clockwise (1986)

'Of course there's Hell. Flames and damnation.' . . . 'And Heaven too,' Rose said with anxiety . . . 'Oh, maybe,' the Boy said. 'Maybe.'

Graham Greene, *Brighton Rock*

'The Monster of the Creation'

Early modern people who worried about atheism were chiefly concerned by the unbelief of anger: by hostility to Christianity, whether incoherent grumbles about priests or open attacks on vital doctrines. It is hardly surprising that these angry unbelievers attracted so much attention, especially since, as we have seen, they had rather more moral backbone than their critics liked to recognise. Even so, they were not on their own a serious threat. It was certainly unnerving if some people withdrew from the great religious struggles of the day and started sniping from the sidelines, but the outcome of a battle is rarely determined by deserters. Christendom was not about to be broken by a fringe of non-participants. It is time to turn our attention to the other, better-concealed, but ultimately more consequential vein of early modern unbelief: the unbelief of anxiety.

In 1628, the English satirist and future bishop John Earle published a character sketch of a stereotypical 'sceptic in Religion'. By now we know what to expect: a blasphemous scoffer and incestuous libertine, boasting of his contempt for God and driven by his sinful lusts.

But no. Earle's 'sceptic' is an agonised vacillator, a man who 'would be wholly a Christian, but that he is something of an Atheist, and wholly an Atheist, but that he is partly a Christian'. As Earle put it in a draft version of the text, 'his whole life is a question'. This sceptic's problems begin with the impossible choice between Catholic and Protestant. He feels the force of both sides' arguments and is wary of simply succumbing to habit or conformity. 'He thinks so many wise men would not believe but on good ground, and so many honest men cannot be on the wrong side' – but he knows there are wise and honest men on both sides. He changes his mind afresh every time he reads something new. He dips his toe into an opinion as 'tenderly as a Cat in the water, and pulls it out again'. His conscience is like a hapless peacemaker trying to intervene in a duel, who is wounded by both sides. But however tentative he may be, he still bridles at any talk of obedience or submission to the Church (any Church). 'He hates authority as the tyrant of reason.' He is so paralysed by the possibility of being wrong that he will never settle on anything as right: 'He finds doubts and scruples better than resolves them, and has always some argument to non-plus himself. The least reason is enough to perplex him, and the best will not satisfy him.'

In the draft version, Earle's central critique of this man's indecisiveness is that 'he is wondrous loath to hazard his credulity, and whilst he fears to believe amiss, believes nothing'. On the face of it, the published version contradicts this: here the sceptic is 'guiltier of credulity than he is taken to be; for it is out of his belief of everything, that he fully believes nothing'. But for all the logical inconsistency, both descriptions ring true. This 'sceptic' is not a hardened scoffer, but a bleeding casualty of the battle for credulity, trapped in the no-man's-land between belief and unbelief. John Donne counselled Christians first to 'stand inquiring' and then to choose their path. This 'sceptic' is rooted permanently to the spot.[1]

Respectable early modern people imagined 'atheists' who never thought about God except to wish he did not exist. Earle reveals another character: the 'atheist' who could think of little else but God, and who feared he did not exist. We do not know whether Earle's portrait was drawn from life – he may possibly have had his Oxford contemporary William Chillingworth in mind. Regardless, he had put his finger on something. His 'sceptic' was full of arguments, reasons and uncertainties, but those opinions are froth which should not distract us. His turmoil was emotional before it was intellectual. The particular theological knots he was tying himself in do not really matter. The point is the mood: agonised indecision. In one important sense, however, Earle's character was misleading, for like the blasphemers and libertines we have already met, he was an adult male of apparently independent means. The real figures behind the caricature came from all social classes and across the age range, and they included a striking number of women.

On her deathbed in 1601, the English Puritan gentlewoman Katherine Brettergh was asked 'whether she did believe the promises of God, nor no?' In her answer, she quoted one of the age's favourite biblical verses, Mark 9:24: 'Lord, I believe; help thou my unbelief.' It was a banal and a momentous sentiment. Banal because, as the marginal notes in her Bible helpfully pointed out, 'my unbelief' could simply mean 'the feebleness, and imperfection of my faith', and it is a truism for Christians that everyone's faith is feeble and imperfect.[2] But since 'unbelief' could also mean much more than that, this biblical proof that belief and unbelief could coexist mattered profoundly. William Perkins, Elizabethan England's greatest Protestant theologian, who died the year after Brettergh, warned that 'these two thoughts, *There is a God*, and *there is no God*, may be, and are both in one and the same heart'. If any of his readers were tempted to reassure themselves that 'they never felt in themselves any such conceits as this, *that there is no God*', Perkins warned them: 'A man cannot always discern what be the thoughts of his own heart.'[3] If you are not crying out to God to help overcome your unbelief, then perhaps your unbelief has already overcome you.

This was not a new problem, but it was a newly acute one. The Reformation started as an argument about the meaning of 'faith'. Protestants loaded more weight than ever before onto that word. As the era's competing churches raced to secure the high ground, their definitions of 'belief' became ever more rarefied. It was no longer simply a matter of holding an opinion. Indeed, *opinion* and *belief* were now seen as opposites, the one provisional, unreliable and human, the other final, certain and divine. Belief became both glorious and unattainable.[4] 'Many think that it is the easiest thing in the world to believe, when as indeed it is the hardest,' chided one preacher. Parroting the Creed does not make you a believer, insisted another. 'To *believe*, is with the heart to assent: it is not with the tongue to recite.'[5] Everyone is at least partly an unbeliever.

This problem was not exclusive to Protestants.[6] It was a French Catholic priest who wrote in 1636 that 'the profession of atheism . . . is a temptation that forms easily in the mind'. When a Catholic such as the brilliant Italian friar Tommaso Campanella set himself to write against atheism, the terrain he covered was very similar to that of his Protestant counterparts: asking how you can be secure in your own faith when every sect trumpets its own certainties, and when most politicians' religion is plainly a matter of convenience rather than of conviction. The difference is that the Catholic Church, unlike most of its Protestant counterparts, had the means to suppress books like Campanella's which asked too many awkward questions.[7]

Even so, this problem was sharpest for Protestants, for whom *faith* was so central. It was sharpest of all for Protestants who did not belong to tightly organised and disciplined churches, in which there was either formal confession of sins (as in many Lutheran churches) or systematic oversight of the moral status of church members (as in many Calvinist churches). Those systems did not solve the problem of belief logically, but they did solve it emotionally, since anxious Christians could outsource their concern about themselves to the ministers who policed them. It was a kind of fideism: you cannot be certain of your own beliefs, but you can place your trust in your community instead.[8]

One large Protestant territory, however, lacked such systems of moral policing entirely: England. Partly for that reason English Protestants had, by the early seventeenth century, developed a strain of obsessively introspective piety distinguished by contortionist feats of self-examination.[9] It is chiefly their story we will be following in the next two chapters, not because England was unique – it was not – but because its peculiarities let us see the case in particularly sharp relief. For at the centre of English Protestants' intense piety was a very particular problem of unbelief.

The preacher at the funeral of another godly matriarch, Elizabeth Juxon, claimed that she had 'groaned many a time under the sense of much unbelief'. But he meant neither that she doubted whether there was a God, nor that she suffered from generically weak faith. He meant something specific: she doubted that she was predestined to Heaven.[10] The Calvinist theology which dominated post-Reformation England taught that all human beings were predestined by God either for Heaven or Hell before the creation of the world, in an unalterable decree. In most Calvinist countries, the anxieties this doctrine fomented were managed by a firm system of church discipline, which reassured those who conformed to it that they were likely to be among God's elect. England, however, had no such system, leaving believers responsible for policing their own piety and managing their own fears. For a significant minority, this task and the anxieties it generated proved overwhelming. Were they or were they not among those predestined to salvation? How could they ever be sure?

Such anxieties were regularly described as a form of doubt or unbelief. The London preacher Obadiah Sedgwick's *The doubting beleever* (1641) is a shrewd and compassionate book of pastoral advice which focuses exclusively on this kind of doubt: what he called 'personal doubtings . . . where not the things in themselves, but in respect of ourselves, are questioned'. Not, is there a God? but, has he saved *me*? – which was still, Sedgwick insisted, a form of unbelief.[11] John Donne distinguished between 'the presumptuous Atheist, that believes no God', and 'the melancholic Atheist that believes no Jesus applied to him' – who believes in Christ but denies that he himself is among the saved. In John Bunyan's *The Holy War*, the city of 'Mansoul' is assaulted by Captain Incredulity and an army of Doubters, in which the 'Resurrection-doubters' and the 'Glory-doubters', who deny the immortality of the soul and the existence of Heaven, fight alongside the 'Election-doubters' and the 'Vocation-doubters', who deny that you yourself have been chosen or called to salvation. And in *The Pilgrim's Progress*, the lord of Doubting-Castle is not Atheist, but the giant Despair.[12]

Since wondering whether you are eternally damned is hardly an attack on Protestant doctrine – if anything the opposite – this conflation of different kinds of doubt may seem perverse. The rationale was that to deny your own salvation was to disbelieve God's promises. Richard Baxter, seventeenth-century England's wisest and most humane Protestant theologian, argued that for Christians to doubt their own salvation was 'to question the truth of Scripture'. He called it a kind of 'reproachful Blasphemy'. This is exactly what a penitent whom we know only as I. G. described.

After some months of fearful despair, she tried to take comfort in the Bible's promises of God's mercy, but words on a page, even a sacred page, were not enough to still her inner struggles. 'I was tempted . . . to think that it was not the Word of God, but my own word': whether because she ultimately believed more in her own worthlessness than in Calvinist doctrine, or because she simply did not dare let herself hope.[13]

I. G.'s sufferings were positively transient compared to Hannah Allen's. As a teenager in the 1650s, Allen went through a period of despair in which she was convinced she was damned. She found a more even keel when she married, but when her husband died in 1664, her spiritual agonies returned worse than ever. She considered suicide, repeatedly harmed herself, and once crawled into a roof void in order to starve to death (her resolve broke after three days). In the end the fog gradually lifted, which she ascribed to God's mercy, her family's love and the passage of time. What matters for us is that during her struggles, her family repeatedly tried to persuade her of God's mercy, but she would have none of it. Once she heard a thunderclap, and told her aunt it was a message from God that she was damned. Surely not, said the aunt: God would not send a miracle to convince someone of their damnation. 'We do not read of such a thing in all the Scripture.' But Allen would not be reasoned with. 'My Answer was, "Therefore my condition is unparalleled; there was never such a one [as me] since God made any Creature, either Angels or Men, nor never will be to the end of the world."' She begged friends not to pray for her, since 'it would but sink me the deeper into Hell'. At first she worried that she had committed the 'unpardonable sin' mentioned in the Gospels, but soon she concluded that that sin was for amateurs and she had committed even worse:

My Sins are so great, that if all the Sins of all the Devils and Damned in Hell, and all the Reprobates on Earth were comprehended in one man, mine are greater. There is no word comes so near the comprehension of the dreadfulness of my Condition; as that, I am the Monster of the Creation.

We might be tempted to laugh at such lugubrious self-importance. But it was in earnest, and it had a purpose. Allen tells us that she 'much delighted' in thinking this way, since she was tempted 'to give up all for lost, and to close with the Devil and forsake my God'. What truly tormented her was her fleeting glimpses of hope. Better to find cold comfort in certainty, and fall back on the devil, who at least never turns away customers. The truly unbearable thought was the possibility that God's mercy might be real.[14] In Allen's case at least, Baxter was right. Doubting her own salvation had metastasised into a thorough denial of basic Christian doctrines.

It was a vicious circle. You fear you are damned, so your faith wavers; and because your faith wavers, you are even more convinced you are damned. In the 1640s, a formerly pious London teenager named Sarah Wight suffered four years of spiritual agonies. As she recalled: 'I could see nothing but Hell, and wrath: I was as desperate, as ever was any . . . I felt myself, soul and body, in fire and brimstone already.' From that agonised conviction, it was only a short step to wonder if 'there was no other Hell, but that which I felt'. At least that held out the hope that death would end her sufferings. On that basis she attempted suicide several times, thinking that 'if I made away [with] myself, there was an end of my misery, and that there was no God, no Heaven; and no Hell'. But the very fact she had such thoughts convinced her that she 'was damned already, being an unbeliever'.[15] Another woman, known to us only as M. K., wrestled with her fears of damnation, and felt as if the devil was saying to her:

Why dost thou thus trouble thy self? Take thy pleasure, do what thou likest. Thou shalt never be called to an account for anything; for as the wise man dieth, so dieth the fool, and both rest in the grave together. There is no God to save thee or to punish thee; all things were made by nature, and when thou diest, there is an end of all thy good and bad deeds.

In desperate straits, unbelief offered a get-out-of-Hell-free card. But M. K. found she could not simply walk away from her faith. Instead she became convinced 'that there was no heaven, no God, no Jesus, no good angels, only a hell there was, and devils to carry me thither'.[16] Donne's distinction between presumptuous and melancholic atheists had dissolved.

Ordinary Christian practice could not survive these agonies. While Hannah Allen's despair was at its worst, she could not stand attending church or hearing others pray. She could not even bear the sight of a book, since books meant Bibles: she once knocked a book out of her own child's hands in distress. In the 1640s a Mrs Drake, another godly gentlewoman convinced that she was 'assuredly damned', told a minister who came to reason with her that she would neither pray nor read the Bible, 'nor ever go to Church again'. Since her damnation was certain, 'she was resolved to spend the remainder of her time in all jollity and merriment, denying herself of no worldly comforts'. For two years, she refused to attend church and scoffed at the ministers who tried to persuade her to. She had, in effect, found a religious reason to be irreligious.[17] Even more well-balanced souls who were tempted to bleak thoughts about their salvation found that 'dullness of devotion' was a natural side effect. Luke Howard, an apprentice shoemaker in the 1650s, suffered lengthy spiritual agonies, and eventually 'sought to make Merry over it, and to take my fill of the World, with all I could enjoy thereof'. He tried to forget God and pursue worldly prosperity. When a preacher stirred his conscience, his response was to hurry away to dinner, 'for I know as much as he can tell me, or more than I or he either can live in'. Howard's conscience caught up with him in the end, but not everyone's did. Richard Baxter sorrowfully recalled a schoolfriend who was intense in his piety and devotions but who then took to the bottle, and despaired at his own sinfulness. Eventually 'his Conscience could have no Relief or Ease but in . . . disowning the Teachers and Doctrines which had restrained him', and he fell away from his faith.[18]

The very fact of falling into despair made some sufferers question their religion. Calvinism teaches that true faith, once found, cannot be lost – in other words, if you fall away, it proves that your faith was false all along. This was logically neat but sometimes impossible to swallow. Dionys Fitzherbert, yet another godly gentlewoman who endured extended spiritual torments, struggled to apply it to her own case. Since she knew how heartfelt and genuine her former faith had been, she was left with only two options: either 'there is no such thing as I did believe, or else the religion that I professed was not true'. At the very least, such beleaguered believers might 'murmur against God as unjust'. Hannah Allen reported 'dreadful Temptations to have hard thoughts of my dearest Lord'. Respectable gentlewomen were not supposed to be angry with God, but when such acute sufferings were mixed with relentless sermons about God's power and justice, how else were they to respond?[19]

Horrid Temptations

Mercifully, these florid outbreaks of suicidal despair were not everyday events, and the problems they reveal were as much psychiatric as theological.[20] But these tender souls were canaries in the mine. They suffered particularly acutely from anxious unbelief, but even the most robust souls could not keep it entirely out of their lungs.

John Bunyan recalled in his autobiography how, as a young man, he had noticed some unexpected thoughts that 'came stealing upon me'. It began slowly, but within weeks

> whole floods of blasphemies both against God, Christ and the Scriptures . . . poured upon my spirit, to my great confusion and astonishment. These blasphemous thoughts were such as stirred up questions in me against the very Being of God, and of his only beloved Son: As, whether there were in truth, a God, or Christ? And whether the holy Scriptures were not rather a fable, and cunning story, than the holy and pure Word of God?

The point, again, is not the substance of his worries but the mood. These 'suggestions', as he called them, 'did make such a seizure upon my spirit, and did so over-weigh my heart . . . that I felt as if there were nothing else'. He compared his struggles against them to a baby's resistance to a kidnapper: spirited, noisy and entirely futile. It felt, he recalled, like a relentless and irresistible assault, and it lasted for about a year.[21]

He was in good company. Seventeenth-century Protestant diaries, autobiographies and correspondence are full of references to 'risings of Atheistic thoughts', 'temptations that there was not a God' or 'this horrid temptation, to question the Being of God'.[22] 'It came questioning into my mind of the truth of God,' wrote the Northamptonshire gentlewoman Elizabeth Isham, 'seeing many would show a reason in nature for almost everything. This temptation came many times unto me.'[23] Richard Baxter recalled that, when he was a newly ordained minister, 'the Tempter strongly assaulted my Faith . . . especially to question the certain Truth of the Sacred Scriptures; and also the Life to come, and Immortality of the Soul'.[24] Those who suffered such shameful assaults often instinctively concealed them. 'I was troubled, but could not acquaint any with my condition,' wrote one woman about her adolescent temptations to unbelief, for 'I did not think that it was so with any other as it was with me.' Another teenage girl beset by 'temptations that there was no God' feared that no one else had ever entertained such appalling thoughts. 'I thought my estate to be singular, and that I should hear Books and Ballads cried of me about the streets.'[25]

In fact, when that girl finally poured out her distress to an aunt, the older woman was able to reassure her 'from her own experience in the like case'. Doubts like these were not discussed openly, especially not in front of children, but nor were they rare. Ministers discreetly advised their flocks about how to deal with them. Blasphemy 'bubbles up within thee', warned the popular devotional writer Daniel Rogers: 'Satan will disquiet thee with Atheisticall thoughts against God, Providence, Scriptures . . . as if they were all but fables.' A bestselling spiritual advice book expected that its readers would suffer from 'vile and unworthy thoughts of God . . . cast in like wildfire by Satan'. The book's index listed both 'Blasphemous thoughts' and 'Thoughts, blasphemous', and in one surviving copy a reader has underlined both entries. 'Art thou tempted to Atheism?' asked another minister: 'why, yet consider that so was Jesus Christ himself' – a claim that required an elastic definition of 'atheism', but was perfect for reassuring people frightened by their own thoughts.[26]

All these people described their doubts in the same way: as having been thrust unwillingly into their minds by the devil. We might be inclined to dismiss that. In fact it is vital for understanding what this kind of unbelief was and why it matters.

First of all, it shows that these narratives are a literary genre, akin to the modern genre of narratives of recovery from mental illness. Like that genre, they suffer from survivorship bias. Early modern Protestants who lost their struggles with atheism did not tell their stories, any more than did those who killed themselves. We have already seen how intertwined physical self-harm and crises of faith could be. Crisis-of-faith narratives are also full of what we might call spiritual self-harm incidents: demonstrative acts of faithlessness, such as trying to burn a Bible or, like Dionys Fitzherbert, openly denouncing your former faith as 'mere delusions and but a dream'. That statement is of a piece with Fitzherbert's conviction during her torments that she had in fact already died. In a spiritual sense it was almost true.[27] Like physical self-harming, such dramatic statements served as an unmistakable sign to others of how intense your sufferings were. They could also be a message to yourself: an attempt to cut through the ever-present pain with a still more intense stab, or even to bring that pain to an end by finally pulling God's judgement down on your head.

In this context, to call your blasphemous thoughts *temptations* was an indispensable distancing technique. It meant they were neither innocent ideas which needed to be considered seriously, nor sins for which you were culpable. They were enemy action: a bombardment which required no response but endurance and resistance. In effect, this was an *ad hominem* argument: if the source of these thoughts was the devil, that told you all you needed to know. One of Satan's regular tactics against the godly, warned a bestselling devotional writer, was

casting into their minds outrageous blasphemies against God [which] will make their hairs to stand on end when they do but think of them, persuading them that they are their own thoughts, and therefore horrible sins, whereas in truth they are but his suggestions . . . Therefore if we do repel and reject them, they are not our sins but the sins of the tempter.

Beleaguered believers are like trees in a storm. They are not to blame if their branches shake, as long as their roots hold firm.[28]

This does also seem genuinely to have reflected such people's experiences. Doubts crept up on them unawares, seeping to the surface or erupting without warning. At the least, the language of temptation tells us that although this phenomenon was widespread, it was no sort of movement or party. If these doubters learned their doubts from other people, they were not conscious of it. I have found no accounts of being tempted into unbelief by others. The recurrent fear that no one else had ever had such terrible thoughts no doubt reflects the experience of feeling God's absence, but it does also suggest that these doubters reached their doubts without outside assistance.

So where *did* these doubts come from? How did the father of lies manage to hook his barbs into so many sufferers? It is easy enough to line up the specific issues and doctrines on which these people were snagged. The presenting issue was often, not whether there is a God, but that perennial pair of secondary questions: the immortality of the soul and the inspiration of the Bible. Richard Baxter, whose wife was tempted to doubt both doctrines in her youth, believed that however logically separate they were, in practice they were inextricable. 'I find none doubt of the Authority of Scripture, but they doubt of the Immortality of the Soul too.'[29] Doubts about immortality were perennial, and surfaced as regularly in this period as before. In 1675, the young New England lawyer Samuel Sewall had a disturbing dream about a boy he knew who had recently died. In his dream, he was carrying the little body up a flight of stairs to Heaven, but 'I went up innumerable steps and still saw nothing, so that I was discouraged, doubting with myself whether there was such a place.' He awoke 'much troubled'.[30] Another young lawyer had had a parallel experience half a century earlier. Simonds D'Ewes attended a friend's funeral in 1624, and naturally wondered to himself whether his loose-living friend would be saved. Suddenly, however, he found his thoughts swerving from that orthodox path, as it struck him that 'now he [the friend] knew whether all those particulars the Scriptures deliver, touching God and the world to come, were true; and . . . whether there were a soul. I was . . . amazed to find myself entangled in these desperate scruples'.[31] Whatever doctrines you believe, there is no denying that death looks very final.

Doubts about the Bible were a more specifically Protestant problem. Protestantism's entire doctrine of authority was compressed between the Bible's covers, and that was a difficult job of containment at the best of times. In the seventeenth century it was made harder both by Catholic attacks and by the accumulation of minor textual puzzles and problems uncovered by biblical scholarship since the Renaissance.[32] Like chisel taps on a case of dynamite, these apparently trivial concerns threatened to blow the whole thing apart. The New England Puritan Michael Wigglesworth spent one Sunday in 1653 being 'sadly assaulted . . . with doubting whether ever word of the scripture were infallible', because of worries about variant versions of the text and about the use of Hebrew vowels.[33] Scholars had been aware of these issues for some time, but they were becoming plainer to everyday believers. Most biblical scholars claimed to be able to discern what the correct version of the text was, but since they could not agree among themselves either on the solution or on the correct method to use to reach it, ordinary readers could be forgiven for concluding that certain knowledge of God's Word was beyond their – and, perhaps, anyone's – reach.[34]

This was a serious matter. Daily Bible-reading was at the heart of Protestant devotional life. If you could not uncomplicatedly trust that the Bible was God's Word, the experience was utterly changed. 'When I had read the word of God,' one woman recalled, the devil 'tempted me with doubts and questions touching some things therein, whether it was truth or not'.[35] The thought was a woodworm quietly eating away the crossbeams of your faith. The tempter's argument was, 'What folly is it to take such pains in hearing the Scripture, and what madness is it so steadfastly to believe it, seeing thou knowest not whether it be God's Word, or the subtle device of man's brain, to keep the people in awe?' Even if it is God's Word, which translation should you choose? 'Some of them must needs be false, and who would ground his faith upon any, until he knows which is the best?'[36] What made these thoughts so insidious was that they turned the problem into an impossible one. No faith could be ventured until all traces of uncertainty were banished. Mary Gunter, a teenage convert from Catholicism, was plagued by the thought 'that the Scriptures are not his word'. Ministers who tried to persuade her that her doubts were unfounded instead made her wonder

> how could she, a silly [ie. uneducated] woman, get the under-
> standing of such deep mysteries? . . . How could she be sure
> that this was the truth which she now professed, seeing there
> are as many or more learned men of the one opinion as of
> the other, and all of them maintain their opinions by the
> Scriptures?[37]

Trying to argue doubts away only made them worse.

One of Gunter's fears was that the Bible was a 'policy', a deliberately manipulative hoax. This venerable theme, revived by Machiavelli, now seemed more compelling than ever. During the Reformation age, Christendom had been splintered into national churches closely controlled by secular governments – none more so than the Church of England. Apparently God's eternal truth changed when you crossed a border, or on the whims of kings and queens. Bishop Earle's 'sceptic' was 'troubled at this naturalness of Religion to Countries, that Protestantism should be born so in England, and Popery abroad'.[38] What if we only believe what we believe out of chauvinism and habit? A popular advice-book warned young Englishmen travelling to the Continent against sampling foreign churches, fearing not so much that they would convert as that they would conclude that all churches had good points and bad points, 'and so, displeased on all sides, you dash upon the rock of Atheism' – a fate to which those who had 'seen many countries' were proverbially prone.[39] Even if you did not give 'perfect credit' to another religion, merely to 'admit of a suspicion that things may be' as others say was to set the woodworm to work.[40]

Nor were different national churches the end of it. Most European territories tried to maintain some religious uniformity within their own borders, but the raucous world of religious diversity would not be shut out. In England, the coming of civil war in the 1640s was accompanied by the collapse of the national church and a sudden, bewildering profusion of sects. Memoirs from this period testify to how 'the diversity of their Opinions . . . occasioned much trouble and disquietness', and describe going 'from one to another . . . wearied in my spirit', or feeling 'tossed to and fro like the waves of the sea'.[41] To choose one sect from among this multitude 'is to throw the dice', despaired one traditionalist.[42] When religions proliferate, preachers warned, Satan's voice will urge you to 'keep thyself quiet and let all alone; hearken not to any of them, or if thou dost, believe them not over hastily . . . Profess not one religion more than another, till thou seest those who are learned agree amongst themselves'.[43] For the devil could be sure that such a day would never come, and that while you waited you would subside into practical atheism.

Alongside the inescapable micro-scale problem – how to live in a religiously divided society – was a less pressing, but more serious macro-scale equivalent: how to live in a religiously divided world. Christians had always known that they only accounted for a fraction of humanity, but the age of exploration confronted them with the vastness of the non-Christian world as never before. A famous summary in the 1620s guessed that no more than a fifth of humanity were Christian, and that many so-called Christians were so beset with 'superstitions' as scarcely to deserve the name. 'That horrible consideration of diversity of Religions' inevitably fostered 'Atheistical spirits'.[44] As Montaigne asked about the cannibals: what reason, laziness aside, do we have to believe that we are right and they are wrong? The era's first major anti-atheist tract warned that some

122

people, when they consider that there are 'both Gentiles and Jews, Turks and Christians in the world, and in divers nations divers Religions, whereof everyone thinketh he serveth God . . . (like men at a stop where many ways meet) . . . do stand still amazed'.[45]

One bestselling preacher actually encouraged this attitude, telling his hearers that their reasons for believing Christianity were no stronger than Jews' or Muslims' reasons for embracing their faiths. He was trying to shock them from the 'slumber' of habitual faith into a more sincere and earnest Christianity, but in fact it was the most sincere and earnest believers who were the most troubled by this question.[46] 'How can you tell,' the devil asked John Bunyan, 'but that the Turks had as good Scriptures to prove their Mahomet the Saviour, as we have to prove our Jesus is?'[47] The question could be answered. Preachers were very confident they could prove Christianity's superiority. But however neat their answers, they could not stop the question from echoing.

Amid all these anxieties which drew early modern Protestants into unbelief, it is worth noticing one supposedly perennial problem which does not seem to have afflicted them. It had been a truism since ancient times, and still is today, that suffering and pain could break Christians' faith, by making them question how a good God could permit such terrible things. Early modern anti-atheist writers sometimes took the trouble to rebut this argument, and one claimed that 'many have made question and doubt of the providence of God' because they see that the wicked prosper and the virtuous suffer.[48] Perhaps so. All I can say is that I have found precious little evidence of it. Our accounts of temptation to unbelief do not ascribe those temptations to worldly suffering. Occasionally we see Christians remonstrating with God for having 'led me into difficulties and perplexing miseries', but that is not unbelief in any sense of the word. The wiser anti-atheist writers believed that 'bitter exclamations' during worldly troubles induced, at worst, an unbelief that lasted only as long as the 'present passion'.[49] In an age which was far more intimately acquainted with quotidian suffering than our own – an age when barely half of children lived to adulthood, and when the best form of pain relief was brandy – we simply do not find evidence that suffering translated into loss of faith.

Yet if we widen the lens from worldly suffering, the picture changes. Both Catholics and Protestants warned that most of humanity would eventually endure an eternity of torment of body and soul in Hell, suffering to which no pain in this world could possibly compare. Churchmen enthusiastically used this doctrine to stir sinners to repentance, but if your conscience was already tender, you could be paralysed or even unhinged by dread. The caricatured atheist-libertines whom we met in the last chapter abandoned their faith out of wishful thinking, so that they could sin with impunity. But wishful thinking could have a more desperate face too. As a child, John Bunyan was 'so overcome with despair of Life and Heaven, that I should often wish . . . that there had been no Hell'. If you have given up hope of Heaven, then mortalism's limited-liability scheme is far more appealing than traditional Christianity. Sarah Wight's repeated insistence in her distress 'that there was no other Hell, but here in the conscience' seems to reflect a desperate desire that it should be so.[50]

The plainest case is that of Ludovic Muggleton, best known for eventually founding the eccentric 'Muggletonian' sect. In the religious turbulence of 1640s London, he moved fretfully from church to church, increasingly convinced that 'I must needs go to Hell'. And so, as the only escape, he longed 'to have said in my Heart, *sure there is no God*'. He could not quite persuade himself it was true, but he did the next best thing. Since he was convinced he was damned, he withdrew from any kind of religious practice, and tried simply to live virtuously on his own terms. It would not save his soul, but it would spare him the misery of continuously contemplating his future torment. 'I found more Peace here than in all my Religion.' In particular, a hope crept up on him: even if there is a

God, perhaps there is no immortal soul? 'I was in good Hope at that time, that there was nothing after Death.' He developed arguments to persuade himself of this, and for three years 'had a great deal of peace of mind in this condition'. 'I dreaded the Thoughts of Eternity . . . I thought, if I could but lie still in the earth for ever, it would be as well with me, as it would be if I were in eternal happiness . . . I cared not for Heaven so I might not go to Hell.'

But one day in April 1651, his long-suppressed belief in eternity came flooding back and his arguments for mortalism suddenly felt flimsy. He cast around desperately, even thinking that, since there had been so 'many Millions of People since the Creation', he might be lucky enough to escape the final judgement due to an oversight. 'God may forget me, and not raise me again, then shall I lie still and be quiet.' Yet he could not cling to that straw, and unwillingly, desperately acknowledged the truth of eternity. As it happened the crisis did not last long, for 'that very same Night the Windows of Heaven were opened to me', and he began his career as a prophet. Naturally, the sect which he created abandoned the traditional concept of Hell.[51] His solution was unique; his problem was all too common.

The one plain example known to me of an English Protestant tempted to abandon his faith due to worldly suffering comes from an even more unusual individual. Thomas Traherne was a meditative, riddling priest and poet who quietly discovered deep wells of inner peace in the midst of his country's turmoil. But, as we will expect by now, he was also tempted by unbelief. On one occasion, he tells us, he 'reasoned' with himself thus:

If there be a God, certainly He must be infinite in Goodness . . . How comes it to pass therefore that I am so poor? of so scanty and narrow a fortune, enjoying few and obscure comforts? I thought I could not believe Him a God to me, unless all His power were employed to glorify me.[52]

So here, at least, we have the classic problem of suffering: but the key detail is that this supposed incident happened when Traherne was four years old. And if he was almost alone in having doubts sparked by suffering, he was certainly not alone in falling into doubt as a child. We have already met several teenagers who, like the Devon gentlewoman Elizabeth Gifford, were troubled by 'thoughts of Atheism'.[53] The pioneering surveyor Richard Norwood was aged about seven when he fell 'several times' to 'reasoning . . . about whether there were a God'.[54] Like many adults, Norwood's doubts began with questioning his own salvation. Offhand adult assurances that God loved him felt flimsy. He began to read the Bible in earnest, but when he eagerly shared his scriptural discoveries with his parents,

> they made me little answer . . . but seemed rather to smile at my childishness. Upon which and the like occasions I often doubted whether things were really so as I conceived them or whether elder people did not know them to be otherwise, only they were willing that we children should be so persuaded of them, that we might follow our books the better and be kept in from play. And thus did atheism show.[55]

As they grow up, all children learn that they have been mistaken, or lied to, about a great many things. When they were told about their invisible God, the thought, 'is this true?', must sooner or later have crossed the minds of many (most? all?) children. Our adult wrestlers with doubt were surprised by the strength of the sudden temptations that they met. But they will most likely have discovered, and overcome, unbelief in themselves before.

These anxious doubters were not bold pioneers of freethinking. If they were atheists, they were reluctant, even horrified ones, drawn despite themselves into entertaining thoughts that they wished would go away. They saw their 'temptations' as irrational. 'I am darkened in understanding,' one serving-maid confessed, 'and I am tempted to believe there is no God.'[56] The darkening and the temptation were inseparable.

Every Bible reader knew that, if you say in your heart that there is no God, that makes you a fool. And so, while these insistent thoughts might come clothed in the 'pretence of sober Reason', anyone with the patience and determination to examine those wrappings would find them threadbare.[57] The temptation to atheism for earnest seventeenth-century Protestants was like fear of flying in our own age. With our rational minds we know that a plane will not simply fall out of the sky, but that knowledge is not much help as we sit white-knuckled through a nasty bout of turbulence. When they were able to calm themselves and gather their thoughts, these men and women knew that there was a God, that the Bible was his Word and that human souls were immortal. Perhaps those truths were counterintuitive, but so were, for example, many mathematical theorems. 'Many things, which seem incredible, are true,' cautioned the formidable classical scholar Meric Casaubon, 'and many things false, which are very credible': put that way, the point is hard to deny. Our doubters knew what they believed. Their problem was 'the prevalency and victory of our sensitive part over our reason'.[58] Like most of us, they struggled to hold on to the truths they knew.

The clearest sign of this is how they tried to fight back against such temptations. Their first resort was reasoned argument: reminding or reassuring themselves of why their nagging and superficially plausible doubts in fact made no sense. The seventeenth century's legion of anti-atheist writers bristled with arguments to prove their case. (I could easily have doubled the length of this book by summarising them.) Some arguments felt tendentious even in their own time – such as the tales of divine retribution against atheists which some enthusiasts assiduously gathered, or the widely made argument that, since witches and demons are real, God must be too.[59] Other points became less convincing the more they were repeated, such as the ancient, circular argument that since religion is universal to humanity, atheism must be unnatural.[60] In particular, a barrage of historical, literary, logical and moral evidence was deployed to defend the Bible: much of it powerful, some of it not.

But rather than being drawn into the individual skirmishes of the seventeenth century's war on atheism, we should step back to see the overall shape of the struggle. The attack on atheism was not a drilled, precise intellectual assault.[61] It was a chaotic, energetic and indiscriminate charge by disorganised volunteers who were profoundly committed to the cause and blithely assured of victory.[62] Martin Fotherby's *Atheomastix* (1622) took over 200,000 words to lay out its case, but he was only beginning. According to the structure he laid out, the published text only covered the first sixteenth of the total argument he planned to make. Mercifully he did not live to complete it. Spotting such a colossal white elephant on the battlefield should alert us to the fact that these weapons were not seriously intended to defeat the enemy. The anti-atheists themselves had not actually been persuaded that God is real by meeting accused witches or by examining the Bible's history. Most of these arguments were throwaway debating points, or auxiliary rationalisations used to bolster convictions they had actually reached by other means.

Nor were they very effective practical defences against temptation. Baxter and a few others insisted on their merits, but the consensus is against him. The abstract thought that there were rational arguments for faith was comforting; the arguments themselves, less so.[63] Bunyan's account of his struggle with atheism is typical. 'Sometimes

I have endeavoured to argue against these suggestions . . . but alas! I quickly felt, when I thus did, such arguings . . . would return again upon me.' Elizabeth Wilkinson 'had continual reasonings within me' against her atheistical thoughts, 'and yet still for a long time I was troubled'. Anyone can argue with temptation. Few of us can reason it into silence. Wiser divines knew that argument could be counter-productive: those tempted to unbelief 'grow sicker by seeing the medicine', not least because flimsy or ill-considered arguments risked discrediting themselves. And indeed, it seems that few things were more likely to foment doubts than reading anti-atheist arguments. Elizabeth Isham's lengthy struggle with atheism was sparked by reading a 'reasoning with an atheist' written by a popular poet. The radical William Walwyn was disturbed by 'mere notional, indigested arguments' deployed to prove the being of God and the authority of Scripture. It was not only, he wrote, that 'I did never believe through . . . any natural argument or reason', but that 'I rather find by experience, most, if not all arguments, produced' to argue for faith in fact serve 'in prejudice thereof'. The eighteenth-century philosopher who claimed that 'nobody doubted the existence of the Deity until . . . lecturers had undertaken to prove it' was being mischievous, but some real sceptics reported coming to their opinions in this way – including the grandfather of American independence, Benjamin Franklin.[64]

Veterans of the battle against unbelief agreed that, since their enemy was irrational, there was little use in bombarding it with rational arguments. Michael Wigglesworth resolved 'to fight against . . . unbelieving thoughts, not by debating with them (for so they are too hard for me) but by slighting them and not attending to them'. Others redefined their struggles in medical terms – for this was an age that saw 'melancholy' as an imbalance of bodily humours, not a psychological disturbance. Atheism, one minister reckoned, 'is but a spiritual madness, arising from the abundance of such distemper in the soul, as in proportion answers to melancholy in the body'. It made sense that in 1597 a noblewoman suffering from 'melancholy', who 'thinks the devil doth tempt her to do evil to her self, and . . . doubteth whether there is a God', took her problem not to a minister of religion, but to London's premier astrologer, Simon Foreman.[65]

Arguing with someone as quick-witted as the devil is a fool's game. Better to change the subject, persist in the faith, and wait for the storm to pass. 'If we will but study and endeavour to please our God,' wrote a Dutch preacher whose work was popular in England, 'and fulfil his will and conform ours to his, then our minds would be troubled with none of these questions.' Faith, after all, is a gift from God, so our responsibility is simply to wait and remain ready to receive. The Bible's story of doubting Thomas tells us that, although he did not believe, he continued faithfully to keep company with the other apostles until his doubts were brought to an end.[66]

The radical preacher John Saltmarsh put it vividly: 'The way to be warm, is not only to ask for a fire, or whether there be a fire or no, or to . . . wish for a greater; but to stand close to that fire there is, and to gather heat.'[67] A fair amount of testimony bears him out. Elizabeth Isham argued with her doubts, but she also knew, or professed to know, that her only hope of a lasting victory lay in prayer.[68] Mary Gunter finally triumphed over her doubts when 'she tied herself to a strict course of godliness, and a constant practice of Christian duties' – and in particular to a hearty daily diet of Bible reading. Others credited their recovery to immersing themselves in devotional books.[69] When the pious Scots lawyer Archibald Johnston of Wariston spent an afternoon trying to counsel two ladies 'about the temptations that there was not a God, and to self-murder', his method was to pray with them and to read aloud from a popular guide to pious living.[70] The technique was to treat broken faith like a broken limb: set it in a rigid cast of conventional pious practice and hope that it would eventually heal.

Sometimes it worked; sometimes not. For example, receiving Holy Communion was said to be one of the most powerful means to strengthen faith. 'So often as we feel these doubtings,' a Sussex minister urged his flock, 'let us draw near to the holy Sacraments, and thereby seek strength and increase of faith.'[71] But what if you sought faith there and did not find it? Richard Farnworth took his first communion in the 1640s after weeks of preparation, trembling with terror at his unworthiness and hoping for assurance of grace. Instead, 'After I had received . . . I sat pondering of it in my heart, and waited in expectation in myself, to receive some divine operation, and spiritual change, and to receive assurance of the pardon of sin; but none came in.' As he dwelt on this frightening emptiness, at last 'I saw . . . that it was not the body and blood of Christ, but a carnal invention.'[72] Trying to jump-start your faith by going through the motions could end up simply draining away what life remained in it.

The most powerful weapons against temptation to unbelief were neither trite rationalisations nor these techniques of self-manipulation, but 'arguments' whose effectiveness lay in their combination of logical force and emotional punch. The two key responses are summed up by the poet and unorthodox Protestant John Milton: 'God has imprinted so many clear signs of himself in the human mind, and so many traces of himself throughout all nature, that no sane person can be unaware of God's existence.'[73] Beneath all the throwaway debating points, it was these two convictions that had real weight to them, and that storm-tossed believers could use as ballast to bring themselves back to an even keel.

To take Milton's second point first: the appeal to nature and the created order was a classic rational argument for the existence of God, but it was more than just that. Virtually every anti-atheist writer used some version of the argument, and it is important for us to appreciate how compelling it was in this age. The only available account of how the universe came to be which did not depend on a Creator was Epicurean atomism, which was at best a very partial and unsatisfactory doctrine. But what made an appeal to the witness of Creation so powerful was that it seemed intuitively as well as logically true. 'What man is there,' asked one anti-atheist in 1634, 'that beholding the frame of this world, may not perceive that there is a God?' It was an argument which everyone could understand. When Dionys Fitzherbert told those caring for her that prayer was futile, for 'there is no such thing' as God, a servant promptly replied: 'No? . . . Who then made you and fashioned the members of your body?'[74]

In the midst of her turmoil, the woman whom we know as M. K. rose early one morning and 'went up into the highest room that was in the house'. She was sorely tempted to leap to her death, and she 'looked forth at the window to see if I could see God'. She could not; but she could see something. 'I beheld the Trees to grow, the Birds to fly, the Heavens how they were hanged, and all things that were before me; then I thought *they could not make themselves.*' For her, it was a turning point. The existence of trees, birds and stars was hardly news to her, but at that moment of raw vulnerability, to have her eyes opened to their intricate majesty was an epiphany. Similarly, when Elizabeth Walker was tempted to atheism, 'the Lord was pleased to obviate that Temptation by my meditating on the Creation', and especially on the flowers which her father cultivated, in which she beheld 'God's curious workmanship'. The mood is calmer than in M. K.'s case, but the sense of awe, here intertwined with her love for her father, is the same.[75] And as in the case of Jane Turner, who 'went in the fields . . . to confirm my self in this truth, that there is a God', this was a conviction reached as much through the senses as through reason.[76] For Elizabeth Isham, the value of meditating on the witness of creation was not merely that it proved there is a Creator, but that, when she considered the natural world, 'I am amazed; for thou doest great things and unsearchable, yea marvellous things without number.'[77] What began as logic could end as worship.

Thomas Traherne's meditations describe how, from his infancy, the wonder of Creation had both enraptured him and filled him with eager curiosity. As a small boy, 'my Soul . . . would be carried away to the ends of the Earth: and my thoughts would be deeply engaged with enquiries'. The 'ends of the Earth' was not a figure of speech: the problem vexed him. Was there a wall at the edge of the world? Or a cliff? Did Heaven perhaps come down, touching the world 'so near, that a man with difficulty could creep under'? And what was beneath the earth: pillars? Dark waters? If so, what was beneath them? He knew that none of his guesses were adequate, but he could not puzzle it out. At last, someone told him the answer, and its simplicity and beauty surpassed any of his speculations. 'Little did I think that the Earth was Round.' That moment of astonished discovery has been shared by generations of children, but if we are to believe him, the young Traherne was a little more unusual in drawing a theological lesson. When he understood the truth,

> I knew by the perfection of the work there was a God, and was satisfied, and rejoiced. People underneath, and fields and flowers, with another Sun and another day, pleased me mightily: but more when I knew it was the same Sun that served them by night, that served us by day.[78]

In the modern age, the majesty and strangeness of the cosmos still has a powerful emotional tug, but that tug has usually been towards atheism rather than towards God. Neither emotional reaction is 'correct'. Traherne simply reminds us how different the same facts can appear to different eyes.

One of the most thoughtful meditations on the natural world's role in the dance between belief and unbelief is found in the 1625

Treatise Containing the Originall of Vnbeliefe, by the Newcastle minister Thomas Jackson. He agreed that the natural world refuted atheism more by refreshing the soul than persuading the mind, and was positively lyrical about 'the pleasant spectacle . . . which woods and shady fountains afford'. He even suggested that atheism might be seasonal. 'If other men's minds be of the same constitution with mine, our apprehensions of the true God as Creator, have a kind of spring, when he renews the face of the earth.' There is no way to know whether he was right, but the notion is not ridiculous. The point is that, for Jackson as for many others, unbelief was not rational scepticism, but 'a spiritual madness', akin to melancholy.[79]

He would say that, wouldn't he; but hear him out. Prevailing medical orthodoxies blamed melancholy on an imbalance of the body's humours. Jackson argued that the commonest cause of atheism was a similar imbalance in material conditions. The soundest believers, he suggested, were those who had sufficient for their daily needs, but no excess. Utter indigence 'starves the natural notions or conceits of God, which must be fed with sense or taste of some goodness'. Unless you have some savour of God's grace in your everyday life, it is hard to believe that that grace governs all creation. More to the point – and it was widely accepted that this was the more serious problem – excessive affluence 'chokes' the same natural notions. The souls of the rich are so cloyed with artificial pleasures, and so beset with trivial worries, that they lose their taste for true joy. If the rising tide of atheism was to be turned, Jackson believed, it would not be by philosophical disputation, but by directing unbelievers' attention to their own hearts, so that they 'might behold the image of God engraven in them'.[80]

In other words, Milton's appeal to the witness of nature in the end brings us back to his first and most fundamental point: that the human mind itself testifies to God. At the root of everything was the appeal to inward experience. 'It is ingraven in all hearts, that there is a Deity.' 'God is to be felt . . . in every man's conscience.'

'The Being and Attributes of God were so clear to me, that he was to my Intellect what the Sun is to my Eye.'[81]

If you dig deep enough into every argument that anxious doubters used to persuade themselves back to faith, sooner or later this is what you find: they knew there was a God because they just knew. In modern terms, hopelessly irrational; for them, the very heart of reason. As in mathematics, some things are simply too self-evident to be logically proven. We know that a part is less than a whole not through deduction, but through intuition – 'common sense', as the first and most influential anti-atheist treatise put it. Perhaps you can laboriously construct a proof to demonstrate the fact, but the project is as ridiculous as trying 'to enlighten the Sun with a candle'. As with the arguments for God, these rationalisations do not actually *persuade* anyone. Whereas those who try to deny self-evident truths, whether in mathematics or theology, 'show themselves to be wranglers and unworthy of all conference, as contenders against their own mother wit . . . There is no reasoning against those which deny the Principles'.[82] If God's being is utterly self-evident, the subject simply cannot be debated. Where would you begin? It is no accident that the analogy of the sun in the sky was so often used. What can you say to people who deny that there is such a thing, other than to reject their error and pity their blindness?

This made it entirely logical to treat unbelief as a monstrous anomaly. Perhaps, some anti-atheists suggested, our own sins blind us to God, on the principle that moral and intellectual corruption are linked – and indeed, those wrestling with unbelief sometimes worried that their doubts were a sign of, or a judgement on, their other sins.[83] A more extreme version of the same argument was that atheists 'scarcely seem to hold the place of human beings'. 'He pretending Atheist', John Donne insisted, 'must be no man, must quench his reasonable soul, before he can say to himself, there is no God.'[84] The much-repeated claim that atheists are subhuman was more than just abuse, and more than just a pretext for

135

atheism as a crime. It was a solution to the puzzle of how anyone could maintain something so obviously false.

But if you found that you could not see it – if all you could make out above you were dark skies – this was no comfort. 'Some secret Instinct whispers me that there is a God,' declared a fashionable book of the 1690s; 'I . . . have endeavoured all I could, and still want the power of being an Atheist.'[85] Lucky for him, many readers would have replied; they found it all too easy. The heart of the question is: why, during the seventeenth century, did people who knew all the arguments that there is a God stop finding God's reality intuitively obvious? Why did people who knew that the wind would not disappear under their wings begin to be gripped by an unexpected fear of falling? 'I find,' wrote the fretful New England Puritan Michael Wigglesworth, 'that the clearest Arguments that can be cannot persuade my heart of belief [in] the being of a God, if God do not let the beams of his glory shine into it.'[86] Why, among seventeenth-century Protestants, did those beams of glory begin to fade?

There was something in the air; it was the spirit of the age – those are useless claims, but they are also true, and we should not kid ourselves that we can pin that spirit to a card and anatomise it. Still, we have learned some things from our tour of Protestant unbelief. The anxiety and intensity of Protestant piety made doubt a serious part of the religious ecosystem. The despair with which a great many Protestants sometimes wrestled could easily shade into doubt of various kinds, whether because God's mercy seemed too good to be true, or because his justice seemed too terrible to contemplate. Once it was there, the methods used to deal with it made it worse. Trying to silence the voice of temptation by arguing with it was a very Protestant response, but an inherently self-defeating one. Debate is, by its nature, open-ended, and the certainty it pursues vanishes over the horizon like a mirage. Doubters set off in pursuit of it, only to find themselves lost in shifting sands.

The seventeenth century's emerging crisis of faith was not an intellectual one. The problem of suffering, the most evergreen rational argument against Christianity, does not seem to have had much purchase. And the doubts which were cited – whether there really is an immortal soul, whether the Bible is to be trusted, whether religion is a hoax, or whether there really is a God – were nothing new. The Reformation had not made Christians ask these questions for the first time. Instead, it had taken doubts that had been suffused through the Church and distilled them. It mobilised doubt as a weapon and encouraged ordinary believers to do the same, in the hope that they would make their way through to a reflective and experienced faith rather than a simple and trusting one. But the journey was a dangerous one. Individual believers were compelled to confront their doubts, and to ask on exactly what foundation their long-professed beliefs actually stood. The whole process brought unbelief out into the open: and it did so deliberately, on the principle that you should keep the devil where you can see him.

And so the implicit doubts that had long pervaded Christendom became explicit. The aim was not to turn believers into unbelievers. It was to turn naive believers into sophisticated, self-aware believers, who had confronted temptation and overcome it. Very often it worked. But as we will see in the next chapter, becoming a sophisticated believer was neither a simple nor a controllable transformation. The process had costs, and casualties.

5

Seeking and Losing Faith

'Whereof one cannot speak, thereof one must be silent.'
Ludwig Wittgenstein, *Tractatus Logico-Philosophicus*

'It's a Great Matter to Believe there is a God'

While religious establishments were panicking about the mostly imaginary atheism of amoral Machiavellian libertines, a quite different form of unbelief was bubbling up under their noses: an unbelief of anxiety, assaulting earnest Christians from within. It is not what either the anti-atheists of the time, or historians of atheism since, lead us to expect, but it makes a certain amount of sense. In early modern times, atheism and unbelief were active stances. They required some commitment, given that custom, habit, society and law all made a quiet religious conformity the path of least resistance. Those with no interest in religion might neglect it, but they would not take a stand against it. They might be bad Christians, but would hardly rise to being anti-Christian. Only those who cared enough to believe also cared enough to doubt.

We have seen how those who suffered from this kind of doubt classed it as a temptation, and tried with mixed success to overcome it. That effort might suggest that their experience does not matter very much. They were unwilling conscripts into atheism's army, and deserted as quickly as they could. But their efforts to realign themselves with God's cause were rarely a simple return to their former duties. Their determination to fight for their faith using the lessons they had learned from their sojourn with unbelief gave the battle an unexpected twist.

Christians commonly assume that doubt is a bad thing. According to thirteenth-century canon law, someone who doubts the faith is by definition an infidel. 'Doubting Thomas' has never been a compliment. According to one exhaustive treatise on that famously sceptical apostle, his reluctance to believe Christ's resurrection 'tendeth . . . wholly to his discredit', for doubt is the most terrible and pervasive of all sins. 'To be doubtful in religion,' warned another moralist, 'is to be certain of the greatest punishment.'[1] This is why early modern books of prayers so regularly featured prayers against doubt, and why doubters feared judgement for their faithlessness.

But anyone who stopped to think about the matter realised that this was inadequate. Even canon law was more nuanced than it appeared. Medieval theologians distinguished between 'deniers' and 'doubters', the former deserving condemnation, the latter sympathy.[2] Doubt was, as we have seen, a temptation, not a sin. And when God permits the devil to tempt his people, he does so for a reason. Temptation is not simply a meaningless attack to be repulsed. It is a trial by combat: a training arena from which the victor emerges stronger. It is to be feared, but it is also an opportunity to be grasped.

The much-quoted Bible verse – 'Lord, I believe; help thou my unbelief' – implies that faith and doubt are not alternatives but companions, inevitably intertwined. This is true in the obvious sense that Christians' faith is weak and incomplete. For seventeenth-century commentators, however, the deeper point was that this mixture was a good thing. If you believe your faith is strong, then what you have is not faith at all, but 'a vain cloud of presumption'.[3] Only hypocrites claim that they never doubt, warned Elizabethan England's theological giant William Perkins. 'True faith, being imperfect, is always accompanied with doubting, more or less.'[4]

'Faith when it is at its strongest is but weak,' agreed his more trad-itionalist contemporary Richard Hooker, 'yet . . . when it is at the weakest, so strong, that . . . it never faileth.' It is when you are most aware of the weakness of your own faith that you are most likely to throw yourself wholly on God's help: so you can be 'faithful in weakness, though weak in faith'.[5] Behind that preacher's flight of fancy stood a more hard-edged observation. 'Undoubtedly he that never doubted, never believed' – it was a much-repeated truism. If you do not feel any pain, you must already be dead. If you do not feel vertigo when you look down, you must be at the bottom of the pit.[6] As the shrewd Puritan Richard Sibbes reassured his readers, 'nothing is so certain as that which is certain after doubts. Shaking settles and roots.' One grateful reader underlined those words.[7] Doubt was not exactly *good*. But it was inevitable, and its fire tempered and purified those who passed through it.

Even laying aside these theoretical arguments, the plain fact was that everyone doubted. 'What experienced Christian doth not suffi-ciently know, that the dear children of God are subject to these pangs?'[8] The great Edinburgh preacher Robert Bruce, whose pulpit oratory supposedly made King James VI weep tears of repentance, repeatedly insisted that 'as faith is on the one part, so doubting is on the other'. Indeed, he claimed, 'the best servants of God, are exercised with terrible doubtings in their souls, with wonderful stammerings, and they will be brought at some times, as appears in their own judgement, to the very brink of desperation.'[9] Christians should not flee from doubt. They should set their feet, spit on their hands and grapple with it.

As the intensity of Bruce's language suggests, he spoke from experience. According to his biographer,

He . . . had been oft assaulted about that great foundation truth, the being of a God, which cost him many days and nights wrestling. When he came up to the pulpit, after he had been silent a little, as was his usual way, he could have said sometimes, 'I think it's a great matter to believe there is a God.'[10]

This hard-won triumph made him a more admirable spiritual exemplar than if he had spent his life in blithely untroubled faith. Protestants, whose religion was grounded in scepticism, were trained not to ignore or suppress their doubts, but to lean into them in the hope and expectation that this was the road to a firmer, more mature, post-atheistic religion. Very often it worked, producing the result which Bruce exemplified, and which most of the troubled souls we met in the last chapter eventually reached: a recognisably orthodox Protestant faith, sometimes tougher for being battle-hardened, sometimes weaker for being wounded. But not always.

The Spiritualists' Progress

Like all revolutions, the Protestant Reformation was always threatening to spin out of control. The magisterial theologians who ended up dominating Protestantism, above all Martin Luther himself, were always fighting on two fronts: against the pope, but also against the people Luther called 'fanatics' – the perverters of the Reformation who threatened to dissolve Christendom into anarchy. These radicals were and are often collectively called 'Anabaptists', since many of them taught that baptism should be restricted to adults who positively chose it: a position which contradicted not only the Christian practice of infant baptism dating back to the second century or before, but also the idea of a universal Church which embraced an entire society. However, not all the radicals were Anabaptists. In 1530 the German preacher Sebastian Franck proposed another category. He was, he said, a 'spiritualist'.[11]

Franck had begun preaching Luther's message in Nuremberg in

1525, but quickly became convinced that Luther's purge of superstition did not go far enough. Luther argued that Christians were saved by faith, rather than by anything they did, since any outward piety could be faked by hypocrites. And yet he insisted that churches, liturgies, sacraments and many traditional Christian pieties ought to continue, making (as it seemed to Franck) only superficial changes. The serpent was not being crushed: it was only shedding its skin. True religion, Franck believed, was a matter of the heart alone. He took his lead in part from an anonymous fourteenth-century treatise which Luther had rediscovered and published in 1516, before the Reformation crisis broke. Luther called this treatise *Theologia Germanica*, and claimed that he had learned more from it than from any book beside the Bible and the works of St Augustine. But it was Franck and his fellow 'spiritualists' who truly ran with its teachings.

The central principle of the *Theologia Germanica* is the need for the 'inward man' to transcend the 'outward man', and ultimately to 'wholly and absolutely cast off himself, so . . . he should be void of himself and one with Christ'. Such a person will be 'a deified, or a divine man . . . illuminated and enbeamed with divine light, and kindled with the eternal and divine love'. The book accepts, a little grudgingly, that such full perfection is unattainable in this life. But while it concedes that 'no man is void of sin', it adds, 'howsoever it be, this is evident, that the nearer any man approacheth to this obedience, so much the less sin is in him'. It accepts the value of outward rites and ceremonies for those making their first steps towards godliness, but implies that they are a stage that might one day be outgrown.[12] The result is a heady, rarefied spirituality which can be contained within orthodox Christianity, but which also incubates a restless radicalism. You would not need to be a particularly excitable reader to conclude that every outward form of piety – everything that is normally meant by *religion* – exists in order to be left behind.

In 1529 Franck resigned his preaching post in Nuremberg and moved to the cosmopolitan city of Strasbourg. The cacophony of sects and preachers he found there, all claiming the mantle of true reformation, appalled him. 'It is impossible,' he wrote, 'that one God, . . . baptism, Supper and gospel can exist in so many repugnant churches.' Instead of throwing his weight behind one of them, or founding an alternative movement of his own, he settled on a much more disconcerting idea: that the one true Church of Christ no longer existed on earth at all. It had, he now believed, disappeared centuries ago, when the last of Christ's original apostles died: 'The outward church of Christ . . . went up into heaven and lies concealed in the Spirit and in truth . . . For fourteen hundred years now there has existed no gathered church nor any sacrament.' This breathtaking claim allowed him to dismiss all the churches in existence without suggesting that God had failed his people. Rather, it was God's will that 'the church is today a purely spiritual thing'. The *Theologia Germanica* had shown that outward religion could be transcended. The time to do so was now: 'All outward things and ceremonies . . . have been done away with and are not to be reinstituted . . . Nothing has been taken from the child except its doll with which it has played long enough.'

The implications were dramatic. All religious observance should stop immediately. No baptisms, no other sacraments, no ministers and preachers, no churches and services. Franck did not even encourage his readers to meet informally to support and encourage one another. And while he remained convinced that the Bible was God's Word, he was increasingly reluctant to lean on its precise text, which he called 'the rind of Scripture', 'the covering of . . . letters', turning instead to its hidden spirit, which 'none but those who are taught of God himself can understand'. This meant abandoning not just each particular Christian church, but Christianity as a whole. He distanced himself from the traditional doctrines of the Trinity and of Christ's Incarnation. True religion lay not in such stale formulae, but in the inner journey to perfection. In which case it only made sense to conclude:

> Consider as thy brothers all Turks and heathen, wherever they be, who fear God and work righteousness, instructed by God and inwardly drawn by him, even though they have never heard of baptism, indeed, of Christ.

Franck's 'spiritualism' was not atheism. But it could hardly have been more hostile to religion.[13]

The Silesian nobleman Caspar Schwenckfeld took a slightly different route. He was an early convert to Luther's movement, but his growing conviction that outward pieties were merely symbols of inner spiritual truths led him, in 1526, to call for a *Stillstand*: a temporary suspension of the Eucharist until the people could be taught to understand it rightly, and until he himself could be sure of the true rite. 'We abstain at this time,' he wrote, 'in order that . . . we may not be a party to error, idolatry and misuse.' As Donne would say, better to stand still than to take the wrong path. But this was not at all Luther's view, and Schwenckfeld was cut adrift, ending up, like Franck, in Strasbourg. There he met Anabaptists for the first time, and quickly concluded that his *Stillstand* needed to be extended to baptism too. These were dangerous views, and he spent the remaining thirty years of his life in hiding, often on the move, always writing.[14]

Presumably he and Franck knew one another, but there is no proof of that, and their theologies were rather different. Franck believed that the true Church was now and would remain a wholly spiritual entity. Schwenckfeld genuinely saw his *Stillstand* as provisional. Eventually God would send true prophets once again, empowered by the Holy Spirit like the first apostles, and then the *Stillstand* would be over. 'We wait, therefore, eagerly and with sighs until Christ invites his guests through his spirit.'[15] Unlike Franck,

Schwenckfeld encouraged his disciples to meet secretly for discussion and mutual encouragement. Even so, these Schwenckfeldians did not dare to celebrate any sacraments, recognise any ministry, enforce any orthodoxy or practise anything that their contemporaries would recognise as religion.

Both Franck and Schwenckfeld continued to find publishers, but their movements were less the first sparks of a fire than the first straws in a wind. Later generations of radicals might read their works, but were not necessarily their disciples. The spiritualists were especially widely read in the Netherlands, both by professed radicals and by more slippery figures. The great Dutch ethicist Dirck Volckertsz Coornhert said that the *Theologia Germanica* was his favourite book, full of 'pearls, gold and gems'. Like Franck, he believed that none of the churches of his own day was the true Church of Christ. Like Schwenckfeld, he suggested the creation of what he called a *stilstandskerk* as an interim measure until God saw fit to restore the real thing.[16]

These theories were first put into practice, not because of an intellectual breakthrough, but because of a political crisis: a bitter schism in the Dutch Calvinist church over the theology of predestination in the 1610s, which ended with a decisive victory for the predestinarians. In defeat, some anti-predestinarians drifted towards radicalism. One anti-predestinarian congregation near Leiden began holding clandestine meetings for reading, prayer and discussion, with no minister leading them. True Christians, they now thought, should enjoy strict equality, with everyone entitled to speak freely. In 1621 they set up a 'free prophecy' group in the village of Rijnsburg, open to anyone. Its monthly meetings lasted deep into the night. Other meetings or 'colleges' sprang up in imitation, drawing both on disillusioned anti-predestinarians and on old-school radicals. By the 1640s, these 'Collegiants' had a foothold in most Dutch cities. They had their own loose orthodoxies – pacifism, opposition to infant baptism, a certain rationalism – but the only fixed point was the commitment to mutual tolerance and spiritual equality.[17]

We do not know whether Adam Boreel joined the Collegiants when he studied at Leiden in the late 1620s; it seems plausible. His documented involvement with them only dates from 1645–6, when his own newly formed 'colleges' in Middelburg and Amsterdam joined with the original movement in what was effect a second foundation. Boreel was a phenomenon: a disciple of Coornhert's and a Hebrew scholar who believed passionately that atheism could be beaten back and Christianity renewed, but only if a great many dangerous errors were cleared out of the way first.[18]

Boreel laid out his views in a weird, crabwise style in his manifesto *To the Law and to the Testimony* (1645).[19] Its starting assumption is that the first apostles' preaching was 'wholly, intrinsically, undoubtedly, and merely true'. Their hearers could therefore be 'infallibly assured of the truth of that word' – so much so that even a 'doubting examiner, after a due search, might be infallibly assured that no error . . . was to be found there'. Having set such a high bar, Boreel then, inevitably, asks how Christians today might attain that same level of invincible certainty. It takes him a great many tortuous pages of logical sifting to reach the obvious conclusion: they can't. Therefore, since ministers can never be fully certain whether they are preaching in accordance with God's will, or simply 'as it seemeth good to themselves', their ministry is 'tainted' and their churches corrupted. Such pseudo-churches 'ought to have been very shy of preaching in the name of God'. And yet they continue, outrageously, to claim divine authority for themselves. Therefore, Boreel insists, all those who care for true Christianity ought 'to separate themselves from such societies . . . accounting them no longer Churches of God, but malignant societies; whereinto the soul of a man fearing God . . . ought not to enter'. He is rather more vague about what these scrupulous objectors should do instead. They ought to worship 'privately . . . making use of the Scripture', but he struggles to reconcile the plain fact that the Bible requires collective worship with his deduction that no one can be sure that any form of worship is valid. So he concludes tentatively that it may be 'profitable' to join a community which worships tolerantly, using the unadorned words of Scripture, and 'with an ear always open readily and thankfully to receive better information'.[20]

This austere vision was realised in the refounded Collegiant movement, and was to have enduring consequences. But Boreel's reinvention of Franck and Schwenckfeld's spiritualist minimalism resonated beyond the Netherlands. Quite how his ideas first reached England is unclear. There were family connections: Boreel's father had been part of a Dutch embassy to England in 1613, and had been knighted by King James I. At some point in the 1630s Boreel himself came to study in England. Almost all we know about this visit is that he was 'noted for zeal' in religion, and that, according to the hostile witness who is our only source for this episode, he was arrested for being an enthusiast and prophet. After a few months English friends secured his release, and he was expelled from the country. But when England fell into civil war in the 1640s, Boreel became so deeply involved with a clique of prominent English and Scottish defenders of Christian rationalism that he even took the trouble to learn the English language. His most constant English correspondent, Samuel Hartlib, was a formidable networker, theologian and scientist, and is the most obvious conduit through whom Boreel's ideas could have reached an English audience, but by no means the only one: plenty of English radicals had spent time in the Netherlands.[21] What we know is that Boreel's book appeared in an English translation – the only translation ever made from the original Latin – as early as 1648; but that well before then, English radicals had embraced his ideas and gone beyond them.

Protestant radicalism came slowly to England. Only in the 1580s did a handful of English Protestants who had run out of patience with their state church's rigid conformism form separatist congregations, chiefly in exile in the Netherlands. Most of these separatists remained more or less within basic Christian orthodoxy, but a few explored wilder shores. In around 1590, an English separatist named Henry Barrow – soon to be executed for his heresies – denounced various even more extreme radical views held by some of his compatriots. Among these was the claim that Roman Catholic baptisms were invalid.

It was no trivial point. If that was so, then none of the first generation of Protestant Reformers had been baptised at all. And since everyone accepted that 'none unbaptised may be a minister or baptise', no mere Reformation could put this matter right. The chain had been broken, the true Church of Christ had entirely vanished from the world, and so things would remain 'until some second John the Baptist or new Apostles be sent us down from heaven'.[22] As soon as we read that, it seems obvious where this argument is going. People told to look for new apostles will inevitably find them. Those who declare that new apostles are needed will probably volunteer their own services. A former servant named William Hacket who decided that he was John the Baptist was executed for blasphemy in 1591. Edward Wightman, who in 1612 became the last person burned for heresy in England, believed that he was not only the new John the Baptist but also the incarnation of the Holy Spirit. Whatever this is, it is not unbelief.[23]

But attacking baptism could, in theory, lead in another direction. Wightman seems to have been inspired by another radical, Bartholomew Legate, who went to the fire a few weeks before him. There is not much hard evidence as to Legate's beliefs, although we know that one of his brothers had refused to have his child baptised.

What we have is a detailed, gossipy account by a former separatist named Henoch Clapham of a faction which he called the 'Legatine-Arians', who 'deny all Baptism and Ordination, till new Apostles be sent'.[24] In a fictionalised dialogue Clapham published in 1608, a 'Legatine-Arian' declares that 'there is no true Baptism upon the earth'. When another character protests that Christ's apostles had conducted true baptisms, the Legatine-Arian replies that the apostles had been 'furnished with the gift of Miracles, for the persuading of their hearers' – otherwise no one would have believed them. Whereupon he turns to the argument Barrow had summarised some years earlier: having been fatally corrupted by centuries of enslavement to the pope, the true Church cannot simply re-establish itself by an act of will. Only God can refound his Church. The logic was stark. 'New Baptism there cannot be, till there come new Apostles. New Apostles there cannot be, who are not endowed (from above) with miracles.'[25]

If we had to guess the next line, we would assume the Legatine-Arian would proclaim his own sect's miracles or anoint himself as a new apostle. But he says something altogether more surprising. 'Miracles we hear of none.' Some sects claim to have had visions: he dismisses them as 'idle dreams'. 'Consequently', there is 'no true Baptism in the earth, nor any one true visible Christian' – not even himself. The other characters in the dialogue are nonplussed. One asks the 'Legatine' to pray with him. He refuses: to do so 'should imply, that you and I were in communion or Christian fellowship', and as the world currently stands 'there can be no such fellowship; and therefore no such prayer'. Another character, half-persuaded, asks if he can join the Legatine's congregation, only to be told: 'How sillily you speak. I have all this while taught you, that there is no Church.'[26]

Perhaps the real Legate was not quite so blank in his denials. One witness claimed that he and his brothers believed their surname, which means 'envoy' or 'ambassador', to 'foreshow and entitle them, to be the new Apostles' – although that is exactly the kind of story a hostile witness might invent.[27] Even so, Clapham's account shows that early seventeenth-century England could at least conceive of an exceptionally austere and minimalist spiritualism which cannot meaningfully be described as a 'religion'. What he described was more than merely an abandonment of all Christian practice. Even if such spiritualists really did expect that new apostles would appear, a God who allows his Church to dissolve into utter depravity and leaves his people with nothing at all for centuries on end is pretty ineffectual. Praying to him hardly seems worthwhile. According to one report, Legate did not pray to Christ for seven years before his death.[28] By Clapham's account, Legate believed that God was almost entirely absent from the world, that there was no immediate prospect of that changing, and that humanity had no choice but to carry on regardless. Whether the mood of this stark vision was bleak or liberated, we do not know. But while it was not 'atheism' in the strict modern sense, we can see why contemporaries might have used that word.

Scholars of the subject reckon that Legate's ideas had no more than a 'fleeting influence'. That may be so, but they may have also been a link in the chain. The source of these doctrines is a mystery, but the Legate family came from Essex and included wealthy cloth merchants who traded with the Netherlands. Equally, our only hint that he had any followers is one opaque report of a meeting with 'a Gentleman-like man' who seems to have been one of their disciples.[29] But some of the ideas which surfaced in the 1620s and 1630s do sound oddly familiar.

London's underworld of religious radicalism was an eclectic one, whose common theme was a shared hunch that Spirit-filled Christians could overcome their innate sinfulness more readily than strict Calvinists imagined. Orthodox preachers called this 'Familism', since it echoed the Dutch sect the Family of Love, which had taught that believers could achieve such a close spiritual union with Christ that they would be 'Godded with God'. What made these new 'Familists' dangerous was that they attracted jaded mainstream Protestants who could be tempted to push the boundaries of their tradition. Foremost among these was John Everard, a renowned London preacher during the 1620s who discovered Sebastian Franck, Familist writings and, not least, the *Theologia Germanica*, which he translated into English. An adventurous preacher in Yorkshire translated it independently around the same time, and by 1634 manuscript copies of both versions were going 'up and down in the City' of London.[30] As other outspoken Protestants steeled themselves to confront King Charles I, these spiritualists were instead aspiring to rise above the fray altogether.

In 1638 an informant provided a detailed account of the 'Familist' groups in London. His allegations went beyond routine claims that they held their goods in common, believed they could attain moral perfection and were eager readers of the *Theologia Germanica*. He accused one group, the 'Familists of the Mount', of denying 'the Resurrection of the body, or any heaven or hell, but what is in this life . . . Heaven is when they do laugh and are merry, and hell when they are in sorrow and pain. And at last they do believe that all things do come by nature'. Another group, the 'Familists of the Valley', were fatalists, believing in God's immutable will, and therefore 'denying all prayers and giving of God thanks for anything, either for this life or the life to come'. They too denied any bodily resurrection.[31]

This informant was not exactly impartial, and it is worth noticing that another witness accused the 'Familists of the Valleys' of *excessive* histrionics in their prayers.[32] But they would not have been the only spiritualists to have felt that ordinary Christian prayer, or orthodox doctrines about life after death, were simply too gross for the elevated purity of their vision.

The following year, John Everard himself was arrested and tried before the court of High Commission. An eyewitness account describes the fifty-five-year-old cleric weeping, pleading with his judges and even begging the bishop of Norwich to stop berating him and simply pass sentence. He would spend a year in prison before being allowed to make a formal recantation; he died not long after his release. Under those circumstances, it would be rash to take the charges against him as proven fact. Even so, they are striking. He supposedly rejected bodily resurrection, denying 'that our bodies nourished of and by beef, mutton, capon and the like could rise again and go to heaven'. Instead, he claimed that all things – including all human beings – are God, merely 'clothed' in their outward appearance, and that at our deaths we 'shall return into God again'. He explicitly denied the existence of Hell. And when the Bible was cited against him, he allegedly claimed that the Bible's teaching about God 'is false if literally understood'. The *Theologia Germanica*, by contrast, was 'the only book for salvation'.[33] His views on the Bible, at least, can be corroborated. In his own writings, Everard distinguished between the Bible's 'dead letter' and God's true Word. 'The Letter . . . is but Chaff which covers the Corn . . . All the Scriptures are symbolical and figurative.' Nor would he allow that the Word was found only between the Bible's covers. Even someone who had never seen or heard the Bible 'may have the inward word, to wit, the law of God written in our hearts'.[34]

So, just as the Protestants whom we met in the last chapter were doggedly resisting temptations to question the Bible, to doubt immortality and to deny God, others were embracing those same questions and doubts. They believed that by doing so they were not rejecting God's truth, but coming closer to it. In bold and restless pursuit of a greater purity, they were eager to leave behind the crass carnalities of a childish faith, just as the first Protestants had abandoned gross superstitions such as transubstantiation. This was not unbelief: it was belief raised to a new height. If reaching that height meant abandoning doctrines and practices which had been Christian shibboleths for centuries – Heaven and Hell, the

Bible and the Church, preaching and prayer – then their boldness in doing so only demonstrated the depth of their faith. And if unenlightened worldlings thought that their faith looked like atheism, what of it: since the time of Christ, such people had always persecuted the truth.

Even so, there was no reason to think that spiritualism would be any more important in England than it had been anywhere else. And then, a few months after Everard's recantation, King Charles I's regime collapsed. What followed would be a decisive gear change in the history of unbelief. At no point during the two decades of war and religio-political turmoil from 1640 to 1660 did England have a government with both the power and the will to impose religious conformity. The result was an exuberant flowering of religious variety without precedent in the Reformation era. Old radicals and new adventurers at the edges of orthodoxy found themselves converging on ideas and practices that look very much like unbelief, and on a scale never before seen.

Historians have long since recognised that the English Civil War was not only the first of the great European revolutions, but also the last of the wars of religion.[35] What made it both of those at once – and what has not been so widely recognised – is that it was also a war of irreligion. England's moral panic about atheism had been simmering for a generation: now it boiled over. The plainest sign of this is in the invective hurled by all sides. Amid the partisan vitriol of the 1640s, each party had its own distinct vocabulary of insults, which immediately identified who a particular pamphleteer was backing. Only one insult was used with equal enthusiasm by everyone: *atheist*.

After all, if someone opposes what you think is obviously right, despite having their error explained to them, naturally you will conclude that they are defying God's will. And plainly no one who truly believes in God would dare do such a thing. English Parliamentarians, convinced that royalists were godless wretches, revelled in stories about soldiers who spoke the king's name with touchy reverence but God's with hair-curling blasphemies. To say nothing of the royalists' actual religion, which to their enemies looked like a parody of true Christianity, so debased that it was tantamount to denying God. Meanwhile, royalists claimed that Parliamentarians' war against superstition had tipped over into open atheism, and that all they really wanted from the Church was plunder. The spectacle of Parliament deciding the nation's religion implied that God was subject to human laws. Royalists imagined Parliament asking, 'Is there a God? Let it be put to vote!' while the king appealed instead to 'the votes of heaven'.[36] And if each side saw atheism in the other, they agreed that the 'lukewarm Neuters' who tried to sit out the conflict were atheists, since anyone who had no opinion about the nation's divisions evidently believed in nothing at all.[37] So the English took up arms in the 1640s to protect true religion, not from corruption or impurity, but from extinction. The nation stood on the brink of an atheistical abyss. It was an apocalyptic moment: the crux of the world's history, playing itself out at Europe's westernmost end.

This war against atheism would not be fought only on the battle-field. The warriors also had to defeat the enemy in their own hearts. Freelancers, volunteers and lone wolves, mostly on the Parliamentary side, pressed towards their own visions of purity. Many of their campaigns do not belong to our story. Some, unwittingly, do.

Most Parliamentarians wanted to replace the reviled church estab-lishment, its made-over medieval churches and its black-gowned priests, with a new church whose ministers were theologically fit for office. But some radicals distrusted university theology and thought that the test of a true minister should be holiness, not education. Others rejected any distinction between ministers and people at all. 'Ministers are abolished as Antichristian, and of no longer use', declared a group of radical soldiers who muscled their way into a pulpit in Surrey in 1649: 'now Christ himself descends into the hearts of his Saints, and his Spirit enlighteneth them with Revelations.'[38] That may not sound like an atheist manifesto, but its effect was to legitimate the kind of anticlerical fury that until now had been associated with libertines. The army officer who said 'their swords shall never be out of their hands, as long as one Priest continued in England' was a fire-breathing radical, not a loose-living blasphemer bridling at self-righteous busybodies, but his words could have borne either meaning. A troop of Parliamentary soldiers quartered in Warwickshire in the mid-1640s were 'constant' in denouncing the region's ministers, 'dissuading the people from going to church', and claiming that they themselves could preach better. Bookstalls heaved with denunciations of the contemptible rituals practised in 'their vile stone Churches', and of the 'atheists and godless persons' who still enslaved themselves to them.[39] But attacking atheism by withdrawing from communal religious observance was, to say the least, a high-risk gambit.

Most radicals, and eventually the republican governments of Oliver Cromwell, favoured some measure of religious toleration. They believed that, as John Milton later put it, 'without . . . liberty, there is no religion, no Gospel; violence alone prevails'.[40] But the horrified traditionalists who saw toleration as a slippery slope to atheism were not wrong. Roger Williams, the period's most famous tolerationist, argued that churches in a nation ought to be like private societies or clubs in a city: free to manage their own affairs, but with no responsibility for 'the essence and being of the City, and so the well-being and peace thereof'. England did not need religion to hold it together. 'The bond of civility' would do the trick.[41]

If toleration eroded religion in theory, it did so all the more in practice. In a free market of religious ideas, consumers get what they want. One pamphlet imagined a browser in London's most notorious radical bookshop asking, 'Have you a Book that declares the Bible not to be the Word of God? . . . any against the Nature and Essence of God? . . . any Book to declare that Christ is not God? . . . any Book that doth deny the immortality of the Soul, Resurrection, Heaven, Hell?' The answer to every question was yes.[42]

Maybe we do not believe the story of the radical who called for toleration for witches, on the grounds that 'they in their conscience hold the Devil for their God'; or of the one who asked, 'what if I should worship the Sun or the Moon . . . or that pewter pot standing by, what hath any man to do with my conscience?'[43] But tolerationists certainly saw free irreligion as a lesser evil than forced superstition. Some argued that, if people had a free choice between religion and atheism, their religion would be more sincere. It is a fair point, but the counter-argument – that this is like a man who 'would have a fair Virgin to lie with him' in order to prove his chastity – also has some force.[44] Tolerationists were deliberately kicking away the props that had long kept most people's religion secure. They were doing it for thoroughly religious reasons, but that does not change the consequences.

Protestants tempted to unbelief were, as we have seen, troubled by two doctrines in particular: the immortality of the soul and the authority of the Bible. English radicals in the 1640s deliberately assaulted both. In a notorious 1644 pamphlet called *Man's Mortality*, the radical Richard Overton branded immortality a 'Hell-hatched doctrine' invented by the clergy to terrorise the simple into obedience. He argued that the 'soul' is a pagan, not a Christian concept, and ridiculed the idea of disembodied survival as nonsensical. Contrary to the howls of horror it provoked, this book was not at all atheistic. The spirit dies with the body, Overton argued, but God will raise both body and spirit to life again at the Day of Judgement, and the saved will then enjoy a (bodily) eternal life in Heaven – just as mainstream Christianity had always taught. He claimed his argument was wholly orthodox. But that was too glib. What becomes of the Christian doctrine of the communion of the saints if the dead saints are merely dead? Does Hell have the same weight in Christians' imagination if it is still awaiting its first inmates? To say nothing of the various biblical texts which seem to teach the opposite, such as Christ's tale of the rich man and Lazarus. Overton's response to that story was to state bluntly that 'there was never such a man . . . or ever such a thing happened . . . [It] was a Parable'.[45] Attack immortality, and pretty soon you are questioning the Bible too.

The claim 'the soul of man is mortal as the soul of a beast, and dies with the body' surfaced repeatedly in the years that followed: sometimes with a promise of a future resurrection, sometimes without.[46] Those who did foresee a final resurrection sometimes argued that only the saved would be raised, and that the damned would simply die rather than being condemned to eternal torment. That doctrine could be defended theologically, and is indeed accepted by a great many Christians in modern times, but it also, quite deliberately, abandoned one of Christianity's most effective tools of social control.[47] An even more dangerous variant was the spiritualist notion that *only* the soul and not the body would be raised. This turned 'resurrection' into an inward, spiritual event, and 'Heaven' and 'Hell' into metaphors for happiness or misery. Those who took this line believed that they were not abandoning traditional Christianity, but instead revealing the profound inner truths that had long lain concealed within it. If they were pressed on what actually lies beyond death – a subject they claimed, implausibly, to find uninteresting – they might maintain that 'every creature is God . . . and shall return into God again, be swallowed up in him as a drop is in the ocean'.[48] One spiritualist said he could no more imagine what he would be after the world's end than he could imagine what he had been before its beginning: 'I am willing to let fall any carnal apprehension of a visible or corporeal enjoyment of God . . . I am content to be nothing, that he may be all . . . I cannot conceive any other resurrection, than of carnal to be made spiritual.'[49] He may have been denying the traditional doctrine by transcending it in the most rapturous and spiritual terms, but he was denying it all the same.

Naturally this same set of impulses called the Bible's literal authority into question. When orthodoxy's defenders quoted Scripture to refute radical claims, radicals who refused to back down were forced to expand their quarrel to include the Bible itself. 'This is Scripture to you,' said one mortalist confronted with conventional proof-texts, 'but not to me': how could orthodoxy's defenders answer that?[50] The radicals picked up long-standing niggles about textual variations, problems of translation and apparent contradictions – issues which biblical scholars had known about and had been successfully managing for centuries – and turned them into real arguments for the first time: not because they were newly persuaded by these old chestnuts, but because, unlike their predecessors, they genuinely needed arguments against the Bible. They did not exactly reject it, but they felt they had outgrown it. It was a 'human tradition', the tool of self-serving priests. Defenders of toleration disliked how the Bible was quarried for 'Laws or Rules, to judge, persecute and condemn one another'. So they insisted that it was 'mysterious and dark', and no sure basis for doctrine.[51] Anyone who claimed a direct revelation from God had to deny that the Bible was the exclusive repository of such revelations. They might well conclude that their own new visions made older revelations redundant.

The soldiers in Surrey who mocked churches and ministers in 1649 also declared that the Bible 'is abolished: It containeth beggarly rudiments, milk for Babes. But now Christ is in Glory amongst us, and imparts a fuller measure of his Spirit to his Saints than this can afford'. They underlined the point by burning a Bible before the people.[52] Some radicals distinguished between Scripture as 'history', the dead outward letter recording what God had done in ages past, and Scripture as 'mystery', the inner Word written on the hearts of God's people here and now.[53] None of this was atheist scoffing: it was, as one orthodox preacher sardonically observed, 'higher flown, more Seraphical' than that.[54] Yet the effect – to lend credence to every burgeoning doubt about the Bible – was the same.

Once you have begun cracking open the husks of traditional Christian doctrines in order to reveal their inner spiritual kernels, how do you know when to stop? As early as 1644, an anonymous pamphlet claiming to be 'set forth by a mad man' interpreted the entire Bible as an allegory of one believer's inner spiritual struggle.[55] This sort of talk quickly zeroed in on a single question. Christianity is a historical faith, which looks 'for great matters from one crucified at Jerusalem 16 hundred years ago' (as it then was). Was that an allegory too? According to Gerrard Winstanley, famous for leading a utopian commune in Surrey in 1649–50, 'Jesus Christ at a distance from thee, will never save thee; but a Christ within is thy Saviour.' *Christ* has here become a universal spiritual principle, not the distant historical figure of the preacher from Nazareth. The renegade Quaker who said that 'your faith stands in a man that died at Jerusalem, and there was never any such thing' was apparently not claiming that there was no historical Jesus – that belief would not surface until modern times[56] – but rather that his life had no enduring spiritual significance. Others believed in Jesus in the same way they believed in Queen Elizabeth I, 'because Chronicles make mention of her'.[57] Some radicals even questioned Jesus' moral authority, saying that 'if Christ were on earth now, he would be ashamed of what he did before', or even that 'Christ's righteousness was a beggarly righteousness'. All the better to put their own fresh revelations on a higher plane.[58]

Could this journey into ever more rarefied and allegorised spiritualism end in actual, 'hard' atheism? It came close. Winstanley tried to rebut the 'report . . . that I deny God', but he had a funny way of going about it. To explain that 'I use the word Reason, instead of the word God' was not much of a defence. Admittedly, by 'Reason', or 'the Spirit Reason', he did mean something ineffable, rather than simply a logical process, but at most this was pantheism, or something like Kant's categorical imperative.[59] And we do have

159

reports of radicals claiming that 'there is no God, or if there be a God, the Devil is a God' – or even saying, 'Where is your God, in Heaven, or in Earth, aloft or below, or doth hee sit in the clouds, or where doth hee sit with his — ?' The last word was presumably 'arse': our witness found it 'too horrid and obscene' to repeat.[60] Most likely this out-of-context comment reflected the speaker's impatience with spiritually inadequate concepts – 'your God' – but it could also be that, having pursued truth up and up the mountain, he and those like him had at last found the summit bare. Either way, they had left Christian orthodoxy far behind them.

Seeking a Rock to Build On

Most English men and women were horrified by this eruption of radicalism, but not all of them panicked. In 1646 Samuel Bolton – a prominent London preacher, Master of Christ's College, Cambridge, and a member of the Westminster Assembly established by Parliament to create a post-war religious settlement – published a guide to surviving an age of 'abounding errors'. The burgeoning sectarian chaos, he suggested, was a test: a means for those who had spent their lives blithely claiming to be Christians to discover whether it was true. He cited Jesus' parable of the house built on sand, the weakness of whose foundations is only revealed when the storm comes. England was now living through just such a storm:

> When a man sees abundance of opinions abroad, one saith this, another that, sure it will make a man to put the question to himself: upon what foundation do I stand? What is my bottom? And how can he have any rest till he have gotten a better foundation to build on, a foundation which none of these opinions can shake and unsettle?

There would be casualties. 'Many fair buildings . . . fall down, and [are] not able to stand out the blast of trial and temptation, because they are houses built on the sands.' The vain and hypocritical Christian, whose faith has never had a secure foundation, will find that 'the multitude of opinions doth draw him away, or else Atheist him'. Such people will be revealed for the unbelievers they have always truly been. But for the true believer, sectarian cacophany has the opposite effect:

> It will make [such] a man to enquire after the rock, and endeavour to build there . . . The multitude of opinions . . . doth *un-atheist* him, put him upon the search and examination what is the truth of God . . . These things do fire him out of his formality, and he can have no rest till he come to some bottom to stand on.[61]

Christians, then, ought not to respond to the storm by hunkering down inside their inherited orthodoxies. Instead, they should let the storm do its work of washing away ill-founded habits and notions. If cracks started to appear in their temple, they ought not to patch it up, but abandon it or even tear it down. And before they thought about rebuilding, their chief duty was to dig: to work down through as many layers of shifting sand as necessary until their shovels finally rang on bedrock.

Bolton hoped to use this storm as the Reformation had used the scepticism which it weaponised: to turn lazy, habitual Christians into earnest, engaged but still orthodox Christians. But not everyone stuck to the script. In England during the 1640s and 1650s, on a scale which Christendom had never before seen, bands of earnest excavators began churning up the landscape of traditional religion. Many of them found their rocks and started to build again, but soon others – or they themselves – began to worry that this foundation, too, might be shakier than it seemed. And in the process the traditional ritual, devotional and intellectual structures of the faith were undermined or deliberately demolished.

This was an age which loved categories, and so it coined a word for such people: *Seekers*. Seekers are usually spoken of simply as another exhibit in revolutionary England's sectarian zoo, along with Ranters, Quakers, Fifth Monarchists, Muggletonians and the rest, but this is misleading. They were a mood, not a sect, and by their nature they resist definition. Until the mid-1640s, 'seeker' was a banal term for a Christian striving to discern and follow God's will. When a 1643 pamphlet said, of the Westminster Assembly, that 'the whole *Assembly* are . . . *Seekers* unto God night and day', it was paying them a rather bland compliment.[62] The word would soon become spicier.

When church discipline collapsed in 1640, a significant minority of English Puritans withdrew, relieved, from the half-reformed established church to form 'independent' congregations. But hypersensitised consciences soon fretted that these congregations, too, were sodden in the dregs of superstition. The young Kentish gentlewoman Mary Springett and her husband, who 'scrupled' at common Puritan practices like psalm-singing, 'looked into the independent way', but they 'saw death there'. Of all the issues about which the 'independents' began to discover qualms, the most momentous was baptism. Many of them began to wonder if baptism ought to be reserved for those old enough to declare their own faith. Tempting as it was, this doctrine was fundamentally at odds with the ideal that the Church should extend to every member of society. In 1644 a group of Parliamentary soldiers in Huntingdonshire heard that a baby was about to be baptised in the parish church. They blocked the road, and some of them 'got into the Church, pissed in the Font, and went to a Gentleman's stable in the Town, and took out a horse, and brought it into the Church, and there baptised it'. It hardly matters whether this was gratuitous desecration, or whether they were trying to demonstrate that infant baptism was a grotesque parody of God's true ordinance. The assault on long-standing Christian practice was equally severe either way.[63]

But denouncing infant baptism was the easy part. If you were reforming baptism, how could you be sure that your new practice was correct? When 'dippers' immersed believers in freezing ponds – usually by night to avoid attracting attention, and sometimes naked so that they could be quickly dried and dressed in warm clothes afterwards – were they actually following God's ordinance? Could they be sure? Mary Springett and her husband were initially drawn to the new baptism, but they 'found it not to answer the cry of our hearts'. The radical prophet Sarah Jones wrote in 1644 that some people were looking for more than just a purified baptismal rite. 'Some are seekers out of a Baptism, looking for Elijah, as John the Baptist, to bring it from heaven, forsaking all fellowship till Christ shall send forth new Apostles to lay on hands.' Old spiritualist ideas were suddenly newly relevant.[64]

Luke Howard, a shoemaker's apprentice from Dover, joined the radicals and was baptised one February 'when the Ice was in the Water'. He embraced the rite 'with great Joy, in hope I had found him, whom my Soul loved'. But over the months that followed, the bitter divisions between baptistic groups, and the immorality he saw among them, made him fear that his baptism was merely a 'carnal ordinance'. The crunch came when he was asked to baptise a new convert, and had to refuse. He could not administer baptism to others when 'I was not satisfied in my own.' He explained to his dismayed fellow believers that 'I saw myself out (and them also) of the Faith of the Gospel, and that if ever I do come to know it; I shall know it as plain as my Natural Eyes knows that Door.'

Anyone who, after the emotional intensity of a clandestine baptism, found that their inner life was not in fact permanently transformed might worry that they 'had grasped but at a Shadow, and catched nothing but Wind'. By 1645 several formerly zealous Baptists had reached this conclusion. Having left his community,

Howard wrote, 'I gave my self up to a seeking state again, and became as Dead to all Forms, as if I had never been amongst them.'[65]

What was this 'seeking state'? There are two kinds of answers, focusing on what Seekers believed, and how they lived. Their beliefs are surprisingly clear and consistent, given that this was a movement defined by dissent and dissatisfaction. They rejected not only baptism but also ministry of any kind. Seekers were, one of their number explained, 'a people who deny all Ordinances': not because rites and ministry were inherently wrong, but because they had not yet found rites and ministry that were demonstrably in keeping with God's will. When they looked at the churches, whether the old establishments or the new radical congregations, Seekers saw 'a Giftless Ministry' and 'a Powerless People'. These institutions called themselves God's churches, but there was no evidence to bear that out, and all too many signs that God had in fact abandoned them to corruption. The only path left was austere self-denial like that attributed to Legate earlier in the century. Seekers insisted that they would accept no one's authority unless accompanied by 'a gift of Healing, a gift of Miracles, a gift of Prophecy', like the first apostles. And yet they gave no credence to any rumours of such gifts in their own times, insisting that if and when they came, they would be utterly unmistakable. In the meantime, Seekers were resolved 'not to go about to build, and set up ways, by their own mistaken, miscalled, and misunderstood gifts: but to wait upon the Lord'.[66]

Clement Writer, a litigious clothier from Worcester, was one of the first to be labelled a 'Seeker' in this sense, and one of the first to defend the position. His 1646 book *The jus divinum of presbyterie* is strongly reminiscent of Boreel's *To the Law and to the Testimony*, both in the way its unusual question-and-answer structure sidles towards its conclusion, and in the argument itself. It is not a translation of Boreel but is perhaps an imitation of him. Yet we know of no direct contact between them. Boreel's book appeared in Latin in 1645 but not in English until 1648, and we know that Writer could not read Latin. Moreover, Writer's argument goes further. He rejects all Christian ministry, including water baptism, unless authorised by 'mighty works which . . . none could do, but by the special power of God'. Christ, he points out, told his apostles to wait to begin their ministry until they were clothed with power from on high. Those apostles' would-be successors should exercise the same restraint.[67]

Writer's critics called him 'an Anti-Scripturist, a Questionist and Sceptic, and I fear an Atheist'. In trying to rebut that charge, he ended up at least partly conceding it, for it turned out he had the same scruples about the Bible as he had about churches. If a preacher told him to obey the Scriptures, 'I must ask him . . . what Scriptures?' The originals, when nothing remained but 'the copies of the copies'? Greek and Hebrew texts that 'a mere Englishman' could not read? A translation? – in which case which one? Texts whose interpretation was, at best, 'mysterious and dark'? There was no rock to be built on here. The Bible's authority, Writer argued, rests purely 'upon its own piety and wisdom', and it is to be interpreted entirely through 'the Law of Nature written in our hearts, or the love and goodness of God'. So the Bible cannot infallibly teach us any doctrines at all. Its only true message is one of 'mutual charity and toleration'.[68] His fear of being deceived by error meant that, as a pious duty, he refused to embrace any firm truth.

Mary Springett shows us what this religion of anxiety meant in practice. After her husband's death in 1644, 'I changed my ways often, and ran from one notion to another, not finding satisfaction or assurance.' Paralysed with uncertainty, she ended her own and her household's daily prayers. In place of a regular round of structured devotions, she was now beating desperately at God's door: 'Most of my time in the day was spent either in reading scriptures, or praying . . . I durst not go into my bed till I had prayed, and I durst not pray till I had read scripture and felt my heart warmed thereby.' Her former piety now seemed to her mere hypocrisy. She was 'ashamed to be accounted religious', and grew to 'loathe' anyone who claimed to be: they 'were worse than the profane, [for] they boasted so much of what I knew they had not attained'. And so she arrived at the archetypal Seeker position:

> I began to conclude that the Lord and his truth was, but that it was made known to none upon the earth . . . There was nothing manifest since the Apostles' days that was true religion . . . I knew nothing to be so certainly of God, as I could shed my blood in defence of it.

It was braver and more truly pious to admit her utter ignorance of God than to worship some imaginary substitute. And so 'I . . . resolved in my heart I would . . . be without a religion until the Lord manifestly taught me one.' She had become a devout and expectant atheist.[69]

For a while Springett gave herself to 'mirth and carding, dancing, singing and frequenting music meetings . . . and jovial eatings and drinkings'. Pious gentlewomen did not do such things, but if all piety was a corrupt sham, why not? The problem was that Springett was not cut out to be a libertine. She continued to brood on her spiritual troubles, and to have vivid, disturbing dreams on the subject. In one, she was told that Christ had returned and was in the next room, but that even so she must compose herself, sit and wait for him to come to her. When she eventually remarried, what drew her to Isaac Penington was that 'he saw the deceit of all notions' and 'refused to be comforted' with easy answers.[70]

The Seekers' hopes were real. They seem genuinely to have believed that the time would come when God would send a new dispensation. The apocalyptic chaos around them implied that it might come soon. The difficulty with this hope was not merely that it became thinner the longer it was delayed, but that it did not solve the problem of what to do in the meantime. One obvious answer

was for like-minded Seekers to meet for discussion or even f[or]
prayer. We do have some accounts of this happening, but they a[re]
problematic. They generally come from Quakers, and Quake[rs]
tended to regard Seekers as Quakers in embryo, waiting merely t[o]
be 'convinced' by a Quaker preacher that what they were seekin[g]
was the light of Christ that had always been within them. The
Seeker meetings these accounts describe sound suspiciously like
exact anticipations of Quaker practice.[71] There are a few other
mentions of a Seeker 'society . . . who worshipped God only by
prayer and preaching', or simply of Seekers meeting for mutual
encouragement, like the Dutch Collegiants.[72] But these groups were
not merely informal; they actively resisted formality. One former
Seeker described an itinerant preaching ministry, during which he
periodically met like-minded folk: 'We fed one another with words,
and healed up one another in deceit, and all laid down in sorrow.'
It was a shifting, irregular debate, not a pattern of worship.[73] And,
like Mary Springett, many Seekers struggled alone. Being a Seeker
was almost defined by withdrawing from settled religious practice
and 'waiting upon the Lord'. When Luke Howard left the Baptists
behind, 'I mourned in secret with Tears . . . in a waste Howling
Wilderness, where I could find no Trodden Path, nor no Man to
lead me out.' After passing through various sects, the Derbyshire
shepherd John Gratton eventually 'left . . . all Churches and People,
and continued alone, like one that had no Mate or Companion
. . . I believed God had a People somewhere, but I knew not who
they were, and was now afraid to join with any, lest they should
not worship God aright'. He would not join any more sects 'for
fear of being deceived'. The scruples that paralysed Seekers' devotion
paralysed their sociability too.[74]

The same scruples troubled them even if they tried to practise
what was left of their faith alone. Regular prayer and Bible reading,
the staples of Protestant piety, felt like empty formalities. Radicals
denounced their former devotional routines: 'when I used all these

duties, I had not one jot of God in me.' When a seventeen-year-old named Edward Burrough tried to steel himself to prayer in 1650, he heard an inner voice reproving him: 'Thou art ignorant of God, thou knowest not where he is, nor what he is; to what purpose is thy Prayer?' This 'broke me off from praying [and] I left off reading in the Scripture', cutting the last moorings still tying him to Christian convention.[75] One Seeker rejected all outward religious forms, even praying alone with her husband, on the grounds that she was 'above Ordinances, above the Word and Sacraments, yea above the Blood of Christ himself'. A sympathiser wrote that Seekers 'are entered into their rest, they cease from their labours . . . all external forms . . . duties of prayer, etc'.[76] As an act of faith, they had renounced religion.

Seekers struggling to know how they should live converged on a bold answer: to transpose their religion into a moral key. One woman, told by a radical preacher that nothing of what she believed was certain, asked what, in that case, she should do. He replied, 'if you live honestly and modestly, you shall do well enough'. Some suggested that instead of meeting for worship, Seekers ought to gather periodically to discuss 'what is good for the Commonwealth, [and] read some good moral things' such as the works of Plutarch or Cicero.[77] The Renaissance had sown the notion that God's law in our hearts could transcend Christianity: now it was flowering. The utopian visionary Gerrard Winstanley, a Seeker fellow-traveller, did recommend prayer – but added that to truly pray was 'to pay the king of righteousness his due', that is, to conduct yourself honestly, to 'till the ground according to Reason', and to recognise and root out evil within yourself. 'He that is drawn up thus to Reason within himself, and to see himself, this man is praying continually.' Muttering words into the air, by contrast, 'only worships the Lord with wind'.[78]

This was all the more compelling because many Seekers' discontent with established religion was driven by anger as well as by anxiety.

Some were provoked by the failure of ministers and people to live up to the moral codes they proclaimed. One reason that so many Seekers – including Mary Springett – eventually became Quakers is that the Quakers truly did seem to model the ferociously exacting morality which their souls sought. But Seekers were more than just rebels against hypocrisy. Many of them came to find Calvinism repugnant in theory as well as in practice: its intolerance, its doctrines of predestination and eternal damnation.[79] As Clement Writer put it, if all doctrine and authority was uncertain, the only certainty left was God's law written onto every human heart. That was the only yardstick against which churches, their doctrines and their Gods might be measured. The radical argument that there is no Hell, for example, was not really based on the various biblical quotations marshalled to make the case, but on moral intuition. 'It is not for the glory of God to impose such a punishment upon any . . . That belongs to cruelty, [and] is abhorred by the light of nature.'[80] The only way to truly follow God was to abandon dogmatism. The price was to redefine 'following God' simply and entirely as striving to adhere to a supposedly universal moral law. That may be magnificent, but it is not religion.

It was also impossible. Apart from anything else, while most seventeenth-century people believed natural law existed, they could not quite agree on its contents. For example, could war and violence ever be justified? In an age of civil conflict, it was not an abstract question.[81] And then there was sex. John Milton launched his public career by arguing for the legitimacy of divorce, and he would later defend polygamy.[82] In 1649–50 respectable England was swept by a panic about so-called Ranters, who supposedly denied that 'one man [ought] to be tied to one woman, or one woman to be tied to one man . . . It is our liberty to make use of whom we please'.[83] Whether or not that was true, many radicals certainly rejected the conventions of godly morality as hypocritical legalism. They danced, gambled, drank, smoked and sometimes more, both to celebrate their God-given freedom and to shock respectable prudes who needed to be shown what real grace meant. 'To the pure all things, yea all acts were pure.'[84]

And if the principle was not intended to abolish sexual restraint entirely, some individuals were keen to use it that way. Orthodox moralists revelled in stories such as that of the Seeker who persuaded his fiancée to sleep with him, saying 'that marriage was but an idle Ceremony' – only to abandon her when she fell pregnant, so that 'instead of one Seeker there were two'.[85] We do not need to believe every scurrilous story to accept the point. If you climb above all devotional practice, all communal religious life, all doctrinal fixed points and even all moral conventions, then no matter how sincere your principles are, you will be left very exposed. To maintain this rarefied trans-religious spirituality, and live your life in the unblinking, invisible light of Reason, is not easy. It is no surprise that some of those who set out up this mountain struggled to actually make homes for themselves above the treeline.

To see this at work, consider the fullest, most compelling, and most unreliable and slippery narrative of the Seeker experience. By the time he wrote *The lost sheep found*, Laurence Claxton had become a Muggletonian. Looking back from that perspective, he described his former life as a series of picaresque scandals. Like so many others, he had progressed restlessly from one sect to the next, but as he told it, his earnest spiritual quest became increasingly self-serving. Expelled from a preaching post for his radical views, he fell into Baptist circles in Suffolk. He married a young woman from this community in a private ceremony in her house, on the grounds that 'marriage is no other, but a free consent in love each to the other before God'. After a brief period of imprisonment, 'I took my journey into the society of those people called *Seekers*', finding meetings that used the term for themselves. Preaching to them, he discovered, was a route to both adulation and cash. He began 'to travel up and down the country, preaching for monies'. He sent money home to his wife, but also 'satisfied my lust' with other young women who were drawn by his doctrines. At this stage, he tells us, he still believed the 'high flown notions' of freewheeling spiritual liberty that he preached, but as he became more skilled at preying on his audiences' pockets and their chastity, 'I concluded all was a cheat, yea, preaching itself.' Naturally, he redoubled his efforts. He fell in with a group of London radicals, telling them that 'till you can lie with all women as one woman, and not judge it sin, you can do nothing but sin'. And, so he claimed, the women came. 'I had Clients many . . . I was not able to answer all desires.' Eventually scandal caught up with him and he fled the city. By this stage he was convinced that 'there was no such thing as theft, cheat, or a lie, but as man made it so'. What began as a theological speculation about Christian liberty became an eminently useful practical principle. He now believed that when he died, 'I should know nothing after . . . my being was dissolved.' And so he aimed merely 'to eat and to drink, and to delight my soul'.[86]

Eventually he began to offer astrological and magical services, and 'made many fools believe in me'. He evidently still had some vestiges of belief himself, however, since he tells us he made several attempts to conjure the devil. When these failed,

> I judged all was a lie, and that there was no devil at all, nor indeed no God, but only nature, for when I have perused the Scriptures I have found so much contradiction . . . that I had no faith in it at all . . . I really believed no Moses, Prophets, Christ, or Apostles, nor no resurrection at all.

Not that this interrupted his preaching career. He was quite ready to feign belief 'for my own advantage'. He was only derailed when he met, and was reduced to 'a trembling condition' by, the Muggletonian prophet John Reeve.[87]

It is a profoundly untrustworthy and self-serving account which revels in the contrast between cynical sectarian corruption and visionary Muggletonian purity. But its narrative arc from idealism through opportunism to cynicism is plausible enough. If you have abandoned all the structures and constraints of your old religion, what is to stop you? Another exhausted Seeker, Luke Howard, eventually decided 'to make Merry . . . and to take my fill of the World, with all I could enjoy thereof: Then I said within my self, I will now be as Proud and as Fine in Apparell, as I possibly can be'.[88] Vain and empty, yes, but what else was there? The 'Atheist' in Bunyan's *The Pilgrim's Progress* tells Christian and Hopeful bitterly that he has 'been seeking . . . twenty years', to no avail. He left home and all he had in pursuit of a fruitless quest. But now 'I am going back again, and will seek to refresh myself with the things that I then cast away.'[89] However enthusiastically Seekers dug in search of bedrock, those who only found layer upon layer of mud and swamp were almost bound to despair of their quest in the end. In which case, with all the old structures of their faith long since overthrown and their pit only getting deeper, what was left but to return exhausted to the surface and enjoy what was left of the daylight as best they could?

And so, at the farthest point out, the Seekers' painfully earnest scruples and the libertines' worldly cynicism met and mingled. Francis Osborne, whose *Advice to a son* (1656) became notorious as an amoral libertine's manifesto, mocked the Catholic claim that St Peter was the prince of the apostles. Instead, he urged his readers 'with our *Seekers* to place St *Thomas* in the Chair; believing, like him, no more than lies patent to human understanding, which is as much as can decently be imposed upon a new believer without a Miracle'.[90]

Seekers used that precise argument to justify their scrupulous inaction. Osborne used it to justify living exactly as he liked. As we look from Seeker to libertine, and from libertine to Seeker, already it is becoming difficult to say which is which.

6

The Abolition of God

Ah, but a man's reach should exceed his grasp,
Or what's a heaven for?

                    Robert Browning, *Andrea del Sarto*

The Three Impostors

The book's existence had been rumoured for centuries. Finally, in 1680, *Of the Three Great Impostors* appeared in print, issued by an impeccably respectable Lutheran publisher in the city of Kiel. It was a tease, of course. Christian Kortholt, the city's theology professor and the book's author, was not in fact denouncing Moses, Christ and Muhammad, but a newer trio: two Englishmen and a Dutchman. These three impostors were the seventeenth century's equivalent of the twenty-first century's New Atheist 'four horsemen': symbols of a wider shift in the mood, and signs to be spoken against.[1] Between them, they sum up the gathering changes we have been tracing in this book, changes which, by the second half of the seventeenth century, were emerging into the open.

The least-known member of Kortholt's trio is Edward Herbert, baron of Cherbury, whose modern reputation has been eclipsed by his younger brother, the poet George Herbert. The two brothers were close, but could hardly have been more different. The quiet, sickly George was a famously devoted pastor, firmly but eirenically Protestant. Edward was a scholar, but also a politician, diplomat, courtier, musician and, not least, a bold and accomplished soldier, quick-tempered and sometimes recklessly frank. It was while serving as English ambassador in Paris that he published *On Truth* (1624), a shockingly sceptical philosophical essay. However, he was prudent enough not to openly question Christianity, and the more candid autobiography he wrote soon after remained unpublished while he lived. When civil war broke out in 1642 Herbert, now in his sixties, refused to take sides. Instead, he retired to work on what would become his last great book, *On Pagan Religion*, finished in 1645. He died three years later: the book was not published until 1663.

Between them, the autobiography and *On Pagan Religion* show how Herbert earned his place in Kortholt's axis of atheism. From his boyhood onwards, Herbert tells us, 'a great number of doubts began to occur to me'. It is by now a familiar story. His particular stumbling block was the moral one. He could not reconcile the doctrine of Hell with his intuition that, if a sinner 'did not mean infinitely to offend . . . God will not inflict an infinite punishment upon him'. Likewise, he found Calvinist predestination impossible to believe, since it consisted of 'base and unworthy thoughts about the most gracious and good God'. Some would have fought back against the dreadful temptation of these thoughts. Herbert was more inclined to follow where they led him. While still a teenager, he tried to puzzle out the real truth of religion, making use of a favourite anti-atheist argument: that every human society had acknowledged gods. If that is so, he wondered, what characteristics are common to human religion in every age and every country? If the local oddities of each religion could be scraped away, perhaps he could reveal beneath them doctrines 'so universally taught that they were not questioned or doubted in any . . . religion'.[2] The treatise on pagan religion, then, was not merely a historical exercise. Herbert was sinking mineshafts to confirm that he had found bedrock.

His actual conclusions now seem rather bland. He became convinced that all religions taught that there is a God who deserves worship, who commands virtue and who both rewards and punishes humanity. These became the 'articles' of his faith. Herbert has been called the father of deism, but proper deists would have found all this disappointingly conventional. Two things gave it a dangerous edge. One, ironically, was Herbert's discretion. His own religious practice, he explained, was to hold to those core 'articles', but also, as best he could, to 'embrace and believe all that the Church in which I was born and brought up did uniformly teach'. Conforming to the Church of England was his duty as a patriotic Englishman. But since that church's doctrines went far beyond his 'articles', he believed its teachings 'either piously upon the Authority of the Church, or at least doubting piously when proofs were not sufficiently made and confirmed unto me'.[3]

This was Montaigne's fideism reworked for an unbeliever. Rather than simply submitting to the Church's authority, he left open the option of 'doubting piously': that is, conforming outwardly with inner mental reservation. Some unbelievers concealed their doubts cynically. Herbert had found a way of doing so on principle, and the principle was capable of quietly hollowing out whole churches. 'Doubting piously' perhaps makes him a truer ancestor of modern Anglicanism than his poet brother.

That dangerous conformity sat uneasily alongside Herbert's response to the obvious problem with his system. If those core 'articles' are humanity's universal religion, why is it that every actual human society has embellished them with so many other doctrines and ceremonies? Herbert knew exactly who to blame for this: 'That race of clever priests who . . . thought that they could dazzle people's minds . . . [and] expected to get more profit and larger allowances for themselves from the various rites, ceremonies, and sacred mysteries which they invented.' In particular, he claimed, the controversial and divisive doctrines which had so often caused religious strife were created by priests in a deliberate attempt to stir up mutual hatreds and so to entrench their own power. Ancient pagan priesthoods had done it and, he believed, Christian priests did exactly the same. So Herbert's core articles of faith are universal principles, but religion, explicitly including Christianity, is a conspiracy.[4] Anxious doubts and moral outrage had joined forces. Herbert took the Machiavellian claim that religion is a political trick and dressed it in pious clothing. He was wise not to publish any of this in his lifetime.

Kortholt's second Englishman was less discreet. Thomas Hobbes was so notorious that 'he cannot walk the streets, but the Boys point at him saying, There goes Hobbes the Atheist!' It was probably not exactly true. Hobbes conformed outwardly to the Church of England for most of his life, and may even have attended its traditional worship in the 1650s, when it was illegal to do so. But his reported claim that he 'liked the religion of the Church of England best of all other' sounds more like an aesthetic choice than a confession of faith. Perhaps he shared Herbert's ethic of 'doubting piously'. He certainly shared Herbert's dislike of priests. His reported comment to the clergy of various denominations who pestered him on his sickbed – 'Let me alone, or else I will detect all your cheats from Aaron [the founder of the Jewish priesthood] to yourselves' – could have come from Herbert. The sustained vitriol of the fourth and final section of his *Leviathan* (1651), an extended howl of rage against the Catholic clergy under the title 'The Kingdom of Darkness', makes Herbert look mild.[5]

Hobbes' reputation for atheism rested chiefly on *Leviathan*, and especially on the half of the book which is supposedly devoted to religion. His attack on biblical authority became notorious: no one had ever denied in print before that the Bible's first five books were written by Moses. But as ever, this was not about disinterested biblical scholarship.[6] Hobbes' two-pronged attack on both biblical and clerical authority has something Seekerish about it. His persistent theme throughout the religious passages of *Leviathan* is the impossibility of certain religious knowledge. No human claim about God – whether made by priests or by the Bible's human authors – is or can ever be beyond question, even if apparently authorised by miracles. Private individuals, including churchmen, may believe such claims, but they cannot force anyone else to agree. They can only persuade, as the first apostles did. Seekers used this sense of provisionality to argue that no religion was possible. Hobbes gave the argument a simple twist. He had spent the first half of his book arguing for the absolute sovereignty of secular governments. He now claimed that, since absolute religious truth is unknowable, secular governments' sphere of control ought to extend over religion too. He does not argue that they have some secret religious knowledge: merely that they are no more likely to be wrong than anyone else, and that no one can prove that they are wrong. He is particularly hostile to any notion of a separate spiritual authority. '*Temporal* and *spiritual* government, are but two words brought into the world, to make men see double, and mistake their lawful sovereign.' A professedly Christian sovereign is 'the supreme pastor of his own subjects' as well as their ruler: not because God can be assumed to have put him in power, but because the mere fact of being in power bestows on itself religious as well as political authority. Hobbes does allow that 'belief and unbelief can never follow men's commands', but only in the most minimal sense. Governments cannot regulate beliefs, but they can absolutely regulate speech and outward action. If all other truths are provisional, political power is all that remains.[7]

Looked at through one eye, this is an anticlerical variant of Montaigne's fideism, or indeed a natural extension of the 'Anglican' position, associated with the Elizabethan theologian Richard Hooker, that monarchs in Parliament have authority not only over the bodies but the consciences of their subjects.[8] But through the other eye, it is the royalist caricature of Parliamentarian relativism – 'Is there a God? Let it be put to vote!'[9] – come to life, or else an attempt to turn Machiavellian cynicism into something praiseworthy. It is not merely that Hobbes believed that religious truth was fundamentally inaccessible, a view that the Seekers shared. What is truly shocking is that this did not trouble him. He had apparently left anxiety behind him. He does seem to have believed that there is a God – otherwise we have to dismiss an implausible amount of his writing as a smokescreen – but he was not especially interested in the question, except insofar as he was suspicious of anyone claiming to act in God's name. The deity he truly revered was political power, the Leviathan itself. The reputation for atheism that this won him was not unjust. But his ideas were easier to condemn than to refute.

Herbert and Hobbes, important as they are, were mere supporting players to Kortholt's third impostor. If modern atheism has a single acknowledged intellectual founder, it is Baruch Spinoza. According to the foremost modern historian of Enlightenment radicalism, Jonathan Israel, 'no one else . . . remotely rivalled Spinoza's notoriety', and with good reason:

> Spinoza's prime contribution to the evolution of early modern Naturalism, fatalism, and irreligion . . . was his ability to integrate within a single coherent or ostensibly coherent system, the chief elements of ancient, modern and oriental 'atheism'. No one else in early modern times did this, or anything comparable . . . [He] fundamentally and decisively shaped a tradition of radical thinking which eventually spanned the whole continent.

At first glance Spinoza seems to belong to a different story from the one this book has been telling: a Dutch Jewish philosopher whose journey towards radicalism began when he questioned his own community's orthodoxies in 1655, at the age of twenty-two. The following year he was expelled from the Amsterdam synagogue. These early clashes eventually bore fruit in his *Theologico-Political*

Treatise (1670), a devastating attack on the authority of the Bible, on any notion of the supernatural, on any attempt to override human reason and, in particular, on clerical authority or any kind of theocracy – a preoccupation he shared with Hobbes, although he was also very critical of Hobbes' political absolutism. Spinoza's claim that 'nature is self-moving, and creates itself' was not atheistic in the strict sense – it is closer to pantheism – but his reputation as the founding father of modern unbelief is well deserved.[10]

For our story, Spinoza's significance lies in what happened after he was excommunicated in 1656: he fell in with Amsterdam's most intellectually open religious community, Adam Boreel's Collegiants. He did so at a moment of particular religious flux, when a pair of English Quaker missionaries had come to Amsterdam, and the Collegiants recognised the Quakers' 'inner light' as congruent with their own quasi-mystical commitment to 'reason'. The young Spinoza quickly became a part of this milieu. He collaborated with the Quaker missionary Samuel Fisher, working with him to translate an early Quaker pamphlet into Hebrew, in the (vain) hope of winning Jewish converts: it was Spinoza's first ever published work. In 1660, Fisher wrote a long, chaotic but incisive attack on biblical authority which anticipated many of Spinoza's later arguments: there is no knowing who learned what from whom, but plainly the two men were intellectually close. In 1658 another Quaker missionary wrote that Spinoza was 'very friendly' to their cause. The influence was not forgotten. Crucial chapters of the *Theologico-Political Treatise* borrowed from the Quaker Margaret Fell. But by then, Spinoza's friendship with the Quakers had fallen foul of a bitter rupture between the Quakers and the Collegiants. The root of the quarrel was not, as is still sometimes suggested, that Collegiant rationalism and Quaker mysticism were polar opposites, but that they were so nearly the same thing that their remaining differences were intolerable. Even so, Spinoza cleaved to his Collegiant friends, in particular to one Pieter Balling, who would translate Spinoza's first original book into Dutch. Spinoza remained personally close to Balling and to several other leading Collegiants throughout his life. When he moved out of Amsterdam in 1660–1, he chose as his rural refuge the village of Rijnsburg, the heartland of the Collegiant movement, founded there four decades earlier.[11]

Spinoza was never a Christian. But he was a Collegiant fellow-traveller: an affinity which would never have required him to contemplate anything so crassly carnal as a baptism. His early critique of both Christianity and Judaism was very much of a piece with the Collegiant, Seeker and Quaker critique of 'religion'. The philosophical heft he brought to the table was new, but the moral force behind it was not. A vital part of this is that, despite or perhaps because of his Jewish background, Spinoza had an extraordinarily positive view of Jesus, whom he called 'not so much the prophet as the mouthpiece of God'. He unproblematically used the momentous title *Christ* for him – no small step for a Jew to take – and repeatedly emphasised that Jesus' teaching and moral vision were so far above anyone else's that 'the voice of Christ may be called the voice of God'. For all his biblical scepticism, he was happy to accept the basic accuracy of the Christian Gospels. The main exception to that is his blanket rejection of miracle stories, but here, too, his reasoning was driven more by theology and ethics than by any quasi-scientific scepticism. The reason he believed that 'nature cannot be contravened' was that the alternative is 'to assert that God has created nature so weak . . . that he is repeatedly compelled to come afresh to her aid': miracles were theologically incoherent. In fact, because a miracle would be 'in contravention to God's nature and laws . . . belief in it would throw doubt upon everything, and lead to atheism'.[12] Any Collegiant or Seeker might have said the same.

In 1662 Pieter Balling, Spinoza's translator and friend, published a remarkable little Dutch book titled *The Light upon the Candlestick*, translated into English the following year. Starting from the impossibility of finding religious certainty in any church or sect, Balling exhorted each reader instead 'to turn into the Light that's in him'. Like Dirck Volckerstz Coornhert, whom we met in Chapter 3, Balling deliberately avoided citing the Bible at any point in his text: he wanted Reason to stand unaided. At most, he allowed for the possibility that some readers might, by means of the light within them, recognise 'the Book called the BIBLE' as having 'an harmony with . . . God'. As to what this 'light' is, he stated breezily that 'it's all one to us whether ye call it Christ, the Spirit, the Word, etc.', but he makes clear that ultimately this 'light' is moral intuition. 'It is properly the nature of this Light infallibly to discover sin and evil.'[13]

The book has caused considerable confusion – Balling wrote it as an intervention in the hairsplitting Collegiant–Quaker dispute, but it is so close to Quakerism that it has often been mistaken for a Quaker text. Its real importance, however, is that this is the point where Seekerism and Spinozism met and meshed, and the Anglo-Dutch ferment of Protestant doubt and questioning that had been coming to a simmer for decades reached boiling point. The book allows for virtually nothing recognisable as Christianity, Judaism or even 'religion'. Yet the mystical rationalism that it advocates is driven, above all, by the strength of its moral vision. And even as it rejected every trace of 'religion' as the word was normally understood, the book's final words lambasted 'all fools that say in their heart there is no God'.[14]

From Then to Now, I: Anger

And so the years around 1660 are when our main story ends: for this is when unbelief finally came out into the open and claimed philosophical respectability for itself. The intellectual history of atheism that follows from then until now is both important and fascinating, but we should not let it fool us. Behind and beneath it lies the deeper, emotional history we have been tracing. Its two streams now mingled and reinforced one another. On one side was the stream of anger: the unbelief of suspicion and defiance, refusing to be taken in or ordered around by priests and their God. That kind of unbelief was eyecatching, but it only became dangerous when it began to assert an ethical framework of its own. The Reformation, by choosing scepticism as its key religious weapon, in effect required believers to transition to a different kind of post-sceptical faith, a journey many of them struggled to complete. Protestants expected their faith to be settled and assured, but their intense self-reflectiveness sometimes made this desperately difficult to achieve. Hence the surge in the second emotional stream of unbelief: the stream of anxiety, in which earnestly pious men and women found themselves beset with fears and uncertainties which could not be reasoned away, because they were not in the end based on reason. Instead, some of these unwilling sceptics dealt with their anxieties in the classic Protestant way: by turning their doubts into a tool, and using it to dig down in the hope of rebuilding their faiths on a sound footing. As their anxieties dissolved one certainty after another, they were left with nothing except their commitment to their moral vision, which increasingly seemed not only to be Christianity's heart but also – as the Renaissance humanists had unwittingly implied – to be detachable from the Christian tradition itself. They turned that moral intuition against the tradition that had taught it to them, criticising Christianity for its failure to embody the ethics of Jesus Christ. And so the two streams came together. The moral force of the unbelief of anger and the moral urgency of the unbelief of anxiety mixed into a gathering flow of insistent, ethically driven doubts that began carving Christendom's old-established landscape into something new.

This is a Protestant-led story, but it could not be confined to the Protestant world. Catholics' and Protestants' existential struggle kept

them in lockstep with one another. For a sign of how the same currents were tugging on Catholicism, consider Blaise Pascal, whose complex, passionate Catholicism was aligned with the unorthodox, Calvinist-influenced movement known as Jansenism. We have already met his very particular perspective on the seventeenth century's anxieties about religious certainty. His treatise against atheism was never completed, and perhaps never could have been: the hundreds of fragments he prepared towards it were published under the bland title *Pensées* a few years after his death in 1662. A dominant theme of these 'thoughts' is the futility of argument. Philosophical proofs 'are so remote from human reasoning and so involved that they make little impact', even if you could be sure of the reliability of your own logic. As to arguments for God from nature, he points out that the Bible never tries to make that case. Such 'proofs' may be edifying for believers, but telling actual atheists that God is self-evident in nature 'is giving them cause to think that the proofs of our religion are indeed feeble . . . Nothing is more likely to bring it into contempt in their eyes'. He is not claiming that nature proves there is *not* a God. It is worse than that: nature is ambiguous. It gives us 'too much to deny and not enough to affirm', so leaving us merely with 'doubt and anxiety'. For Pascal, those lost in this trackless desert should give up their doomed mirage-chasing, and wait for their only hope of escape: a divine guide.

> We know the truth not only through our reason but also through our heart . . . Those to whom God has given religious faith by moving their hearts are very fortunate . . . but to those who do not have it we can only give such faith through reasoning, until God gives it by moving their heart, without which faith is only human and useless for salvation.

There is no point, said the mathematical giant of his age, in relying on the 'mathematical mind'. For all its achievements that mind

struggles reliably to discern truths. The 'intuitive mind' would have to serve instead.[15]

This counsel of despair mirrors his Protestant counterparts' conclusion: in the end, either you see God or you don't. Either way, reasoned arguments will not persuade you to change your mind. Whichever side of the divide you have landed on, you will construct arguments to defend your position, but you should not mistake those *post hoc* rationalisations for your true reasons. It was this impasse that sparked Pascal's most notorious theological gambit: his wager.

The wager had in fact already been around for at least a century, having first been popularised by the rationalist Protestant radical Faustus Socinus.[16] Its crude form warned atheists that they stood to gain nothing if they were right, but risked eternal damnation in Hell if they were wrong, and so urged them to believe out of raw self-interest. The problems with this crass argument were obvious, not least that it proposed a nakedly pragmatic 'faith' that hardly deserves the name. Pascal adapted it not to browbeat atheists, but as a thought-experiment for those paralysed by the impossibility of certainty. There may or may not be a God, he concedes:

> But to which view shall we be inclined? Reason cannot decide this question. Infinite chaos separates us. At the far end of this infinite distance a coin is being spun which will come down heads or tails. How will you wager?

Perhaps you would prefer not to gamble? Too late: once you are born, 'there is no choice, you are already committed'. But although the odds are utterly unknowable, the stakes are not, and so Pascal the mathematician can offer at least one kind of certainty. We are offered the chance to stake something temporary – our earthly lives – for something eternal. And even at vanishingly long odds, a rational gambler would risk any finite stake for a chance of an infinite reward.[17]

It is a clever, bloodless argument. Pascal does not expect anyone to be persuaded by it. Quite the opposite: he is very clear about the futility of such arguments. His point is that unbelievers may accept his logic, may even 'want to be cured of unbelief', but even so find that true faith is beyond their reach. In which case, the answer is evidently not 'multiplying proofs of God's existence' but recognising that 'if you are unable to believe, it is because of your passions'. The wager, then, is a call not to conversion, but to self-examination. It confronts unbelievers with the fact that even a logically watertight reason to believe would not change their minds. It proves that we are immune to proof. In the end, for believer and unbeliever alike, 'the heart has its reasons of which reason knows nothing'.[18]

Pascal framed the problem brilliantly. By its nature, he could not solve it. His contemporaries, and his successors down to the present, are compelled to wager on a coin toss, or set of dice rolls, which we cannot see and at whose odds we can scarcely guess. And so, like any real gambler, we wager not with our heads but with our hearts and our guts. What alternative is there?

As a forest of explicitly anti-religious arguments springs up from the later seventeenth century onwards, it can sometimes be difficult to see the wood for the trees, let alone to trace the subterranean currents of emotion that continued to nourish them. Still, we have already seen enough to know where to look. Our two intermingled streams of unbelief, anger and anxiety, both continued to flow, merging into a persistent moral force. There are so many and varied unbelieving voices in the centuries between then and now that any selection at all risks distortion. All we can do in the remaining pages is to listen to a handful of those voices, telling old stories in new ways.

That unbelief remained angry is unmistakable. There was mockery, which since the Renaissance (and before) had been an invaluable means of sidestepping difficult questions. If you can make religion look ridiculous, you are saved the trouble of either proving it false or proving something else true, and you reserve the option of covering your tracks by claiming that you were only joking. And making religion look ridiculous is sometimes so easy that it is irresistible. Charles Blount, an English deist of the late seventeenth century, would eventually go on to write openly against Christianity, but he began with an anonymous work, *Anima Mundi* (1679), whose 'defence' of the immortality of the soul was deliberately framed to make it look absurd. A more mischievous and explosive joke was played by Johann Joachim Müller, grandson of a renowned Lutheran anti-atheist who, so rumour claimed, had once seen or perhaps even owned a copy of the mythical *Of the Three Impostors*. In 1688 young Müller was invited to take part in an academic debate by Johann Friedrich Mayer, an ultra-orthodox Lutheran pastor in Kiel whose own interest in *Of the Three Impostors* verged on the obsessive. It was too much to resist. In his presentation in Kiel, Müller electrified the audience by quoting from the notorious, imaginary book. On his departure, he left behind a gift for Mayer: a copy of the manuscript for which the Christian world had been hunting for so long. Mayer believed it was authentic, and knowing how dangerous it was, kept it close. Copies only began to circulate widely after his death in 1712. Müller had of course concocted the whole thing, and eventually admitted as much. Still, it was more than just a throwaway prank. The book fits into a long-standing culture among German law students of writing absurdist spoofs, such as a notorious 'debate' nearly a century earlier about whether or not women were human. Those students had not seriously been denying women's humanity, any more than Müller was seriously denouncing Christ as an impostor. But you do not play jokes like that unless you think they are funny. At the least, you want your audience to laugh rather than to be outraged. Very likely you want them to wonder, if only for a moment, whether you are right.[19]

Spoofing religion has remained a constant theme of unbelief down to the present. The most famous example is probably still Voltaire's Dr Pangloss, whose 'metaphysico-theologo-cosmolonigology' convinced him that the world is as perfect as could be, and even that his own syphilis was a price worth paying so that the world might have cochineal. The modern era's most compelling literary meditation on belief and unbelief, Dostoevsky's *The Brothers Karamazov*, has a neat example of the genre, put into the mouth of the debauched father, Fyodor Karamazov, who admits blithely that he expects to be dragged down to Hell with hooks when he dies:

> And then I think: hooks? Where do they get them? What are they made of? Iron? Where do they forge them? Have they got some kind of factory down there? You know, in the monastery the monks probably believe there's a ceiling in hell, for instance. Now me, I'm ready to believe in hell, only there shouldn't be any ceiling; that would be, as it were, more refined, more enlightened, more Lutheran.[20]

Even in nineteenth-century Russia, 'Lutheran' could be a code word for 'half-atheist'. It is a straight line from here to the flowering of religious mockery in modern times, which has given us Alan Bennett's 'Take a Pew' in *Beyond the Fringe*, *Monty Python's Life of Brian*, and the incomparable *Father Ted*: more merry absurdism and gentle ridicule than vicious satire, but containing occasional, unmistakable flashes of real anger.

As ever, the primary target of that anger is not God himself, but his earthly representatives. The anticlericalism which animated unbelievers from the Middle Ages to Herbert, Hobbes and Spinoza has remained an engine of atheism down to the present, and not everyone finds the subject funny. The 'infamous thing' which Voltaire's motto '*écrasez l'infâme*' demanded must be crushed was the deadening and sometimes deadly power of the clergy. The real problem with a tyrannical conception of God, he warned, was that it 'invites men to become tyrants' in his name. The same mood is even plainer in Thomas Paine's *The Age of Reason* (1794), the first anti-Christian bestseller, a book said to have triggered Bible-burning parties on both sides of the Atlantic. Paine's fury was directed not at God, but at churches, which he called

> human inventions, set up to terrify and enslave mankind, and monopolize power and profit . . . I do not believe in the creed professed by the Jewish Church, by the Roman Church, by the Greek Church, by the Turkish Church, by the Protestant Church, nor by any church that I know of. My own mind is my own church.

That was not a metaphysical position; in fact, beneath it all, Paine's substantial religious views were surprisingly conventional. It was, as befits one of the heralds of the American revolution, a declaration of independence. And it is a sentiment we can imagine Christopher Marlowe expressing two hundred years earlier.[21]

Two notorious nineteenth-century examples tell the same story. Thomas Huxley is now best known as 'Darwin's bulldog', although the myth of his triumph over the hapless bishop of Oxford in a debate over evolution in 1860 has grown in the telling. Huxley was certainly more outspoken on religious matters than Charles Darwin himself, and famously coined the term 'agnostic' to describe the scientific unbelief he advocated. But he was also an odd, and very English, kind of unbeliever. The opposite of agnosticism, as he saw it, was not Christianity, theism or religion as such, but 'Ecclesiasticism, or . . . Clericalism'. He despised Bishop Wilberforce's title and his officiousness at least as much as his opinions. Remarkably, Huxley claimed to be defending 'the foundation of the Protestant Reformation', by which he meant the 'conviction of the supremacy of private judgement' – in contrast to the 'effete and idolatrous sacerdotalism' which he believed had overtaken the Church of

England in his own age.[22] That was not at all what the first Protestant Reformers had thought they were doing, but Huxley did have a point. He was deploying the same merciless scepticism which the Reformers had weaponised and popularised, and against their traditional targets.

Huxley's much less respectable contemporary Mikhail Bakunin, the Russian anarchist and revolutionary, had a very different perspective but strikingly similar concerns. His essay 'God and the State', written during the revolutionary false dawn of the Paris Commune in 1871, boils with rage at 'every religious system' ever invented. Their 'very nature and essence . . . is the impoverishment, enslavement and annihilation of humanity for the benefit of divinity'. And so his fury turned first of all to the slavemasters who had perpetrated this crime: 'Whoever says revelation says revealers, messiahs, prophets, priests and legislators inspired by God himself . . . All men owe them passive and unlimited obedience; for . . . against the justice of God no terrestrial justice holds. Slaves of God, men must also be slaves of Church and State.'

One result was that Bakunin, like Huxley and Fyodor Karamazov, could not help but insert himself into the unending conflict between Catholic and Protestant. For him, the essence of religion was to enslave humanity to priests. So he concluded, with wonderfully circular logic: 'That is why Christianity is the absolute religion, the final religion; why the Apostolic and Roman Church is the only consistent, legitimate, and divine church.' Since Catholicism alone had truly embraced religion's tyrannical destiny, it was the only religion he saw as a worthy enemy. Protestants and theological liberals, 'honest but timid souls' whose God 'is a nebulous, illusory being that vanishes into nothing at the first attempt to grasp it', were beneath his contempt. Like a great many atheist (and anti-atheist) campaigners before and since, Bakunin anointed his most extreme and caricatured opponents as the only ones who needed to be taken seriously, thus avoiding any risk of engaging with people whose more subtle or inconvenient ideas might deviate from the scripts he had written for them.[23]

In all these cases, the charge was not that clergy were peddling foolish notions of an imaginary God. It was that they were using those notions in order to subjugate, exploit and oppress the people. This was not about metaphysics; it was about wealth and power, and the criticism was moral, not philosophical. It was in line with the traditional Protestant criticism of clerical power, which Protestant radicals had quickly turned onto the new Protestant establishments. And its moral framework was straightforwardly Christian. These critics did not merely observe that churches oppress their people, nor did they follow Machiavelli in seeing this as a shrewd and prudent tactic. They believed that for the strong and cunning to oppress the weak and simple is wrong.

If they did turn their anger from the clergy to God himself, they did so in the same vein. Paine's *The Age of Reason* did not attack the Bible chiefly by amassing textual and historical problems with it, but by declaring it morally unfit for purpose:

> Whenever we read the obscene stories, the voluptuous debaucheries, the cruel and tortuous executions, the unrelenting vindictiveness, with which more than half the Bible is filled, it would be more consistent that we called it the word of a demon than the Word of God. It is a history of wickedness that has served to corrupt and brutalize mankind.

Like Richard Dawkins' pithy claim that 'the God of the Old Testament is arguably the most unpleasant character in all fiction', this works by measuring the Bible against an agreed moral standard and finding it wanting – that standard, certainly in Paine's case, being derived from the Christian tradition itself. As a self-confessed deist, Paine found the Bible blasphemous. It defamed God by portraying him as morally deficient. One of the most common stumbling blocks for Christian belief in modern times – the traditional doctrine of Hell – worked in the same way. It triggered a moral intuition that God simply could not consign a part of his creation to eternal torment. This intuition did not refute the formidable logic of Augustinian or Calvinist theology: it bypassed it. The result has sometimes been materialism or some other mortalist doctrine, but equally often it has been forms of Christianity that reject Hell, or beliefs like spiritualism, which allows for immortality without Hell and which had a powerful appeal in the early twentieth century.[24]

Again, at the apogee of this moral anger, we find Bakunin. He recognised that the problem of the clergy could not be separated from the problem of God. If they really were God's representatives, then they truly would be entitled to enslave humanity. Some writers would have sidestepped at this point into some logical argument that there is no God, but Bakunin recognised that this would be dishonest, and confronted the issue head on:

> If God existed, only in one way could he serve human liberty – by ceasing to exist . . . I reverse the phrase of Voltaire, and say that, *if God really existed, it would be necessary to abolish him.*

On the surface, this is ridiculous: a fulfilment of all the accusations that atheism is a form of wishful thinking. Bakunin's syllogism – 'If God is, man is a slave; now, man can and must be free; then, God does not exist' – absurdly derives a metaphysical claim from a political opinion. He is a new Canute, not merely ordering the tide to turn but the entire sea to dry up.[25] But on a deeper level, this is good moral theology. God is by definition good. But the existence of a God is (Bakunin believes) inherently oppressive and therefore evil. Therefore the very concept of God is self-contradictory. If you accept his premisses, the case is watertight. Once again, however, among those premises is a very particular moral framework, which presumes liberty is an absolute good and subjugation an absolute evil. How far that framework is itself of Christian origin is not especially important. The point is that this is how the atheism of anger works. It is only when its *moral* standards come into conflict with God that God has to be abolished.

From Then to Now, II: Anxiety

Alongside, and intertwined with, the unbelief of anger remains the unbelief of anxiety. The seventeenth century's agonised Puritans, wrestling with doubt, have had countless successors: individuals who have not embraced the fierce certainties of dogmatic faith or of angry unbelief, who are not so much sitting on the fence as impaled on it. Sometimes these agonies have been resolved into more or less settled belief, or unbelief; sometimes doubters have withdrawn, exhausted, from the fray, and made some sort of peace with their uncertainties; sometimes those uncertainties have not been resolved at all. Many of these dramas are documented in a distinctively modern literary form, uniquely well suited to exploring characters' inner turmoil: the novel. Religious anxieties burn through novels such as James Hogg's astonishing *Private Memoirs and Confessions of a Justified Sinner* (1824), the works of George Eliot, or, again, Dostoevsky. The mother in *The Brothers Karamazov* who cannot control her doubts about immortality could have been airlifted directly to nineteenth-century Russia from seventeenth-century England:

> I think, all my life I've believed, and then I die, and suddenly there's nothing . . . What, what will give me back my faith? . . . How can it be proved, how can one be convinced? Oh, miserable me! . . . I'm the only one who can't bear it. It's devastating, devastating![26]

Some achieve unbelief. Some have it thrust upon them.

But as we saw in Chapter 5, those who suffer these agonies are not merely passive. Very often they try to defend or refound their faith, holding on to its core while relinquishing what seems unnecessary or indefensible. This can make it difficult to distinguish between religion's defenders and its adversaries. Spinoza is not the only iconic figure in the history of unbelief who was, at least in his own terms, a believer. Dominic Erdozain's compelling history of anti-Christian thought argues that a whole series of these philosophers were in fact trying to purify Christianity, not to destroy it. Pierre Bayle, the French Enlightenment's first great apostle of liberalism, scourge of attempts to use religion as a tool of social order, was trying to redeem Christianity from cruel distortions, not an atheist prudently maintaining a sham, residual faith. Voltaire echoed Spinoza by rejecting miracles on the grounds that 'the universal theologian, that is, the true philosopher, sees that it is contradictory for nature to act on particular or single views': that is a religious, not an atheistic conviction. Paine wrote his fierce critique of Christianity in *The Age of Reason* 'lest in the general wreck of superstition, of false systems of government and false theology, we lose sight of morality, of humanity and of the theology that is true'.[27]

These thinkers had not rejected Christianity, nor were they unwilling to deal in its currency. They were, however, persuaded that that currency was devalued, and that the guarantees of the churches that claimed to stand behind it might no longer be sound. And as any banker knows, anxieties of that kind are intolerable, whether well founded or not. Rather than trying to shore up faith in those old guarantors, these speculators attempted a bolder gambit: to rebase their religious currency entirely, founding it on the gold standard of natural law and morality rather than the churches' dubious claims to authority. They believed that in doing so they were going back to Christianity's true heart.

Yet some of the results of this rebasing did not look very much like traditional Christianity. The Enlightenment era's single most important philosopher, Immanuel Kant, was a convinced adherent of the new gold standard. His 'categorical imperative', which codified it, still underpins what much of the modern world thinks is self-evident moral common sense. Kant believed himself to be defending God, but where Montaigne had confined his God to an honoured and secluded cloister, 'Kant built a fortress of conscience . . . that swore a rescued God to silence.' In this system, as Erdozain puts it, 'morality has swallowed religion'. Even Ludwig Feuerbach's *The Essence of Christianity* (1841), one of the age's bitterest moral critiques of religion in any form, belongs in the same tradition. By this stage, the battle for credulity has finally been lost and Christianity has eaten itself.[28]

The culmination of this process is in Dostoevsky's *Brothers Karamazov*, when the idealistic Ivan lays out his very distinctive form of unbelief. At first glance it looks like the classic argument from suffering: God could not permit suffering, but suffering exists, therefore there is no God. But this is not Ivan Karamazov's argument. He does not deny God. He even accepts that in the end a higher good may come of suffering. His problem is simply that his moral intuition gags at the very idea:

> If the suffering of children goes to make up the sum of suffering needed to buy truth, then I assert beforehand that the whole of truth is not worth such a price . . . Imagine that you yourself are building the edifice of human destiny with the object of making people happy in the finale, of giving them peace and rest at last, but for that you must inevitably and unavoidably torture just one tiny creature, that same child who was beating her chest with her little fist, and raise your edifice on the foundation of her unrequited tears – would you agree to be the architect on such conditions?

This is not unbelief; it is defiance. His brother Alyosha murmurs that it is 'rebellion'. Ivan himself says, 'It is not that I don't accept God, Alyosha, I just most respectfully return him the ticket.' He finds the universe ethically unacceptable. The God who made it this way is real enough, but Ivan wants nothing to do with him.[29]

And yet, the gold standard against which Ivan Karamazov and all these other moralists were measuring their religion was Christian. Ivan himself could not have made it plainer. Having declared his wish to return his ticket, he launches into his parable of the Grand Inquisitor, in which a (Catholic) inquisitor, who we are explicitly told does not believe in God, berates an incognito Jesus at great length for the foolish impracticality of his morals before condemning him to die. Jesus remains silent throughout, but at the end 'approaches the old man in silence and gently kisses him . . . That is the whole answer'.[30] Ivan is not clinging to Jesus' moral authority while rejecting churches and doctrines. He is rejecting churches and doctrines because of, and by means of, Jesus' moral authority.

Dostoevsky may have given us the most memorable image of this clash between Jesus and religion, but as Erdozain points out, it was hardly original to him. Spinoza set a trend: unbelievers singling Jesus out for praise. Voltaire, especially later in life, treated Jesus with uncharacteristic reverence, as an archetype of true natural religion. Thomas Jefferson claimed to follow what he called 'the Philosophy of Jesus', saying that Jesus would not recognise a single feature of the so-called Christianity erected in his name. Thomas Paine believed not only that 'the morality [Jesus] preached and practised was of the most benevolent kind', but that 'it has not been exceeded by any'. These sceptics may not revere him as the incarnate Second Person of the Trinity, but they plainly see him as unique. John Stuart Mill, the nineteenth-century liberal whose atheism was undoubted, believed that 'the authentic sayings of Jesus of Nazareth' were not merely in 'harmony with the intellect and feelings of every good man or woman', but almost constituted true humanity: 'That they should be forgotten, or cease to be operative on the human conscience, while human beings remain cultivated or civilized, may be pronounced, once for all, impossible.'[31]

Perhaps some of these sentiments were insincere. If so, they were bowing to a cultural fact: for believers and unbelievers alike, Jesus Christ was by far the most potent moral figure in Western culture. Respectable radicals might question his divinity, but only a scoundrel like Nietzsche would question his morality. One raw index of this cultural power was the English fashion for literary 'lives' of Jesus started by John Seeley's *Ecce Homo* (1865) and bolstered by a new wave of questions about the Bible's reliability. Over the next forty years a staggering five thousand such 'lives' were published.[32] If the late Victorian age was losing faith in Christianity, as plenty of Christians feared, it was certainly not losing interest in Christ.

One odd, backhanded testimony to Jesus' cultural power is the persistence among a certain combative strain of atheism of a very odd belief: that Jesus of Nazareth never existed. Historically speaking, this claim is not impossible, but it is pretty implausible: in effect, it requires the existence of a large-scale, entirely successful and oddly pointless conspiracy in the first century. But it is not and never has been intended as a sober historical claim. Napoleon, who is recorded as denying Jesus' existence on several occasions, was not a scholar of ancient history. He simply had one of modern history's most colossal egos, and resented kowtowing to the moral authority of a dead Galilean peasant. The case was made more substantially by Karl Marx's scholarly mentor Bruno Bauer, perhaps the most serious historian ever to deny Jesus' existence. Bauer took this stance because it fitted with his long-standing anti-Christian views, and also with his anti-Semitism, which baulked at accepting a Jewish prophet's position at the heart of western civilisation. A simpler, although equally implausible solution to that particular problem was adopted by Adolf Hitler, who said in private conversation that 'it's certain that Jesus was not a Jew' and in fact that

'Jesus fought against the materialism of his age, and, therefore, against the Jews.'[33]

In our own times, Jesus-denialism has found a more harmless home on the fringes of atheist subcultures. Books such as Kenneth Humphreys' *Jesus Never Existed* (2005) or Joseph Atwill's *Caesar's Messiah* (2005) are openly anti-religious polemics or simple contrarianism rather than sober historical studies.[34] What makes the determined pursuit of this argument interesting is that it is not only implausible: it is unnecessary. Denials of Christianity do not become weaker if you admit that Jesus of Nazareth existed, any more than denials of life on Mars become weaker if you admit that Mars exists. This fringe are following Napoleon by recognising that Christianity's cultural power depends less on philosophical or theological claims than on Jesus' moral authority. Atheism's more level-headed advocates in recent times have preferred to avoid engaging with Jesus at all. An unusual exception is the novelist Philip Pullman's *The Good Man Jesus and the Scoundrel Christ* (2010), an engaging fictionalised separation of the good, ethical Jesus from his bad, religious alter ego. Spinoza would have recognised the distinction. Even in our own times, it seems, the authority of Jesus of Nazareth remains a force to be reckoned with. Rather than criticising or relativising his morals, Christianity's opponents generally feel obliged to avoid him, to co-opt him by claiming his ethical mantle, or in extremis, to abolish him.

From Jesus to Hitler

The wrestling match between belief and unbelief in the Western world has been a long one. Both parties have made numerous premature declarations of victory or defeat, but the struggle has repeatedly proved unpredictable. There is no knowing how things will turn next. Even so, since the mid-twentieth century, something has changed in Europe and North America. 'Religion', said an authoritative commentator on the United States in 1955, 'has become part of the ethos of American life to such a degree that overt anti-religion is all but inconceivable.' Western society was certainly very secular, as Christian commentators lamented, but Christianity continued to define its moral frameworks. And so virtually everyone continued to claim a residual identity as a Christian, apart from the few who had ancestral ties to Judaism or another religion. In the last half-century, that default, universal religious identity has broken down. For the first time, substantial and fast-growing minorities who deny that they have any religion at all have appeared. Even in the overtly pious United States, this is true of over a third of adults born since 1980.[35] The minority of earnest and devout Christians may or may not be shrinking – the picture varies from place to place, and certainly in the United States this group remains large and assertive – but the mass of nominal believers who have formed the majority in most 'Christian' societies for over a century seem rapidly to be shedding their skin. The change is above all a generational one. It seems increasingly plain that the 1960s – or the 'long 1960s' from around 1955 to 1975 – were an inflection point, when a new kind of secularism appeared in western culture.[36] Why?

This book's perspective suggests some answers. For a start, it is worth noticing what has *not* caused this secular surge. Angry unbelief has repeatedly over the past few centuries tried to confront or suppress religion, without much success. The first avowedly anti-Christian movement of modern times, during the wild days of the first French Revolution, served simply to stoke some of the Revolution's staunchest opposition. In the end Napoleon came to terms with the church whose founder he claimed never existed. Twentieth-century Communists' official atheism had, at best, a mixed record of success. Most (not all) Communist regimes permitted some religious practice, hoping that religion would wither under the force of propaganda and discrimination so that it did not have to be forcibly uprooted. However, both legal and illegal religious movements often flourished under Communism and have returned to a prominent socio-political role in a number of post-Communist societies. Even in open societies, campaigning, strident atheism has been no more obviously successful than campaigning, strident movements for religious renewal. In 1925, a group of combative New York atheists founded the American Association for the Advancement of Atheism, with the aim of mounting a 'direct frontal assault' on religion. It generated a good deal of excitement and a number of local chapters, but the 'assault' did not result in any kind of breakthrough. Within a decade it had ceased to function. Like the so-called 'village atheists' whose mulish nonconformity outraged nineteenth-century America; like the rakish 'Hellfire Clubs' which so offended moralists in eighteenth-century England; like the libertines who supposedly thronged sixteenth-century Paris; and like the steady stream of blasphemers who passed through medieval church courts, these people were shocking but not threatening. They were a part of the moral equilibrium of a Christian society.[37] Christianity has endured a good many 'direct frontal assaults' in the past few centuries. They have not proved very effective. If anything, the period since the 1950s has been distinguished by the *absence* of substantial, coordinated anti-religious campaigns. The example of the so-called 'New Atheist' movement spearheaded by Richard Dawkins, Christopher Hitchens and their fellow 'horsemen' in the 2000s suggests that, even now, such campaigns are much better at cheering up atheists than at persuading believers.

Nor does the post-1960s secular turn reflect a contemporaneous collapse in the intellectual case for religion. The 'New Atheists' and most of their fellow-travellers are happy to present themselves as heirs to the Enlightenment critique of religion, or of the nineteenth century's set-piece debates about science. Not much about this case is substantially new, aside from a psychological and neurological dimension. If anything, the humanist-materialist argument against Christianity has weakened over the past century. At the turn of the twentieth century, an educated lay person in Europe or North America might have been expected to believe that the universe is infinitely old and entirely deterministic; that humanity's 'races' are fundamentally different from one another; that the process of evolution is governed by some sort of progressive life force; that the New Testament is a collection of myths created some centuries after the events it claims to describe, and the Old Testament a mere collage of stories shared by peoples across the entire ancient Near East. All those beliefs are inimical to traditional Christianity, and a century on, none of them have stood the test of time.[38] If Christianity has disintegrated intellectually, it happened a long time ago, not during the 1960s.

So if religion has neither collapsed nor been crushed, what has been happening to it? Historians of the 1960s describe a series of tectonic social changes, from the decline of collective identities in increasingly individualistic societies, to the momentous changes in gender roles and in sexual mores that accompanied second-wave feminism, the contraceptive pill and the rise of women's paid employment. However, the most recent study by one of the most trenchant of these historians goes further. Callum Brown's remarkable book *Becoming Atheist* is an oral history of modern unbelief, based on interviews with eighty-five adult atheists across Europe and North America. It is impossible to read his account and deny that religiosity in the Western world has undergone an epochal shift during his interviewees' lifetimes.

Brown's people and their stories are enormously varied, but he observes that they share a remarkably consistent *ethical* code. That code has two key elements. First is the so-called 'golden rule' of treating others as you would like to be treated – a Christian imperative, but not, as Brown points out, an exclusively Christian one.

Then there is a linked set of principles about human equality and bodily and sexual autonomy. Brown calls this ethical framework 'humanism', a term which relatively few of his interviewees volunteered, but which all of them were happy to embrace when offered the chance.[39] What makes this interesting is that Brown's interviewees claimed, without exception, that they were 'humanists' before they discovered the term.

> Humanism was neither a philosophy nor an ideology that they had learned or read about and then adopted. There was no act of conversion, no training or induction . . . A humanist condition precedes being a self-conscious humanist.[40]

This 'humanism' was not a manifesto they had adopted, much less a programme imposed on them. Those of them who had grown up in religious settings had embraced this ethic before they broke with their religion. When the breaking point did come, it was either because of a conflict between their religious and their humanist ethics, or because their humanist ethics made their religion appear redundant. The implication is that, in the West since the mid-twentieth century, growing numbers of earnestly or nominally religious people have adopted an ethic which is independent of their religion, and is in some tension with it: so they have either drifted away from or consciously rejected their religion. This account, with ethics as its driving force, meshes with the story we have been tracing since the seventeenth century.

So where did this diffuse, ubiquitous ethic come from? If Brown's humanists did not even consciously adopt their ethics, how did they reach such a consistently shared position? Brown – a proud humanist himself – suggests that it may arise from 'within human experience', indeed that 'reason alone may construct humanism': an echo of the old argument for God from universal human consensus. It is an appealing idea, but it is demonstrably false.

Modern humanism is, perhaps unfortunately, in no sense an expression of universal human values. Its ethical markers – gender and racial equality, sexual freedom, a strong doctrine of individual human rights, a sharp distinction between the human and non-human realms – are, in a long historical perspective, very unusual indeed. Nor do they stand on a very firm logical base, as anyone who has ever tried philosophically to prove the existence of human rights knows. The fact that those values appear intuitively obvious to Brown, and indeed to me, is not an answer. It is the problem.[41]

Brown does, however, observe that the dominance of these values in Western culture can be dated to 1945, and in particular to 'the notion of human rights which emerged from the Second World War'.[42] As well as being the most catastrophic war in human history, the Second World War and in particular the Nazi genocide was the defining moral event of our age, which reset our culture's notions of good and evil. By the early twentieth century, Christianity's only undisputed role in Western society, its raison d'être, was to define morality. This is precisely what it failed to do in the Second World War, the modern era's most intense moral test. It failed not only in the sense that many churches and Christians were to a degree complicit with Nazism and fascism, but in the wider sense that the global crisis revealed that Christianity's moral priorities were wrong. It now seemed plain that cruelty, discrimination and murder were evil in a way that fornication, blasphemy and impiety were not.

As the post-war generations digested these lessons, they turned the war into the Western world's foundation myth. Cultural conservatives sometimes worry that modern Western societies lack shared sacred narratives, but this is not exactly true. In the same way that Victorian publishers endlessly retold the life of Jesus, post-war films, novels and other media endlessly retold and retell the Second World War. It is the story to which we continually return. Its history retains an unparalleled grip on our imagination because it is our *Paradise Lost*: our age's defining battle with evil.

Once the most potent moral figure in Western culture was Jesus Christ. Believer or unbeliever, you took your ethical bearings from him, or professed to. To question his morals was to expose yourself as a monster. Now, the most potent moral figure in Western culture is Adolf Hitler. It is as monstrous to praise him as it would once have been to disparage Jesus. He has become the fixed reference point by which we define evil. The humanist ethic which Brown summarises is almost a precisely inverted image of Nazism. In the seventeenth century, arguments tended to end with someone calling someone else 'atheist', marking the point at which the discussion hit a brick wall. In our own times, as Godwin's Law notes, the final, absolute and conversation-ending insult is to call someone a Nazi. This is neither an accident nor a marker of mental laziness. It reflects that fact that Nazism, almost alone in our relativistic culture, is an absolute standard: a point where argument ends, because whether it is good or evil is not up for debate. Or again, while Christian imagery, crosses and crucifixes have lost much of their potency in our culture, there is no visual image which now packs as visceral an emotional punch as a swastika.

The plainest evidence that Nazism has crossed the barrier separating historical events from timeless truths is the way it has permeated the modern age's most popular myths. To many people it is incongruous, even embarrassing, that the twentieth century's bestselling work of fiction is an excessively long, unapologetically archaic and sometimes self-indulgent fairy tale written by a philologist who was a very traditional Catholic, and whose most devoted readers were and remain teenage boys. But even if you share the now-receding literary disdain for J. R. R. Tolkien's *The Lord of the Rings*, there is no gainsaying its cultural importance. Tolkien himself had no patience for allegory as a literary form, and vigorously denied that he had written one, but if the War of the Ring does not mirror the Second World War which was raging as he wrote the book, it certainly refracts it, and he privately admitted as much. Tolkien was an early and staunch opponent of Nazism in general and Nazi racial ideology in particular, in part because he felt the Nazi appropriation of his beloved Nordic mythology as a personal affront. But while he never doubted the righteousness of the Allies' cause, he was also a veteran of the Battle of the Somme, and knew that this war was, like any war, 'an ultimately evil job': so he told his son in 1944. And he used his own developing myth to explain what he meant: not only that there were 'a great many Orcs on our side', but that 'we are attempting to conquer Sauron with the Ring'. Such a war might end in victory, but a victory whose effect would be 'to breed new Saurons'.[43]

Whatever we make of that as a political judgement, as a cultural prophecy it has proved uncannily prescient. Western culture has been breeding new Saurons ever since. The figure of the Dark Lord has stalked through the most persistent and popular mythologies of the post-war era, from *Star Wars'* Darth Vader to Harry Potter's Lord Voldemort. The debt these ersatz Hitlers owe to their real-world archetype is sometimes implied, sometimes openly acknowledged, but always plain. These are the myths on which generations of children in the post-Christian West have been raised, transposing the brutal lesson of the Second World War into time-less morality tales. It is a lesson our culture seems determined to teach itself and eager repeatedly to relearn: that this is what true evil looks like, even though in reality evil rarely appears in such unambiguous dress. And while the Christian ethical sensibility which Tolkien embodied still underpins these myths, they have, like the culture in which they have thrived, left that original taproot behind them.

And this is where the emotional history of unbelief currently stands in what used to be Christendom. Perhaps we still believe that God is good, but we believe with more fervour and conviction that Nazism is evil. In post-war humanism, the centuries-old Christian moral revolt against Christianity has finally kicked over the traces and renounced its residual connection to Christian ethics. Or at least, it has tried to. Since this humanism has emerged by processes of intuition rather than of conscious reasoning – since its history is, inevitably, an emotional history – it cannot rid itself of its ancestry quite so easily. It has become almost commonplace to point out that 'secular thought is mostly composed of repressed religion' and that humanism continues to be shaped by Christian moral norms. Combative atheists deplore this and opportunistic Christians celebrate it, but they are agreed about the fact.[44] It could hardly be otherwise. In this sense, the old struggle between belief and unbelief is not over. It has simply entered a new phase.

Still, a new phase it is. Breaking our moral currency's last links to the old gold standard of Christian ethics is unprecedented. Perhaps gold standards are in the end no more rational than any other coin, but underwriting our moral currency with the anti-Nazi narrative instead of with Christianity is an experiment. It is not clear how well or how long that narrative will be able to bear the burden it has been asked to carry. If we are going to choose a historical reference point for absolute evil, then Nazism is certainly hard to beat; but as the Second World War falls off the edge of living memory, will the old stories and convictions retain their power? Are the moral myths we have distilled from them, heady as they are, capable of nourishing an enduring ethical sensibility? Will the lessons we have learned from them continue to seem intuitively and self-evidently true? The stirrings of authoritarian nationalism around the world suggest not. The readiness of some of those nationalists to claim pop-culture myths for themselves – Tolkien's mythology is all too open to racial categories which are, literally, dehumanising[45] – is a warning that emotive myth-making is a game all sides can play. If the common coin of our shared morals comes into increasing question, with contested histories and myths being reduced to scraps of paper, we will have little to underpin our collective ethics except intuition – unless another shared experience, with luck one less terrible than the Second World War, provides renewed values against which our currency can be rebased.

Two things at least are clear. First, Western Christendom is not about to snap back into place. The contemporary humanist surge is not a blip or an anomaly, but a continuation of moral forces that have been at work within the Christian world for centuries. Believers hoping it will go away and normal service will be resumed are deluding themselves. Indeed, they are in some danger of being tempted by authoritarian nationalist voices that want to unlearn the Second World War's moral lessons. When such voices say 'Christian', they mean a tribal identity rather than a universal ethic. That is not merely repugnant. It is self-defeating. Western culture sloughed off this kind of seductive, compromised religion for a reason, and would if necessary probably do so again. In the meantime, religions that dig their heels in to oppose the new moral environment risk taking on the role of medieval blasphemers: to validate a majority culture by offering it exactly the kind of predictable opposition it craves. The religions that will prosper in this environment will be those that work with the grain of humanist ethics, while finding ways to offer something that humanism cannot.

Because, secondly, the humanist surge is not a stable new reality either. The intuitions which make it possible will not flow peacefully, steadily and indefinitely. Our cultures' moral frameworks have shifted before and they will do so again. Our beliefs will, inevitably, follow. Believers and unbelievers alike share an interest in where that story goes next.

Acknowledgements

Like many of the stories of doubt it tells, this book began as a niggling afterthought: a surprised observation, when I was preparing my 2013 book *Being Protestant in Reformation Britain*, that so many of the earnestly pious believers I was studying had consciously wrestled with atheism. I wrote some of this material up as a lecture and began hawking it around, and the more I thought and talked about it, the murkier and more significant the story became. I am grateful for those early audiences' comments, and especially for Lori Anne Ferrell's firm instruction to me to stay on the scent.

Among several important early conversations – with Leif Dixon, Erik Midelfort, Subha Mukerji, Kate Narveson, Susan Schreiner and others – I have to single out Ethan Shagan, whose 2018 book *The Birth of Modern Belief* has developed in parallel with this one. A series of discussions with him culminated in a long lunch in Vancouver in 2015, by the end of which I had the first outline of this book in my head. Without his encouragement and provocation, I would never have had the nerve to tackle a topic like this on the scale it deserves. Any acuity or insight my book may have owes a great deal to him. If you've enjoyed this book, or indeed if you haven't, you should buy his too.

By that time I was already a few months into a Major Research Fellowship awarded by the Leverhulme Trust to work on a somewhat different project, on religious radicalism in mid-seventeenth century England. As I came to the view that that was actually an episode in the history of atheism, I had to explain to the Trust that I now wanted to write something rather different from what I had originally promised. They accepted my change of direction without a murmur, and so I am now grateful to them not simply for their generosity but also for their faith in the way open-ended research works. I hope they feel the result does them credit.

As I felt my way into the subject, I started recklessly accumulating other debts. The ones I recall include Mikki Brock, for the atheistic merchants of Ayr; Mike Driedger, for setting me straight on Dutch mysticism; my student Sally Flannery, for the vivid clarity of her definitions; Tobias Gregory, who led me through Montaigne; Jane Heath, for her many encouragements and for her shrewd advice on matters classical; Tom Holland, for overcoming my reticence about Tolkien; Lucy Kaufman, for a breadcrumb trail in the archives at York; Chris Marsh, for ballad lore; Justin Megitt, for introducing me to the Jesus-deniers; Bill Sheils, for Erasmus, More, Wittgenstein and other level-headed wisdom; Nick Spencer, for some sharp, last-minute insights; Stacie Vos, for the jollity of Mrs Drake; and Maddy Ward, for opening my eyes to Quaker theology. I hope those I have forgotten will forgive me. Felicity Bryan, Joy de Menil and Arabella Pike were able to see, from my initial book proposal, the size and shape that it in fact ought to have: I am grateful to all of them for their patience and wisdom, and also to the two anonymous readers who sharpened the text considerably. Special thanks go to the Huntington Library in San Marino, California, and the Folger Shakespeare Library in Washington, DC, which awarded me one-month residential fellowships in 2016 and 2017 respectively. Those were invaluable oases of time, when the only dilemma was whether to immerse myself in their superb collections or to make the most of the wonderful gatherings of scholars.

A particular word of thanks to three authors I have yet properly to meet: Dominic Erdozain, since my debt to his sweeping *The Soul of Doubt* (2016) will be obvious; John Gray, for his wonderfully spine-stiffening *Seven Types of Atheism* (2018), a blast of fresh air when I needed it; and in particular Francis Spufford, for *Unapologetic* (2012), which proves that talking about belief and doubt in terms of emotions is not only legitimate but necessary. Now I only need to learn to write a tenth as well as they do.

The heaviest burden of writing a book falls on the people who are closest. Ben and Adam have not let me take myself too seriously, and kept me admirably on task in the closing stages. But as always, from first to last, my greatest debt is to Victoria, without whom . . .

Notes

Introduction

1   John Bunyan, *The Pilgrim's Progress*, ed. W. R. Owens (Oxford: Oxford University Press, 2003), 128.

2   On what I mean by 'the West', and the limited implications of this story for the rest of the planet, see below, p. 10–11.

3   http://www.pewresearch.org/fact-tank/2015/05/13/a-closer-look-at-americas-rapidly-growing-religious-nones/ (accessed 31 January 2019).

4   http://www.pewforum.org/2018/05/29/being-christian-in-western-europe/pf_05-29-18_religion-western-europe-00-15/; http://blogs.lse.ac.uk/religionglobalsociety/2016/07/who-are-the-religious-nones-in-britain-atheists-agnostics-or-something-else/ (both accessed 31 January 2019).

5   Charles Taylor, *A Secular Age* (Cambridge, MA: Harvard University Press, 2007), 25.

6   This is a caricature, but the three tendencies I mention – the focus on the period from roughly 1660 to 1900; the focus on intellectual elites, especially a small number of canonical thinkers; and the focus on explicitly anti-Christian positions taken by those thinkers – are persistent features of histories of atheism: a subject which, unlike the history of religion, tends to be seen principally as a branch of intellectual history. See, for example, Alan Charles Kors, *Atheism in France, 1650–1729* (Princeton: Princeton University Press, 1990); Michael J. Buckley, *At the Origins of Modern Atheism* (New Haven and London: Yale University Press, 1987); Wayne Hudson, Diego

Lucci and Jeffrey R. Wigelsworth (eds), *Atheism and Deism Revalued: Heterodox Religious Identities in Britain, 1650–1800* (Farnham: Ashgate, 2014); Gavin Hyman, *A Short History of Atheism* (London: I. B. Tauris, 2010); Jonathan Israel, *Radical Enlightenment: Philosophy and the Making of Modernity 1650–1750* (Oxford: Oxford University Press, 2001). Those who have an eye both to intellectual elites and to mass culture, such as Charles Taylor (a philosopher by training) or Owen Chadwick, in his brilliant *The Secularisation of the European Mind in the Nineteenth Century* (Cambridge: Cambridge University Press, 1975), nevertheless find it difficult to escape the presumption that the elites lead and the masses eventually follow. Israel asserts that intellectual elites 'moulded, supervised, and fixed the contours of popular culture' (*Radical Enlightenment*, 5). The principal exceptions to this rule are the social historians of 'secularisation' (as distinct from 'atheism'), whose chronology is typically different – from the mid-nineteenth century to the present – and for whom intellectual elites are generally less decisive. See, most combatively, Steve Bruce, *God is Dead: Secularization in the West* (Oxford: Blackwell, 2002); also Hugh McLeod, *Secularisation in Western Europe, 1848–1914* (Basingstoke: Macmillan, 2000); Hugh McLeod and Werner Ustorf (eds), *The Decline of Christendom in Western Europe, 1750–2000* (Cambridge: Cambridge University Press, 2003); James Turner, *Without God, Without Creed: The Origin of Unbelief in America* (Baltimore: Johns Hopkins University Press, 1986).

7   Taylor, *A Secular Age*, advances a hugely subtle and sophisticated version of this claim.

8   Kors, *Atheism in France*, 130; Thomas Nash, *Christs teares ouer Ierusalem* (London: James Roberts, 1593), fo. 62r; Alexander Murray, 'Piety and impiety in thirteenth-century Italy', in *Popular Belief and Practice*, ed. G. J. Cuming and Derek Baker (Studies in Church History 8. Cambridge: Cambridge University Press, 1972), 102.

9   Blaise Pascal, *Pensées*, ed. and trans. A. J. Krailsheimer (London: Penguin, 1995), 127.

10 A point made with merciless good cheer in Jonathan Haidt, *The Righteous Mind* (London: Allen Lane, 2012).

11 Here I am picking up a challenge left by Alan Kors in his magisterial *Atheism in France*, which concentrates on the conceptual tools used to build early eighteenth-century atheism, 'leaving to others the psychohistory, social history or metahistory of why atheists chose or were impelled to think in such ways'. He adds: 'As the Benedictine educator Porcheron wrote in 1690, the mind can be compared to "a naked guest who comes to live in a furnished palace". Let us explore some of that furniture together' (p. 6). For myself, I am more interested in the guest.

12 Dominic Erdozain, *The Soul of Doubt: The Religious Roots of Unbelief from Luther to Marx* (Oxford: Oxford University Press, 2016), 5.

13 This remains a controversial field, and I should underline two starting assumptions. First, that as both a cultural and a biological phenomenon, human emotion is susceptible to historical change without being infinitely variable, and reconstructing past emotional cultures is therefore both possible and necessary. Second, that emotion is to a degree collective: our emotions are not only reflected in, but also learned from, interpreted through and given force by our cultural setting. As such they are at least partly accessible to history. Among the most helpful discussions of the field are Barbara H. Rosenwein, 'Problems and Methods in the History of Emotions', *Passions in Context* I.1 (2010), 1–32; Monique Scheer, 'Are emotions a kind of practice (and is that what makes them have a history)? A Bourdieuian approach to understanding emotion', *History and Theory* 51 (2012), 193–220; Thomas Dixon, *From Passion to Emotions: The Creation of a Secular Psychological Category* (Cambridge: Cambridge University Press, 2003), esp. 246.

14 Peter L. Berger, *The Sacred Canopy: Elements of a Sociological Theory of Religion* (New York: Anchor, 1967), 129.

15 Bunyan, *The Pilgrim's Progress*, 128–9.

16 Ethan Shagan, *The Birth of Modern Belief: Faith and Judgement from*

the Middle Ages to the Enlightenment (Princeton: Princeton University Press, 2018), 102–5; cf. Ephesians 2:12.

17 Arnould Bogaert, *A pronostication for diuers yeares . . . translated into Englysh oute of Frenche by Iohn Coke* (London: [R. Jugge for] Wyllyam Awen, 1553), sig. B5v. It did not come into general use in English until the 1560s.

18 John Cheke, tr. William Elstob, 'A Treatise of Superstition', in John Strype, *The Life of the Learned Sir John Cheke, Kt.* (London: for John Wyat, 1705), 250–1, where the translation misleadingly does not differentiate between Cheke's use of Latin and of Greek; cf. John McDiarmid, 'John Cheke's preface to *De Superstitione*', *Journal of Ecclesiastical History* 48.1 (1997), 100–20.

19 Thomas Fuller, *The Holy State* (Cambridge: Roger Daniel for John Williams, 1642), 328–9. For similar distinctions, cf. Francis Bacon, *The Essayes or Counsels, Civill and Morall*, ed. Michael Kiernan (Cambridge, MA: Harvard University Press, 1985), 52–3; Francis Cheynell, *The divine trinunity of the Father, Son, and Holy Spirit* (London: T. R. and E. M. for Samuel Gellibrand, 1650), 439; John Dove, *A confutation of atheisme* (London: Edward Allde for Henry Rockett, 1605), 2–4.

20 The claim that it was merely an 'obscenity', 'used in whatever sense one wanted to give it', is overstated. Lucien Febvre, *The Problem of Unbelief in the Sixteenth Century: The Religion of Rabelais*, tr. Beatrice Gottlieb (Cambridge, MA: Harvard University Press, 1982), 132, 135.

21 For the former, see, for example, John Wingfield, *Atheisme close and open, anatomized* (London: Thomas Harper, 1634), sigs E11v–12r; Christopher Love, *The naturall mans case stated* (London: E. Cotes for George Eversden, 1652), 237–8. For the latter, see, for example, Thomas Collier, *A second generall epistle to all the saints* (London: for Giles Calvert, 1649), 34–7; G. G., *A dispute betwixt an atheist and a Christian the atheist being a Flemming, the Christian an Englishman* (London: s.n., 1646), 2, 13; Francis Cheynell, *The rise, growth, and danger of Socinianisme* (London: for Samuel Gellibrand, 1643), 48–9.

22 John Gray, *Seven Types of Atheism* (London: Allen Lan

23 This I take to be the central point of Haidt, *Righteous*

24 Gray, *Seven Types of Atheism*, 158.

1. An Age of Suspicion

1 Thomas Curtis van Cleve, *The Emperor Frederick II of Hoh*
Immutator Mundi (Oxford: Clarendon Press, 1972), 304–
431–3; Georgina Masson, *Frederick II of Hohenstaufen: A Life* (L
Secker & Warburg, 1957), 228–34; Georges Minois, *The Atheist*
The Most Dangerous Book that Never Existed, tr. Lys Ann Weiss (Cł
and London: University of Chicago Press, 2012), 1–6.

2 Minois, *Atheist's Bible*; Max Gauna, *Upwellings: First Expression*
Unbelief in the Printed Literature of the French Renaissance (Lonc
and Toronto: Associated University Presses, 1992), 24. The earli
proven printing of the book is a French version from 1719, with
likely earlier edition in 1712: Alan Charles Kors, *Epicureans an*
Atheists in France, 1650–1729 (Cambridge: Cambridge University
Press, 2016), 159. There is some evidence of an earlier version in
1650: Minois, *Atheist's Bible*, 74. See also below, pp. 173, 186.

3 Febvre, *Problem of Unbelief*, 352.

4 It should be said that while most medieval Europeans believed that
the earth did not move, they knew it was a globe. For modern flat-
earthers, see, for example, https://www.tfes.org/; http://ifers.123.st/.
I do not recommend spending too long inside these halls of mirrors,
but they should not merely be laughed at. They are our age's simplest
and most harmless example of how to reject and insulate yourself
from your own culture's most basic truisms.

5 Thomas Aquinas, *Summa Theologica*, 1a.2.1–3.

6 Psalms 14:1, 53:1. The two psalms are almost identical throughout.

7 Walter L. Wakefield, 'Some Unorthodox Popular Ideas of the
Thirteenth Century', *Medievalia et Humanistica* new series IV (1973),
25–35 at 26; Alexander Murray, 'The Epicureans', in *Intellectuals and*

Writers in Fourteenth Century Europe, ed. Piero Boitani and Anna Torti (Cambridge: D. S. Brewer, 1986), 149–51.

8   Murray, 'The Epicureans', 156.

9   John H. Arnold, *Belief and Unbelief in Medieval Europe* (London: Hodder, 2005), 220–1; Maureen Flynn, 'Blasphemy and the Play of Anger in Sixteenth-Century Spain', *Past and Present* 149 (1995), 29–56, esp. 41–2, 46–7, 49–50; Gerd Schwerhoff, 'Horror Crime or Bad Habit? Blasphemy in Premodern Europe, 1200–1650', *Journal of Religious History* 32.4 (2008), 398–408, esp. 405–7.

10 Flynn, 'Blasphemy and the Play of Anger', 53.

11 Wakefield, 'Some Unorthodox Popular Ideas', 27–8; Arnold, *Belief and Unbelief*, 225.

12 Stephen Justice, 'Eucharistic Miracle and Eucharistic Doubt', *Journal of Medieval and Early Modern Studies* 42.2 (2012), 307–32, esp. 312.

13 Andrew E. Larsen, 'Are All Lollards Lollards?', in *Lollards and Their Influence in Late Medieval England*, ed. Fiona Somerset, Jill C. Haven and Derrick G. Pitard (Woodbridge: Boydell, 2003), 59–72; Anne Hudson, *The Premature Reformation* (Oxford: Clarendon Press, 1988), 384; John A. F. Thomson, *The Later Lollards 1414–1520* (Oxford: Oxford University Press, 1965), 36–7.

14 Ancient Judaism was divided over the immortality of the soul, but medieval and early modern Jews strongly affirmed it – as we will see in the case of Uriel Acosta: see below, pp. 98–100.

15 Murray, 'The Epicureans', 155, 162; D. P. Wright (ed.), *The Register of Thomas Langton, Bishop of Salisbury 1485–93* (York: Canterbury and York Society vol. 74, 1985), 70.

16 Dove, *Confutation of atheisme*, 68; Murray, 'Piety and impiety in thirteenth-century Italy', 101–2; Murray, 'The Epicureans', 159.

17 Murray, 'The Epicureans', 142.

18 Ibid. 158–9.

19 This argument has been very persuasively advanced by Susan Reynolds, 'Social Mentalities and the Case of Medieval Scepticism', *Transactions*

of the Royal Historical Society 6th ser. 1 (1991), 21–41; see also Arnold, *Belief and Unbelief*, 227–8; Robert N. Watson, *The Rest is Silence: Death as Annihilation in the English Renaissance* (Berkeley: University of California Press, 1994), 28.

20 Wakefield, 'Some Unorthodox Popular Ideas', 27–8.

21 Hudson, *Premature Reformation*, 384–5; Thomson, *Later Lollards*, 79–80; Richard Baxter, *Confirmation and restauration the necessary means of reformation, and reconciliation* (London: A. M. for Nevil Simmons, 1658), 162; William Pemble, *The workes of that learned minister of Gods holy Word, Mr. William Pemble* (London: Tho. Cotes [and Miles Flesher], for Iohn Bartlet, 1635), 559.

22 William of Tyre, *A History of Deeds Done Beyond the Sea*, tr. Emily Atwater Babcock and A. C. Krey (New York: Columbia University Press, 1943), vol. 2, 299–300; cf. Reynolds, 'Social Mentalities', 33.

23 Philippe de Mornay, seigneur du Plessis-Marly, *A woorke concerning the trewnesse of the Christian religion*, trans. Philip Sidney and Arthur Golding (London: John Charlewood and George Robinson, 1587), 153; Paul H. Kocher, 'The Physician as Atheist in Elizabethan England', *Huntington Library Quarterly* 10.3 (1947), 229–49 at 238–9. Kocher's article remains a shrewd overview of this subject.

24 Kocher, 'Physician as Atheist', 232; Ayelet Even-Ezra, 'Medicine and Religion in Early Dominican Demonology', *Journal of Ecclesiastical History* 69.4 (2018), 734.

25 Murray, 'The Epicureans', 162.

26 Nicholas Davidson, 'Unbelief and Atheism in Italy, 1500–1700', in Michael Hunter and David Wootton (eds), *Atheism from the Reformation to the Enlightenment* (Oxford: Oxford University Press, 1992), 55–85 at 64, 67.

27 Thomas Browne, *Religio Medici and Other Works*, ed. L. C. Martin (Oxford: Clarendon Press, 1964), 3.

28 Kocher, 'Physician as Atheist', 229. This is often cited as an old proverb, but the use of the word 'atheist' means it cannot predate the sixteenth century. It seems likeliest that it was coined by the first

person known to have cited it, Sir Thomas Browne: on whom see below, pp. 69–70.

29 Daniel Rogers, *Naaman the Syrian his disease and cure* (London: Th. Harper for Philip Neville, 1642), 220, 588–9; Henoch Clapham, *An epistle discoursing vpon the present pestilence* (London: T. C[reede] for the Widow Newbery, 1603), sig. A3r–v; Thomas Adams, *A commentary or, exposition vpon the diuine second epistle generall, written by the blessed apostle St. Peter* (London: Richard Badger for Iacob Bloome, [1633]), 1545; James Godskall, *The Kings medicine for this present yeere 1604* (London: for Edward White, 1604), sig. E2r. Cf. Francis Herring, *A modest defence of the caueat giuen to the wearers of impoisoned amulets, as preseruatiues from the plague* (London: Arnold Hatfield for William Iones, 1604), sig. A3r.

30 Robert Burton, *The Anatomy of Melancholy*, vol. III, ed. Thomas C. Faulkner, Nicholas K. Kiessling and Rhonda L. Blair (Oxford: Clarendon Press, 1994), 401.

31 Ecclesiasticus 38:1–2.

32 William Bullein, *A dialogue bothe pleasaunte and pietifull wherein is a goodly regimente against the feuer pestilence* (London: John Kingston, 1564), fos 6v–7v.

33 Bullein, *A dialogue*, fo. 8r–v. The claim that some physicians were 'nullifidians' was reprised in Franciscus Arcaeus, *A most excellent and compendious method of curing woundes in the head*, tr. John Read (London: Thomas East for Thomas Cadman, 1588), sig. ¶¶¶3r.

34 Browne, *Religio Medici*, 10, 20; and see below, pp. 69–70.

35 Antoine Adam, *Les Libertins au XVIIe Siècle* (Paris: Buchet/Chastel, 1964), 113–17. The story is questionable not least because it is difficult to identify Basin: a Louis Bazin-Ferret lived in the road Beurrier refers to and died in late 1659 or early 1660, but there is no evidence he was a physician.

36 See pp. 120–1, 158–9.

37 And that in the seventeenth century, by which time they should have known better: Martin Fotherby, *Atheomastix clearing foure truthes,*

against atheists and infidels (London: Nicholas Okes, 1622), sig. B1v.

38 Gauna, *Upwellings*, 59–63.

39 James Hankins, 'Monstrous Melancholy: Ficino and the Physiological Causes of Atheism', in *Laus Platonici Philosophi: Marsilio Ficino and His Influence*, ed. Stephen Clucas, Peter J. Forshaw and Valery Rees (Leiden: Brill, 2011), 25–43 at 39–43.

40 Henk van der Belt, *The Authority of Scripture in Reformed Theology: Truth and Trust* (Leiden: Brill, 2008), 134; George T. Buckley, *Atheism in the English Renaissance* (Chicago: University of Chicago Press, 1932), 73–4.

41 Pliny the Elder, *The historie of the world: commonly called, The naturall historie* (London: Adam Islip, 1634), 3–5, 187; and NB the title of Pliny the Elder, *The historie of the world . . . Translated into English by Philemon Holland Doctor in Physicke* (London: G. B., 1601). Abridged editions often omitted the most blatantly anti-religious passages.

42 Paul Oskar Kristeller, 'The Myth of Renaissance Atheism and the French Tradition of Free Thought', *Journal of the History of Philosophy* 6.3 (1968), 233–43 at 237–8.

43 Alison Brown, *The Return of Lucretius to Renaissance Florence* (Cambridge, MA: Harvard University Press, 2010), esp. viii; Stephen Greenblatt, *The Swerve: How the World Became Modern* (New York: Norton, 2011).

44 Wakefield, 'Some Unorthodox Popular Ideas', 26–7.

45 Chauncey E. Finch, 'Machiavelli's Copy of Lucretius', *The Classical Journal* 56.1 (1960), 29–32; Ada Palmer, 'Reading Lucretius in the Renaissance', *Journal of the History of Ideas* 73.3 (2012), 395–416 at 412–13.

46 Brown, *Return of Lucretius*, 81–2.

47 Niccolò Machiavelli, *The Discourses*, ed. Bernard Crick, trans. Leslie J. Walker (London: Penguin, 1970), 139–43, 149.

48 Niccolò Machiavelli, *The Prince*, trans. George Bull (London: Penguin, 1999), 19, 47. Here I follow – with reservations – the argument laid out in William B. Parsons, *Machiavelli's Gospel: The Critique of Christianity in* The Prince (Woodbridge: Boydell Press, 2016), esp. 1–3, 10–12, 180.

49 Machiavelli, *Discourses* 144; Gauna, *Upwellings*, 66–8.

50 Gray, *Seven Types of Atheism*, 46–7.

51 *The Jew of Malta*, lines 1–2, 9–11, 14–15, in *The Complete Works of Christopher Marlowe*, ed. Fredson Bowers, 2nd edn, vol. I (Cambridge: Cambridge University Press, 1981; cf. 1st edn 1973); British Library, Harleian MS 6848 fo. 185r; and see below, pp. 89–94.

52 Richard Copley Christie, *Étienne Dolet: The Martyr of the Renaissance, 1508–1546* (London: Macmillan & Co., 1899), 461, 480–5; Nicholas Davidson, 'Christopher Marlowe and Atheism' in Darryll Grantley and Peter Roberts (eds), *Christopher Marlowe and English Renaissance Culture* (Aldershot: Scolar Press, 1996), 141.

53 Kors, *Atheism in France*, 221–4; David Wootton, 'New Histories of Atheism', in Michael Hunter and David Wootton (eds), *Atheism from the Reformation to the Enlightenment* (Oxford: Oxford University Press, 1992), 33, 41.

54 Davidson, 'Unbelief and Atheism in Italy', 55.

55 Richard Harvey, *A theologicall discourse of the Lamb of God and his enemies* (London: Iohn Windet for W. P[onsonby], 1590), 95; Dove, *Confutation of atheisme*, 5.

56 Roger Ascham, *The scholemaster or plaine and perfite way of teachyng children* (London: John Day, 1570), fos. 27v–29r. In fact the word came into English from French, which Ascham would not have seen as much of an improvement.

57 Richard Hooker, *Of the Laws of Ecclesiastical Polity: Book V*, ed. W. Speed Hill (Cambridge, MA: Belknap Press, 1977), 24. On the covens, see among others Dove, *Confutation of atheisme*, 17–18; Gauna, *Upwellings*, 74–9.

58 Kors, *Atheism in France*, 66.

59 Palmer, 'Reading Lucretius'.

60 Ada Palmer, 'Humanist Lives of Classical Philosophers and the Idea of Renaissance Secularization: Virtue, Rhetoric, and the Orthodox Sources of Unbelief', *Renaissance Quarterly* 70 (2017), 935–76; Ruben

Buys, *Sparks of Reason: Vernacular Rationalism in the Low Countries 1550–1670* (Hilversum: Verloren, 2015), 180–1.

2. The Reformation and the Battle for Credulity

1   Brad S. Gregory, *The Unintended Reformation: How a Religious Revolution Secularized Society* (Cambridge, MA: Harvard University Press, 2012).

2   John Calvin, *Opera quae supersunt omnia*, ed. G. Baum, E. Cunitz and E. Reuss, vol. 11 (Braunschweig: Schwetschke, 1873), 491.

3   As Max Gauna points out, the parallel is suspiciously close: Gauna, *Upwellings*, 76–7.

4   Jules Bonnet (ed.), *Letters of John Calvin: Compiled from the Original Manuscripts and Edited with Historical Notes, vol. II: 1545–53* (New York: Burt Franklin, 1972), 123–4; François Berriot, 'Un procès d'athéisme à Genève: l'affaire Gruet (1547–1550)', *Bulletin de la Société de l'Histoire du Protestantisme Français* 125 (1979), 577–92 at 579–82.

5   Berriot, 'Un procès d'athéisme', 585–91.

6   John Calvin, *Concerning Scandals*, tr. John W. Fraser (Edinburgh: St Andrews Press, 1978), esp. 57–61, 68.

7   Burton, *Anatomy of Melancholy*, vol. III, 337; McDiarmid, 'John Cheke's preface to *De Superstitione*'.

8   P. S. Allen (ed.), *Opvs epistolarum Des. Erasmi Roterodami* (Oxford: Clarendon Press, 1941), vol. x, 137.

9   *The forme of prayers and ministration of the Sacraments, &c. used in the Englishe congregation at Geneua* (Geneva: J. Crespin, 1556), 5; Lawrence Anderton, *Miscellania or a treatise Contayning two hundred controuersiall animaduersions* (Saint-Omer: English College, 1640), 183.

10 Bacon, *Essays*, 54.

11 Henry More, *An antidote against atheisme* (London: Roger Daniel, 1653), 1–2. John Owen, a contemporary of More's whose Protestantism was of a very different flavour, shared essentially the same analysis,

although he was more sanguine about the scale of the problem: John Owen, *Vindiciae evangelicae or The mystery of the Gospell vindicated, and Socinianisme examined* (Oxford: Leonard Lichfield for Thomas Robinson, 1655), 59.

12 Samuel Harsnett, *A declaration of egregious popish impostures* (London: James Roberts, 1604), 251, quoted in Alexandra Walsham, *Providence in Early Modern England* (Oxford: Oxford University Press, 1999), 232.

13 Pascal, *Pensées*, 28, 182. Cf. Amanda Porterfield, *Conceived in Doubt: Religion and Politics in the New American Nation* (Chicago: University of Chicago Press, 2012), 15–16; Andrew C. Fix, *Prophecy and Reason: The Dutch Collegiants in the Early Enlightenment* (Princeton: Princeton University Press, 1991), 11–12; Buys, *Sparks of Reason*, 236–7; Taylor, *A Secular Age*, 226. It is in this mystical sense that Gerrard Winstanley chose to 'use the word Reason, instead of the word God, in my writings . . . Reason is that living power of light that is in all things; it is the salt that savours all things'. Gerrard Winstanley, *Truth lifting up its head above scandals* (London: [s.n.], 1649), sig. A7r.

14 Vincent of Lérins, *The waie home to Christ and truth leadeing from Antichrist and errour*, ed. and tr. John Proctor (London: Robert Caly, 1554), sig. A7r.

15 For one exception, see Robert Bruce, *Sermons vpon the Sacrament of the Lords Supper* (Edinburgh: Robert Waldegraue, 1591?), sig. L7v.

16 William Peryn, *Thre godlye and notable sermons, of the sacrament of the aulter* (London: J. Herforde, 1546), sig. B1r–v.

17 Richard Smith, *The assertion and defence of the sacramente of the aulter* (London: J. Herforde, 1546), fos 46r–v, 235v.

18 Stephen Gardiner, *A detection of the deuils sophistrie* (London: J. Herforde, 1546), fos 15v, 30r; John 6:52.

19 Anne Hudson, 'The Mouse in the Pyx: Popular Heresy and the Eucharist', *Trivium* 26 (1991), 40–53.

20 Reginald Scot, *The discouerie of witchcraft* (London: William Brome, 1584), 191.

21 Michel de Montaigne, *Essays*, trans. M. A. Screech (London: Penguin, 2013), 167.

22 Samuel Bolton, *The arraignment of errour* (London: G. Miller for Andrew Kembe, 1646), 41; G. G., *A dispute betwixt an atheist and a Christian*, 4.

23 François Berriot, 'Hétérodoxie religieuse et utopie politique dans les « erreurs estranges » de Noël Journet (1582)', *Bulletin de la Société de l'Histoire du Protestantisme Français* 124 (1978), 236–48; Geoffroy Vallée, *La Beatitude des Chrestiens ou Le Fleo de la Foy* (Paris: Librairie de l'Académie des Bibliophiles, 1867), 10; Wootton, 'New Histories of Atheism', 13.

24 Richard Overton, *Mans mortalitie* (Amsterdam: John Canne, 1644), sig. A2v; Jacob Bauthumley, *The light and dark sides of God* (London: for William Learner, 1650), 45; Thomas Edwards, *The third part of Gangraena* (London: for Ralph Smith, 1646), 62; William Erbery, *The testimony of William Erbery, left upon record for the saints of suceeding ages* (London: Giles Calvert, 1658), 84; 2 Corinthians 11:14.

25 Anthony Weldon, *The court and character of King James* (London: R. I., 1651), 156. This is apparently the earliest form of the proverb, 'Fool me once, shame on you. Fool me twice, shame on me': a sentiment which, for once, seems not to have any classical precedents.

26 William Chillingworth, *The religion of protestants a safe way to salvation* (Oxford: Leonard Lichfield, 1638), sig. §§3r–v, p. 80.

27 Joseph Hall, *The Arte of Divine Meditation* (London: Humfrey Lownes, 1606), 8–9; Nicholas Byfield, *The Marrow of the Oracles of God* (London: George Purslow for Ralph Rounthwaite, 1622), 493. Cf. Alan W. Gomes, 'Reason Run Amok? The Protestant Orthodox Charge of Rationalism against Faustus Socinus' in Jordan J. Ballor, David S. Sytsma and Jason Zuidema (eds), *Church and School in Early Modern Protestantism* (Leiden: Brill, 2013), 551–66.

28 For example, Thomas Broke, *Certeyn meditations, and things to be had in remembraunce* (London: W. Seres for J. Day, 1548), sig. A5v.

29 John Foxe, *Actes and monuments of these latter and perillous dayes* (London: John Day, 1563), 868–9.

30 George Herbert, *The Works of George Herbert*, ed. F. E. Hutchinson (Oxford: Clarendon Press, 1941), 200–1.

31 John Dod and Robert Cleaver, *Ten sermons tending chiefely to the fitting of men for the worthy receiuing of the Lords Supper* (London: Roger Jackson, 1611), 109; Christopher Sutton, *Godly meditations upon the most holy sacrament of the Lordes supper* (London: T. Snodham for N. Bourne, 1613), sigs A12r–v, B4r. Cf. Lewis Bayly, *The Practise of pietie* (London: John Hodgetts, 1620), 552, 554.

32 Miles Huggarde, *The displaying of the protestantes* (London: Robert Caly, 1556), fo. 28v; Francis Young, *English Catholics and the Supernatural, 1553–1829* (Farnham: Ashgate, 2013), 27–8.

33 Alec Ryrie, 'Scripture, the Spirit and the Meaning of Radicalism in the English Revolution', in Bridget Heal and Anorthe Kremers (eds.), *Radicalism and Dissent in the World of Protestant Reform* (Göttingen: Vandenhoeck & Ruprecht, 2017), 100–17.

34 Richard Popkin, *The History of Scepticism from Savonarola to Bayle* (Oxford: Oxford University Press, 2003), 69–72; Richard Baxter, *A key for Catholicks, to open the jugling of the Jesuits* (London: R. W. for Nevil Simmons, 1659), sig. b3r; John Owen, *Of the divine originall, authority, self-evidencing light, and power of the Scriptures* (Oxford: Henry Hall, 1659), 202; Chillingworth, *Religion of protestants*, sig. §§3v.

35 Gauna, *Upwellings*, 100–1.

36 Montaigne, *Essays*, 46, 84.

37 Pascal, *Pensées*, 215, 229; and cf. 23, 73, 119, 186, 212.

38 Montaigne, *Essays*, 31, 33.

39 Ibid. 70, 82, 85, 119–20.

40 Popkin, *History of Scepticism*, 56.

41 Montaigne, *Essays*, 70, 172, 187, 222, 427, 449.

42 Minois, *Atheist's Bible*, 65; Joseph Mede, *The works of the pious and profoundly-learned Joseph Mede* (London: Roger Norton for Richard

Royston, 1672), 2; Popkin, *History of Scepticism*, 65–6.

43 Pascal, *Pensées*, 28, 34, 185. The impossibility of absolute scepticism was a truism: see Mornay, *A woorke concerning the trewnesse of the Christian religion*, 12; Meric Casaubon, *Of credulity and incredulity in things natural, civil, and divine* (London: for T. Garthwait, 1668), 4, 155.

44 Montaigne, *Essays*, 220–1, 226.

45 Ibid. 69–70, 119, 192.

46 Popkin, *History of Scepticism*, 59–70.

47 Edward Hyde, *Clarendon: Selections from the History of the Rebellion and The Life by Himself*, ed. G. Huehns (Oxford: Oxford University Press, 1978), 42, 44; Robert Orr, *Reason and Authority: The Thought of William Chillingworth* (Oxford: Clarendon Press, 1967), 14, 17–19; Popkin, *History of Scepticism*, 65–6.

48 William Chillingworth, *The Works of William Chillingworth, MA of the University of Oxford . . . The ninth edition* (London: for Benj. Motte, 1727), vol. iii, 20, 40; R. S[impson] (ed.), *Life of Lady Falkland. From a MS. in the Imperial Archives at Lille* (London: John Chisholm, 1861), 65–6, 72–5; Orr, *Reason and Authority*, 30.

49 S[impson] (ed.), *Life of Lady Falkland*, 75; Orr, *Reason and Authority*, 40; Chillingworth, *Religion of protestants*, 73, 112, 372, 375.

50 Chillingworth, *Religion of protestants*, 73, 96–7, 372; Barbara J. Shapiro, *A Culture of Fact: England, 1550–1720* (Ithaca, NY: Cornell University Press, 2000).

51 Chillingworth, *Religion of protestants*, sig. §§1v.

52 Orr, *Reason and Authority*, 198.

53 Browne, *Religio Medici*, 3, 6, 8, 10, 20–3. *Religio Medici* went through eight editions in 1642–60 and five more over the following century, not counting editions of Browne's complete works.

54 Browne, *Religio Medici*, 9–11, 20.

55 John Donne, 'Satire III', lines 76–82, in *The Poems of John Donne*, ed. H. Grierson (Oxford: Oxford University Press, 1933), 139.

56 Montaigne, *Essays*, 119–22.

57 Jean Bodin, *Colloquium of the Seven about the Secrets of the Sublime*, ed. and tr. Marion Leathers Daniels Kuntz (Princeton: Princeton University Press, 1975), xxi–xxix, xliv, 7, 163–5.

58 Browne, *Religio Medici*, 6–7.

3. The Atheist's Comedy

1   Quoting the first English edition of 1587: Mornay, *A woorke concerning the trewnesse of the Christian religion*, sig. **1r. The count of thirty-seven includes four partial editions in English and Dutch.

2   Thomas Morton, *A treatise of the nature of God* (London: Tho. Creed for Robert Dexter, 1599), 27–8; Dove, *Confutation of atheisme*, sig. A2r; Wingfield, *Atheisme close and open*, sig. A10v.

3   Seth Ward, *A philosophicall essay towards an eviction of the being and attributes of God* (Oxford: Leonard Lichfield, 1652), 11.

4   On the cultural significance of anti-atheism, see especially George Hoffmann, 'Atheism as a Devotional Category', *Republics of Letters* 1.2 (2010), 44–55, and Leif Dixon, 'William Perkins, "Atheisme," and the Crises of England's Long Reformation', *Journal of British Studies* 50.4 (2011), 790–812; also Kenneth Sheppard, *Anti-Atheism in Early Modern England 1580–1720: The Atheist Answered and His Error Confuted* (Leiden: Brill, 2015).

5   National Library of Scotland, MS Wodrow Qu. LXXXIII fos 68–107 at 85r, 86v; Michelle Brock, 'Plague, Covenants, and Confession: The Strange Case of Ayr, 1647–8', *Scottish Historical Review* 97.2 (2018), 129–52.

6   Alexander Henderson, *A sermon preached to the honourable House of Commons at their late solemne fast, Wednesday, December 27, 1643* (London: for Robert Bostock, 1644), 28; John Donne, *LXXX sermons preached by that learned and reverend divine, Iohn Donne* (London: for Richard Royston, 1640), 756; Love, *The naturall mans case stated*, 249–56; Wingfield, *Atheisme close and open*, sig. E12r. The significance of these expansive definitions of 'atheism' for the shifting meanings

of the category of 'belief' are illuminatingly traced in Shagan, *Birth of Modern Belief.*

7 Montaigne, *Essays*, 168–9.

8 Shagan, *Birth of Modern Belief.*

9 Cyril Tourneur, *The Atheist's Tragedy*, in *The Plays of Cyril Tourneur*, ed. George Parfitt (Cambridge: Cambridge University Press, 1978), esp. V.ii.236, 253–5; cf. Cyril Tourneur, *The atheists tragedie: or The honest man's reuenge As in diuers places it hath often beene acted* (London: [Thomas Snodham] for John Stepneth and Richard Redmer, 1611).

10 Tourneur, *Atheist's Tragedy*, I.i.18–19, 29–30, 128–9, IV.iii.117–20.

11 One modern outworking of this problem is entertainingly traced in Haidt, *The Righteous Mind*, 45–7.

12 *The wonderfull example of God shewed upon Jasper Coningham* (London: for Thomas Millington, to be solde at his shop in Cornehill, 1593–1603?). There are eight known editions before 1701 and the ballad became so familiar that its tune became widely known as 'Jasper Coningham'. Professor Christopher Marsh judges it to be among the hundred most popular ballads in seventeenth-century England. Cf. a variant of the same story in *The Punish'd Atheist: Or, The Miserable End of a North Country Gentleman* (London: for J. Blare, 1664–1703?). I am grateful to Professor Marsh for his assistance with these ballads.

13 John Ford, *'Tis Pity She's a Whore*, in *'Tis Pity She's a Whore and Other Plays*, ed. Marion Lomax (Oxford: Oxford University Press, 1995), V.v.33–6.

14 Henry Smith, *Gods arrowe against atheists* (London: John Danter, 1593), sig. B1v.

15 Thomas Nash, *Christs teares ouer Ierusalem* (London: [George Eld] for Thomas Thorp, 1613), 125; John Whitgift, *Works*, ed. John Ayre, vol. 2 (Cambridge: Parker Society, 1852), 483; Samuel Hieron, *A Helpe Vnto Deuotion* (London: H. L[ownes] for Samuel Macham, 1610), 340–2; Samuel Clarke et al., *The Lives of sundry Eminent Persons in this Later Age* (London: Thomas Simmons, 1683), 62; cf. John Craig, 'Psalms, Groans and Dogwhippers: The Soundscape of

Worship in the English Parish Church, 1547–1642' in Will Coster and Andrew Spicer (eds), *Sacred Space in Early Modern Europe* (Cambridge: Cambridge University Press, 2005), 104–23; Leigh Eric Schmidt, *Hearing Things: Religion, Illusion and the American Enlightenment* (Cambridge, MA: Harvard University Press, 2000), 58.

16 Thomas Beard, *The theatre of Gods judgements wherein is represented the admirable justice of God against all notorious sinners* (London: S.I. & M.H., 1642), 88, 133.

17 Tourneur, *Atheist's Tragedy*, II.iv.146–7; Philip Sidney, *The Countess of Pembroke's Arcadia (The New Arcadia)*, ed. Victor Skretkowicz (Oxford: Clarendon Press, 1987), 358–9; Henoch Clapham, *Errour on the left hand, through a frozen securitie* (London: N. O[kes] for Nathaniel Butter, 1608), 53–4.

18 Nash, *Christs teares ouer Ierusalem* (1613), 124; Francis Bacon, *Of the advancement and proficience of learning; or, The partitions of sciences* (Oxford: Leon. Lichfield for Rob. Young, 1640), 9; cf. Bacon, *Essays*, 53; Mornay, *A woorke concerning the trewnesse of the Christian religion*, 10; Anthony Farindon, *XXX sermons lately preached at the parish church of Saint Mary Magdalen Milkstreet, London* (London: for Richard Marriot, 1657), 186.

19 Bacon, *Essays*, 52.

20 Fuller, *The Holy State*, 380.

21 Donne, *LXXX sermons*, 227, 486.

22 Hooker, *Laws of Ecclesiastical Polity: Book V*, 23.

23 Fuller, *The Holy State*, 380; Jeremy Corderoy, *A Warning for Worldlings. Or a comfort to the godly, and a terror to the wicked* (London: Thomas Purfoot, for Lawrence Lyle, 1608), 203; Love, *The naturall mans case stated*, 241. Cf. John Swan, *A true and breife report, of Mary Glouers vexation and of her deliuerance by the meanes of fastinge and prayer* (London?: [s.n.], 1603), 68; Dove, *Confutation of atheisme*, 76; Jean d'Espagne, *Popular errors, in generall poynts concerning the knowledge of religion* (London: for Thomas Whittaker, 1648), 96.

24 Robert Pricke, *A verie godlie and learned sermon treating of mans mortalitie* (London: Thomas Creede, 1608), sig. D4r; Hooker, *Laws of Ecclesiastical Polity: Book V*, 23; Farindon, *XXX sermons*, 51–2.

25 Christopher Marlowe, *Doctor Faustus*, A-text II.i.135, in *Doctor Faustus and Other Plays*, ed. David Bevington and Eric Rasmussen (Oxford: Oxford University Press, 1995); *The arraignment and tryall with a declaration of the Ranters* ([London]: by B.A., 1650), sig. A4v; Burton, *Anatomy of Melancholy*, vol. III, 396; C.J. Betts, *Early Deism in France: from the so-called 'déistes' of Lyon (1564) to Voltaire's 'Lettres philosophiques' (1734)* (The Hague: Martinus Nijhoff, 1984), 23–6.

26 Henderson, *Sermon preached to the honourable House of Commons*, 28–9.

27 *The Works of the Learned and Pious Author of The Whole Duty of Man* (Oxford and London: Roger Norton for Edward Paulet, 1704), vol. II, 111; Fuller, *The Holy State*, 378; Richard Younge ['Iunius'], *The Drunkard's Character* (London: R. Badger for George Latham, 1638), 559.

28 Kors, *Atheism in France*, 28; Thomas Adams, *The gallants burden. A sermon preached at Paules Crosse* (London: W. W[hite] for Clement Knight, 1612), fo. 16r.

29 Robert Persons, *An aduertisement written to a secretarie of my L. Treasurers of Ingland* ([Antwerp]: [s.n.], 1592), 18; The National Archives, Kew, SP 14/4 fo. 189r; Buckley, *Atheism in the English Renaissance*, 149–50; William M. Hamlin, *Tragedy and Scepticism in Shakespeare's England* (Basingstoke: Palgrave, 2005), 49, 53; *Sir Walter Rauleigh his lamentation: Who was beheaded in the old Pallace at Westminster the 29. of October. 1618* (London: for Philip Birch, 1618). The traditional label 'school of night' is taken from Shakespeare's *Love's Labours Lost*, IV.iii.201, although the evidence linking that throwaway phrase to Raleigh's group is thin, to say the least.

30 British Library, Harleian MS 6848 fo. 191r.

31 British Library, Harleian MS 6849 fos 183r–190r.

32 Ibid. fos 184v, 187v–188v.

33 British Library, Harleian MS 6848 fo. 190r.

34 See above, p. 39.

35 *Tamburlaine, Part II*, V.i.186–90; *The Massacre at Paris*, lines 123–6. In *Complete Works of Christopher Marlowe*.

36 Marlowe, *Doctor Faustus*, A-text, I.i.49, 111; I.iii.86–7; II.i.18–19, 120.

37 Robert Greene, *Greenes, groats-worth of witte, bought with a million of repentance* (London: [J. Wolfe and J. Danter] for William Wright, 1592), sigs E4v–F1r.

38 Charles Nicoll, 'Marlowe [Marley], Christopher', *Oxford Dictionary of National Biography*.

39 British Library, Harleian MS 6848 fos 154r, 185r–v.

40 Ibid.

41 Thomas Lodge, *Wits miserie, and the worlds madnesse discouering the deuils incarnat of this age* (London: Adam Islip, 1596), 10.

42 Borthwick Institute, York, MS HC.CP.1590/5, http://dlibcausepapers. york.ac.uk, identifier yorkcp:85885108 (accessed 12 January 2018), fos 1r, 6r; cf. David Cressy, *Travesties and Transgressions in Tudor and Stuart England* (Oxford: Oxford University Press, 2000), 162–70. I am grateful to Lucy Kaufman for this reference.

43 W. Hylton Dyer Longstaffe (ed.), *The Acts of the High Commission Court within the Diocese of Durham* (Durham: Surtees Society 34, 1858), 115–19.

44 Pascal, *Pensées*, 132.

45 Nash, *Christs teares ouer Ierusalem* (1613), 128; cf. Bacon, *Essays*, 53.

46 Tourneur, *Atheist's Tragedy*, I.ii.221–3.

47 See, among many others, *The libertine overthrown, or, A mirror for atheists* (London: J. Bradford, 1690?); Burton, *Anatomy of Melancholy*, vol. III, 338; John Bruce (ed.), *The Works of Roger Hutchinson* (Cambridge: Parker Society, 1842), 138, 140; Adams, *The gallants burden*, fo. 17r; Vallée, *La Beatitude des Chrestiens*, 10.

48 Gauna, *Upwellings*, 75; Calvin, *Opera*, vol. 11, 491.

49 This was not a universal view: some theologians tried to justify some

forms of concealment or deceit. Perez Zagorin, *Ways of Lying: Dissimula* *Persecution and Conformity in Early Modern Europe* (Cambridge, N Harvard University Press, 1990); Stefania Tutino, 'Between Nicoden and "Honest" Dissimulation: The Society of Jesus in England', *Histori Research* 79.206 (2006), 534–53; Andrew Pettegree, *Marian Protestantis Six Studies* (Aldershot: Ashgate, 1996), 86–117.

50 Davidson, 'Unbelief and Atheism in Italy', 79; Adam, *Les Libertin au XVIIe Siècle*, 111–13. Cf. Bacon, *Essays*, 52.

51 What follows draws on his own posthumously published account, as translated into English in 1740: Uriel Acosta, *A Specimen of Human Life*, ed. Peter M. Bergman (New York: Bergman Publishers, 1967).

52 No copies were known to survive until one was discovered in a Danish library in 1990.

53 Acosta, *A Specimen of Human Life*, 11–12, 18–19, 33–4, 37–8.

54 Buys, *Sparks of Reason*, 37–8, 102–3.

55 E[leazar] D[uncan], *The copy of a letter written by E. D. Doctour of Physicke* (London: Melchisedech Bradwood, 1606), 15–16.

56 Tourneur, *Atheist's Tragedy*, esp. I.ii.38, I.iv.128, IV.v.36–40, 54–62. Uniquely among the play's highborn characters, Sebastian always speaks in prose, not in verse.

57 See, for example, Sonnet 146.

58 *Macbeth*, V.v.23–27; *Measure for Measure*, III.i.116–19, 127, 145; *Titus Andronicus*, V.i.71, 73, 79–80, 141–2, 147.

59 George Santayana, 'The Absence of Religion in Shakespeare', in *Interpretations of Poetry and Religion* (New York: Charles Scribner's Sons, 1932), 147–65; *Twelfth Night*, II.iii.145–6.

60 A section of *The Tempest*, II.i, is lightly paraphrased from Montaigne's essay 'On the Cannibals', as printed in the 1603 English version translated by John Florio. Alongside that hard evidence, the subject's most obsessive textual detective has found 'about a hundred close phrasal correspondences' between Shakespeare and the 1603 text, as well as 'a glossary of about seven hundred and fifty words, selected from Florio's Montaigne, which were used by Shakespeare during and

after, but not before 1603': George Coffin Taylor, *Shakspere's Debt to Montaigne* (Cambridge, MA: Harvard University Press, 1925), 5. Whether or not you swallow that argument whole, it is at least highly plausible that Shakespeare's familiarity with Montaigne extended beyond passing acquaintance with a single essay.

61 Santayana, 'The Absence of Religion', 156.

62 David Loewenstein, 'Agnostic Shakespeare?: The Godless World of *King Lear*', in David Loewenstein and Michael Witmore (eds), *Shakespeare and Early Modern Religion* (Cambridge: Cambridge University Press, 2015), 155–71; *King Lear*, IV.i.38–9.

4. The Puritan Atheist

1 John Earle, *Micro-cosmographie. Or, a peece of the world discouered in essayes and characters* (London: W. Stansby for E. Blount, 1628), sigs I2r–I4v; John Earle, *The Autograph Manuscript of Microcosmographie* (Leeds: Scolar Press, 1966), 161–5; and see above, p. 71.

2 William Harrison, *Deaths aduantage little regarded, and The soules solace against sorrow* (London: Felix Kyngston, 1602), part III, 14–15; *The bible and holy scriptures* (Geneva: R. Hall, 1560), New Testament, fo. 22r.

3 William Perkins, *A treatise of mans imaginations* (Cambridge: John Legat, 1607), 33, 51.

4 Shagan, *Birth of Modern Belief.*

5 Nicholas Bownde, *The vnbeleefe of S. Thomas the Apostle laid open for the comfort of all that desire to beleeue* ([Cambridge?]: Cantrell Legge, 1608), 50; Fotherby, *Atheomastix*, sig. B3r.

6 See, among others, the discussions above of Montaigne and of Uriel Acosta.

7 Germana Ernst, *Tommaso Campanella: The Book and the Body of Nature*, tr. David L. Marshall (Dordrecht: Springer, 2010), 129–35; Hoffmann, 'Atheism as a Devotional Category', 53.

8   Kors, *Atheism in France*, 54.

9   I described this culture a little more kindly, and at much greater length, in my *Being Protestant in Reformation Britain* (Oxford: Oxford University Press, 2013).

10 Stephen Denison, *The Monument or Tombe-Stone* (London: Richard Field, 1620), 100.

11 Obadiah Sedgwick, *The doubting beleever* (London: M. F. for Thomas Nicols, 1641), 14–15.

12 Donne, *LXXX sermons*, 402–3; John Bunyan, *The Holy War, made by Shaddai upon Diabolus* (London: for Dorman Newman and Benjamin Alsop, 1682), 294; Bunyan, *The Pilgrim's Progress*, 109–10.

13 Richard Baxter, *The saints everlasting rest, or, A treatise of the blessed state of the saints in their enjoyment of God in glory* (London: Rob. White for Thomas Underhil and Francis Tyton, 1650), 177; Vavasor Powell, *Spirituall Experiences, Of sundry Beleevers* (London: Robert Ibbitson, 1653), 330–1. The text does not explicitly state that I. G. is a woman, but I have presumed so, both because it seems more humane to risk misgendering 'her' than to deny 'her' a gender altogether, and also because 'she' claims to have found special comfort in a vividly female image of God's love: 331.

14 Hannah Allen, *A narrative of God's gracious dealings with that choice Christian Mrs. Hannah Allen* (London: John Wallis, 1683), esp. 4, 10, 15, 23, 42–4, 72. On the unpardonable sin, see Matthew 12:31–2.

15 Henry Jessey, *The exceeding riches of grace advanced by the spirit of grace* (London: Matthew Simmons for Henry Overton and Hannah Allen, 1647), 7, 78, 82.

16 Powell, *Spirituall Experiences*, 173–4.

17 Allen, *A narrative of God's gracious dealings*, 58–9; John Hart, *Trodden down strength, by the God of strength, or, Mrs Drake revived* (London: R. Bishop for Stephen Pilkington, 1647), 13, 23–9: I owe this reference to Stacie Vos.

18 Princeton University Library, MS RTC01 no. 62, fo. 32r; Luke Howard, *Love and Truth in Plainness Manifested* (London: T. Sowle,

1704), 13–15; Richard Baxter, *Reliquiae Baxterianae, or, Mr. Richard Baxters narrative of the most memorable passages of his life and times* (London: T. Parkhurst, J. Robinson, F. Lawrence and F. Dunton, 1696), vol. I, 4. Cf. Elizabeth Stirredge, *Strength in Weakness Manifest* (London: J. Sowle, 1711), 26.

19 Katherine Hodgkin (ed.), *Women, Madness and Sin in Early Modern England: The Autobiographical Writings of Dionys Fitzherbert* (Farnham: Ashgate, 2010), 194; Sedgwick, *The doubting beleever*, 64–9; Allen, *A narrative of God's gracious dealings*, 15.

20 Quite how unusual they were, and how much Calvinist theology exacerbated them, remains open to dispute: Ryrie, *Being Protestant*, 27–32; John Stachniewski, *The Persecutory Imagination: English Puritanism and the Literature of Religious Despair* (Oxford: Clarendon Press, 1991).

21 John Bunyan, *Grace abounding to the chief of sinners in a faithful account of the life and death of John Bunyan* (London: for Nath. Ponder, 1692), 46–9, 51.

22 *The Diary of Michael Wigglesworth 1653–57: The Conscience of a Puritan*, ed. Edmund S. Morgan (New York: Harper and Row, 1965), 45; *The Diary of Sir Archibald Johnston of Wariston, vol. II: 1650–1654*, ed. David Hay Fleming (Edinburgh: Scottish History Society, 1919), 259; Jane Turner, *Choice experiences of the kind dealings of God* (London: R. Hils, 1653), 25.

23 Princeton University Library, MS RTC01 no. 62, fo. 31r.

24 Baxter, *Reliquiae Baxterianae*, vol. I, 21.

25 Samuel Clarke, *A Collection of the Lives of Ten Eminent Divines, Famous in their Generations* (London: for William Miller, 1662), 516; Anthony Walker, *The Holy Life of Mrs Elizabeth Walker* (London: J. Leake, 1690), 19–20.

26 Rogers, *Naaman the Syrian*, 287; Richard Sibbes, *The bruised reede, and smoaking flax* (London: [M. Flesher] for R. Dawlman, 1631), 138 (the marked copy is at the Folger Shakespeare Library, call no. STC 22480.2); Love, *The naturall mans case stated*, 259.

27 Jessey, *The exceeding riches of grace*, 60; Hodgkin (ed.), *Women, Madness and Sin*, 192.

28 John Downame, *The Christian warfare* (London: Felix Kyngston, for Cuthbert Burby, 1604), 84, 267–8.

29 Baxter, *The saints everlasting rest*, sig. bb2v; Richard Baxter, *A breviate of the life of Margaret, the daughter of Francis Charlton . . . and wife of Richard Baxter* (London: for B. Simmons, 1681), 68–9. The trinity of doubt – God, soul, Bible – was neatly summed up in the full title of Seth Ward's 1652 book *A philosophicall essay towards an eviction of the: Being and attributes of God. Immortality of the souls of men. Truth and authority of Scripture.*

30 In the dream he eventually reached 'a fair chamber with goodly lodgings', but with the logic of dreams, this turned out to be a room at Harvard, and his attention turned to how the scholars had used pulleys to bring furniture up to such a height. Halsey Thomas (ed.), *The Diary of Samuel Sewall 1674–1729*, vol. I (New York: Farrar, Straus & Giroux, 1973), 12.

31 James Orchard Halliwell (ed.), *The Autobiography and Correspondence of Sir Simonds D'Ewes* (London: Richard Bentley, 1845), vol. I, 251–2.

32 See above, pp. 32–3, 59.

33 *Diary of Michael Wigglesworth*, 49.

34 Crawford Gribben, 'Bible Reading, Puritan Devotion and the Transformation of Politics in the English Revolution', in Robert Armstrong and Tadgh Ó hAnnracháin (eds), *The English Bible in the Early Modern World* (Leiden: Brill, 2018), 150–1. For divergent scholarly views of the subject, see John Goodwin, *The divine authority of the Scriptures asserted* (London: A.M. for Henry Overton, 1647), 9–17; Owen, *Of the divine originall*, esp. 173; and for an uneducated radical's reaction, see Thomas Collier, *A general epistle to the universal church of the first born* (London: Giles Calvert, 1648), 33–8.

35 Powell, *Spirituall Experiences*, 143–4.

36 Downame, *The Christian warfare*, 323, 346–7.

37 Thomas Taylor, *The pilgrims profession. Or a sermon preached at the funerall of Mris Mary Gunter* (London: I. D[awson] for Io. Bartlet, 1622), 144–5.

38 Earle, *Micro-cosmographie*, sig I3r.

39 Francis Osborne, *Advice to a son; or Directions for your better conduct* (Oxford: Henry Hall for Thomas Robinson, 1656), 67, 76–7; Lodge, *Wits miserie, and the worlds madnesse*, 17.

40 Ward, *A philosophicall essay*, 2.

41 John Toldervy, *The foot out of the snare. Or, A restoration of the inhabitants of Zion into their place* (London: J. C. for Tho. Brewster, 1655), 2; Richard Farnworth, *The heart opened by Christ; or, The conditions of a troubled soul that could find no true rest* (London: [s.n.], 1654), 9; Bauthumley, *The light and dark sides of God*, 78.

42 Jeremy Taylor, *Treatises of 1. The liberty of prophesying, 2. Prayer ex tempore, 3. Episcopacie* (London: for R. Royston, 1648), preface 33, part I, 2.

43 Downame, *The Christian warfare*, 355.

44 Burton, *Anatomy of Melancholy*, vol. III, 342, 399.

45 Mornay, *A woorke concerning the trewnesse of the Christian religion*, sig. **4v.

46 William Pinke, *The Tryall of a Christians syncere loue vnto Christ* (Oxford: John Lichfield for Edward Forrest, 1631), part II, 4, 10–14.

47 Bunyan, *Grace abounding*, 47.

48 Wingfield, *Atheisme close and open*, sig D9v. Cf. similar sentiments in Thomas Fuller, *The just mans funeral. Lately delivered in a sermon at Chelsey* (London: William Bentley for John Williams, 1649), 13; Burton, *Anatomy of Melancholy*, vol. III, 400; Lodge, *Wits miserie, and the worlds madnesse*, 65.

49 Thomas (ed.), *The Diary of Samuel Sewall*, vol. I, 35–6; Thomas Jackson, *A Treatise Containing the Originall of Vnbeliefe* (London: I. D. for John Clarke, 1625), 28.

50 Bunyan, *Grace abounding*, 4; Jessey, *The exceeding riches of grace*, 7, 11. Watson, *The Rest is Silence*, argues that early modern England was

gripped with a fear of annihilation and of mortalism, but this seems to me exactly backwards: it was a doctrine for which many people scarcely dared hope.

51 Lodowick Muggleton, *The acts of the witnesses of the spirit in five parts* (London: [s.n.], 1699), 17–32.

52 Thomas Traherne, *Centuries, Poems and Thanksgivings*, ed. H. M. Margoliouth (Oxford: Clarendon Press, 1958), vol. I, 119.

53 Clarke, *A Collection of the Lives of Ten Eminent Divines*, 516; and see above, pp. 113, 116–17.

54 Ryrie, *Being Protestant*, 433–4.

55 Wesley Frank Craven and Walter B. Hayward (eds), *The Journal of Richard Norwood, Surveyor of Bermuda* (New York: Bermuda Historical Monuments Trust, 1945), 5, 7–8.

56 Jessey, *The exceeding riches of grace*, 45.

57 Baxter, *Reliquiae Baxterianae*, vol. I, 21.

58 Casaubon, *Of credulity and incredulity*, 24–5, 155; Farindon, *XXX sermons*, 53.

59 Beard, *The theatre of Gods judgements*, 90–1; University of Sheffield, Hartlib MS 29/6/20A, 26/8/1A–6B; *The Diary and Correspondence of Dr. John Worthington*, ed. J. Crossley, vol. I (Chetham Society 13: Manchester, 1847), 346; Adams, *The gallants burden*, fo. 16r; Baxter, *The saints everlasting rest*, 245 (Baxter's full argument deducing God's being from the devil's is laid out on pp. 236–45); Dove, *Confutation of atheisme*, 33; Browne, *Religio Medici*, 29.

60 Sheppard, *Anti-Atheism in Early Modern England*, 65–6. See, among many others, Fotherby, *Atheomastix*, sig. B1r; Dove, *Confutation of atheisme*, 27; Smith, *Gods arrowe against atheists*, sig. B4r–v; Mornay, *A woorke concerning the trewnesse of the Christian religion*, 9; Walter Charleton, *The darknes of atheism dispelled by the light of nature* (London: J.F. for William Lee, 1652), 4; Wingfield, *Atheisme close and open*, sig. D11r.

61 Unlike, for example, the Catholic use of fideism to attack Protestantism: see above, p. 65.

62 Sheppard, *Anti-Atheism in Early Modern England.*

63 Baxter, *The saints everlasting rest*, 179–81; Baxter, *Reliquiae Baxterianae*, vol. I, 21–2, 128; cf. the exercise in Folger Shakespeare Library, MS V.a.520 fos 19v–20v.

64 Bunyan, *Grace abounding*, 47; Clarke, *A Collection of the Lives of Ten Eminent Divines*, 512; Jackson, *A Treatise Containing the Originall of Vnbeliefe*, 9; More, *An antidote against atheisme*, sig. A7r–v; Princeton University Library, MS RTC01 no. 62, fo. 31r; William Walwyn, *A still and soft voice from the scriptures, witnessing them to be the word of God* (London: [s.n.] , 1647), 11–12; Katherine Calloway, *Natural Theology in the Scientific Revolution* (London: Pickering and Chatto, 2014), 4; Benjamin Franklin, *The Autobiography and Other Writings*, ed. Alan Houston (Cambridge: Cambridge University Press, 2012), 46. The philosopher was Anthony Collins.

65 *Diary of Michael Wigglesworth*, 84; Jackson, *A Treatise Containing the Originall of Vnbeliefe*, 10; Bodleian Library, Oxford, MS Ashmole 226 fo. 233r.

66 Huntington Library, HA Religious Box 3 no. 14, fo. 4v; Bownde, *The vnbeleefe of S. Thomas*, 26 (cf. John 20:24–9).

67 John Saltmarsh, *Free grace, or, The flowings of Christs blood free to sinners* (London: for Giles Calvert, 1646), 95.

68 Princeton University Library, MS RTC01 no. 62, fo. 31v.

69 Taylor, *The pilgrims profession*, 150–2; Allen, *A narrative of God's gracious dealings*, 5–6; Clarke, *A Collection of the Lives of Ten Eminent Divines*, 516–17.

70 *The Diary of Sir Archibald Johnston of Wariston, vol. II*, 260.

71 William Attersoll, *The badges of Christianity. Or, A treatise of the sacraments* (London: W. Iaggard, 1606), 63; Ryrie, *Being Protestant*, 344–7.

72 Farnworth, *The heart opened by Christ*, 7–8.

73 John Milton, *De Doctrina Christiana*, ed. and tr. John K. Hale and J. Donald Cullington with Gordon Campbell and Thomas N. Corns (Oxford: Oxford University Press, 2012), 25.

74 Wingfield, *Atheisme close and open*, sig. D1v; Hodgkin (ed.), *Women, Madness and Sin*, 192.

75 Powell, *Spirituall Experiences*, 176; Walker, *The Holy Life of Mrs Elizabeth Walker*, 19.

76 Jane Turner, *Choice experiences of the kind dealings of God*, 25.

77 Princeton University Library, MS RTC01 no. 62, fo. 31v.

78 Traherne, *Centuries*, vol. I, 119–20.

79 Jackson, *A Treatise Containing the Originall of Vnbeliefe*, 9–10, 190, 195–6.

80 Ibid. 10, 22, 24.

81 Adams, *The gallants burden*, fo. 16r; Smith, *Gods arrowe against atheists*, sig. B2r; Baxter, *Reliquiae Baxterianae*, vol. I, 22.

82 Mornay, *A woorke concerning the trewnesse of the Christian religion*, 1.

83 Sheppard, *Anti-Atheism in Early Modern England*, 142.

84 Hooker, *Laws of Ecclesiastical Polity: Book V*, 22; Donne, *LXXX sermons*, 227. Cf. Mornay, *A woorke concerning the trewnesse of the Christian religion*, 2; Dove, *Confutation of atheisme*, 2; Morton, *A treatise of the nature of God*, 30–1; Casaubon, *Of credulity and incredulity*, 155.

85 Jean de la Bruyère, *The characters, or, The manners of the age* (London: for John Bullord, 1699), 418, 427.

86 *Diary of Michael Wigglesworth*, 45.

5. Seeking and Losing Faith

1 Bownde, *The vnbeleefe of S. Thomas*, 10, 33; John Trundle?, *Keepe within Compasse: Or, The worthy Legacy of a wise Father to his beloued Sonne* (London: [G. Eld] for John Trundle, 1619), sig. A4v. This quotation is a little unfair to Bownde, whose approach was in fact more nuanced: Patrick S. McGhee, 'Unbelief, the Senses and the Body in Nicholas Bownde's *The vnbeleefe of S. Thomas* (1608)', in *Doubting Christianity: The Church and Doubt*, ed. Frances Andrews, Charlotte Methuen and Andrew Spicer (Studies in Church History 52, 2016), 266–82.

2   Robert N. Swanson, 'Doubt and Assurance in Medieval Catholicism', in *Doubting Christianity*, 190.

3   Joseph Hall, *Epistles, the second volume: conteining two decads* (London: A. H[atfield] for Eleazar Edgar and Samuel Macham, 1608), 172.

4   William Perkins, *An exposition of the Lords prayer* (London: [J. Wolfe for] Robert Bourne and John Porter, 1593), 161; he was explicitly cited on this point in Robert Linaker, *A comfortable treatise, for the reliefe of such as are afflicted in conscience* (London: W. Stansby for John Parker, 1620), 93–4.

5   Richard Hooker, *A learned and comfortable sermon of the certaintie and perpetuitie of faith in the Elect* (Oxford: Joseph Barnes, 1612), 7, 10.

6   Attersoll, *The badges of Christianity*, 62; cf. Richard Rogers et al., *A garden of spirituall flowers* (London: W. White for T. Pavier, 1616), sig. C1r; Hall, *Epistles, the second volume*, 171.

7   Sibbes, *The bruised reede*, 68; underlining in the Folger Shakespeare Library's copy, call no. STC 22479. Cf. the same sentiment in Baxter, *Reliquiae Baxterianae*, vol. I, 22.

8   Denison, *Monument or Tombe-Stone*, 100; cf. John Andrewes, *The Conuerted Mans New Birth* (London: N. Okes, 1629), 27; Sedgwick, *The doubting beleever*, sig. A6v.

9   Robert Bruce, *Sermons Preached in the Kirk of Edinburgh* (Edinburgh: Robert Waldegraue, 1591), sigs I7r–8r, K1v; Bruce, *Sermons vpon the Sacrament*, sig. T2r.

10 William Cunningham (ed.), *Sermons by the Rev. Robert Bruce, Minister of Edinburgh* (Edinburgh: Wodrow Society, 1843), 144.

11 Confusingly, the same word is used for those in the nineteenth and twentieth century who believed it was possible to speak with the spirits of the dead: these two kinds of spiritualism are completely unconnected.

12 Here quoting the English edition of 1648, itself based on the Latin edition of 1558: *Theologia Germanica. Or, Mysticall Divinitie* (London: for John Sweeting, 1648), 12, 29, 59–63, 92.

13 Douglas Gwyn, *Seekers Found: Atonement in Early Quaker Experience* (Wallingford, PA: Pendle Hill, 2000), 57–9; Sebastian Franck, 'A Letter to John Campanus', in George Hunston Williams and Angel M. Mergal (eds), *Spiritual and Anabaptist Writers* (London: SCM Press, 1957), 149–50, 155–6; R. Emmet McLaughlin, 'Spiritualism: Schwenckfeld and Franck and their Early Modern Resonances', in John D. Roth and James M. Stayer (eds), *A Companion to Anabaptism and Spiritualism* (Leiden: Brill, 2007), 119–61 at 138–9.

14 Gwyn, *Seekers Found*, 52–7; McLaughlin, 'Spiritualism: Schwenckfeld and Franck', 125–33.

15 Gwyn, *Seekers Found*, 52.

16 Ibid. 63; McLaughlin, 'Spiritualism: Schwenckfeld and Franck', 140–3; Buys, *Sparks of Reason*, 201.

17 Here I am following the very useful account in Fix, *Prophecy and Reason*, 37–42.

18 Fix, *Prophecy and Reason*, 90–3.

19 [Adam Boreel], *Ad legem, et ad testimonium* ([s.l.]: [s.n.], 1645). Below I follow the 1648 English translation: *To the law, and to the testimonie or, A proposall of certain cases of conscience by way of quaere* (London: George Whittington, 1648).

20 Boreel, *To the law, and to the testimonie*, esp. 5, 28, 37–8, 83, 92–3, 96.

21 Walther Schneider, *Adam Boreel: Sein Leben und seine Schriften* (Giessen: Otto Kindt, 1911), 41–2, who bridles at the charge of 'enthusiasm'; University of Sheffield, Hartlib MS 3/3/32B, and cf. 3/3/60B, on Boreel's command of English. On his English links in general, see Rob Iliffe, '"Jesus Nazarenus Legislator": Adam Boreel's Defence of Christianity', in Silvia Berti and Françoise Charles-Daubert (eds), *Heterodoxy, Spinozism and Free Thought in Early Eighteenth-Century Europe* (Dordrecht and Boston: Kluwer, 1996), 375–96; Ernestine van der Wall, 'The Dutch Hebraist Adam Boreel and the Mishnah Project', *Lias* 16 (1989), 239–63.

22 Henry Barrow, *A brief discouerie of the false church* (Dordt?: [s.n.], 1590?), 115.

23 Ian Atherton and David Como, 'The Burning of Edward Wightman: Puritanism, Prelacy and the Politics of Heresy in Early Modern England', *English Historical Review* 120.489 (2005), 1215–50 at 1234–5.

24 Atherton and Como, 'Burning of Edward Wightman', 1237–9; Henoch Clapham, *Antidoton or a soueraigne remedie against schisme and heresie* (London: [Felix Kingston for] John Wolfe, 1600), 33. The tag 'Arian' refers to the Legates' denial that Christ was divine.

25 Henoch Clapham, *Errour on the right hand* (London: W. White, 1608), 29–31. Cf. the briefer report from John Etherington, which in essence agrees with Clapham's testimony: *A discouery of the errors of the English Anabaptists* (London: W. Jones for Robert Bird, 1623), 76–7.

26 Clapham, *Errour on the right hand*, 31–2, 37–8.

27 Etherington, *A discouery*, 77.

28 Thomas Fuller, *The church-history of Britain from the birth of Jesus Christ until the year MDCXLVIII* (London: for John Williams, 1655), book X, 62.

29 Thomas Gataker, *An answer to Mr. George Walkers vindication* (London: E.G. for F. Clifton, 1642), 38–9; David Como, 'Legate, Bartholomew', *Oxford Dictionary of National Biography*.

30 David Como, *Blown by the Spirit: Puritanism and the Emergence of an Antinomian Underground in pre-Civil-War England* (Stanford: Stanford University Press, 2004), esp. 38–41, 54; Nicholas McDowell, *The English Radical Imagination: Culture, Religion and Revolution 1630–1660* (Oxford: Clarendon Press, 2003), 36–7; University of Sheffield, Hartlib MS 29/2/22A; Elizabeth Allen, 'Everard, John', *Oxford Dictionary of National Biography*. Roger Brereley's translation (British Library, Sloane MS 2538) was eventually published in 1648, superseding Everard's rather clunkier version (Folger Shakespeare Library, MS V.a.222; Cambridge University Library, MS Dd.xii.68).

31 The National Archives, Kew, SP 16/520 fo. 126r–v.

32 Stephen Denison, *The white wolfe, or, A sermon preached at Pauls Crosse* (London: George Miller, dwelling in Blacke-Fryers, 1627), 39.

33 British Library, Additional MS 11045, fos 37r–38r; Bodleian Library, Oxford, MS Tanner 67 fos. 143r–144v.

34 John Everard, *The Gospel-Treasury Opened* (London: I.O. for Rapha Harford, 1659), part II, 103–4; Cambridge University Library, MS Dd.xii.68 fos 41r–42r.

35 John Morrill, 'The Religious Context of the English Civil War', *Transactions of the Royal Historical Society* 5th series, 34 (1984), 155–78.

36 Huntington Library, MS HM 46532, and cf. the better-known variant version published in Alexander Brome (ed.), *Rump: or An exact collection of the choycest poems and songs relating to the late times* (London: for Henry Brome and Henry Marsh, 1662), 64; Charles I, *His Maiesties letter to the maior of Bristol* (Oxford: Leon. Lichfield, 1642), 2.

37 See, for example, Rogers, *Naaman the Syrian*, 254, 347–8; Edward Calver, *Englands sad posture; or, A true description of the present estate of poore distressed England* (London: Bernard Alsop, 1644), 37–8.

38 'Theodorus Verax' [Clement Walker], *Anarchia Anglicana: or, the history of independency. The second part* ([s.l.]: [s.n.], 1649), 152–3.

39 Edwards, *The third part of Gangraena*, 20–1; *A discovery of the great fantasie, or, Phantasticall conceitednesse* (London: T.P. and M.S., 1642), 12, 18.

40 Milton, *De Doctrina Christiana*, 9.

41 Roger Williams, *The bloudy tenent, of persecution, for cause of conscience* (London: [s.n.], 1644), 25–6.

42 William Grigge, *The Quaker's Jesus* (London: M. Simmons, 1658), 57–9.

43 Edwards, *The third part of Gangraena*, 187.

44 Baxter, *The saints everlasting rest*, 178.

45 Overton, *Mans mortalitie*, esp. sig. A2v, 31; cf. Luke 16:19–31. On the essential orthodoxy of this Christian mortalism, see Norman T.

Burns, *Christian Mortalism from Tyndale to Milton* (Cambridge, MA: Harvard University Press, 1972), esp. 157.

46 Thomas Edwards, *The first and second part of Gangraena* (London: T. R. and E. M. for Ralph Smith, 1646), 22; cf. *A relation of severall heresies . . . Discovering the originall ring-leaders, and the time when they began to spread* (London: by J. M., 1646), 10.

47 See esp. Samuel Richardson, *A discourse of the torments of hell* (London: [s.n.], 1660).

48 Edwards, *The first and second part of Gangraena*, 17.

49 Bauthumley, *The light and dark sides of God*, 23, 55–6.

50 Edwards, *The first and second part of Gangraena*, 34.

51 Thomas Edwards, *Gangraena, or, A catalogue and discovery of many of the errours, heresies, blasphemies and pernicious practices of the sectaries of this time* (London: for Ralph Smith, 1646), sigs H3v, L2r; [Clement Writer], *The Jus Divinum of presbyterie* (London: [s.n.], 1655), 87–8.

52 'Theodorus Verax', *Anarchia Anglicana*, 153.

53 For example, Bauthumley, *The light and dark sides of God*, 72: this distinction would become a mainstay of Quakerism.

54 Edwards, *The first and second part of Gangraena*, 14.

55 *Divinity and philosophy dissected, and set forth, by a mad man* (Amsterdam: [s.n.], 1644), esp. 59.

56 See below, p. 196–7.

57 Edwards, *The first and second part of Gangraena*, 18; Winstanley, *Truth lifting up its head*, 12; George Fox, *The Journal of George Fox*, ed. Norman Penney (New York: Cosimo Books, 2007), 37; Edwards, *Gangraena, or, A catalogue and discovery*, sig. P4v.

58 John Holland, *The Smoke of the Bottomlesse Pit* (London: for John Wright, 1651), sig. A3r; Edwards, *The third part of Gangraena*, 107.

59 Winstanley, *Truth lifting up its head*, esp. sigs. A7v–8v, 2, 10.

60 Edwards, *The third part of Gangraena*, sig. d3v; Edwards, *The first and second part of Gangraena*, part 2, 134.

61 Bolton, *Arraignment of errour*, 22.

62 *Powers to be resisted, or, A dialogue arguing the Parliaments lawfull*

resistance of the powers now in armes against them (London: Henry Overton, 1643), 48.

63 David Booy (ed.), *Autobiographical Writings by Early Quaker Women* (Aldershot: Ashgate, 2004), 81–2; Matthew Bingham, *Orthodox Radicals: Baptist Identity in the English Revolution* (Oxford: Oxford University Press, 2019); Edwards, *The third part of Gangraena*, 17–18.

64 Booy (ed.), *Autobiographical Writings*, 82; S[arah] J[ones], *To Sions louers, being a golden egge to avoid infection* (London: [s.n.], 1644), sig. A2v.

65 Howard, *Love and Truth in Plainness Manifested*, 8–11; cf. Stephen Crisp, *A memorable account of the Christian experiences, Gospel labours, travels, and sufferings of that ancient servant of Christ, Stephen Crisp* (London: T. Sowle, 1694), 13; Laurence Claxton, *The lost sheep found: or, the prodigal returned to his father's house* (London: printed for the author, 1660), 19; Edwards, *Gangraena, or A catalogue and discovery* sigs K4v, L1v, L3v.

66 John Jackson, *A sober word to a serious people: or, A moderate discourse respecting as well the Seekers, (so called) as the present churches* (London: J. Cottrel for James Noell, 1651), 2, 18, 49–50, 53; Edmund Calamy, *The great danger of covenant-refusing, and covenant-breaking* (London: M. F. for Christopher Meredith, 1646), 27.

67 [Clement Writer], *The jus divinum of presbyterie* (London: s.n., 1646), esp. 12, 34; Luke 24:49. For Writer's reputation see Edwards, *Gangraena, or, A catalogue and discovery*, sig. M1v; Baxter, *A key for Catholicks*, 333.

68 Edwards, *Gangraena, or, A catalogue and discovery*, sig. M1v; Writer, *Jus divinum* (1655), 28, 66–71, 87–8.

69 Booy (ed.), *Autobiographical Writings*, 82–4, 88.

70 Ibid. 83–4, 87.

71 William Penn, preface to George Fox, *A journal or historical account of the life, travels, sufferings, Christian experiences and labour of . . . George Fox* (London: for Thomas Northcott, 1694), sigs B1v–C1r; cf. Norman Penney (ed.), *The First Publishers of Truth* (London and

Philadelphia: Friends' Historical Society, 1904), 54–5, 106, 235, 243–4, and many other examples.

72 Claxton, *The lost sheep found*, 19; Jackson, *A sober word to a serious people*, 3.

73 Francis Howgill, *The inheritance of Jacob discovered. After his return out of Ægypt* (London: for Giles Calvert, 1656), 11.

74 Farnworth, *The heart opened by Christ*, 12; Howard, *Love and Truth in Plainness Manifested*, 12–13; John Gratton, *A Journal of the Life of that Ancient Servant of Christ, John Gratton* (London: assigns of T. Sowle, 1720), esp. 16, 28, 31–2.

75 Edwards, *Gangraena, or, A catalogue and discovery*, sig. N1v; Edward Burrough, *The memorable works of a son of thunder and consolation . . . Edward Burroughs* ([London]: [s.n.], 1672), sig. E1v.

76 Thomas Parker, *The copy of a letter written by Mr. Thomas Parker . . . to his sister, Mrs Elizabeth Avery* (London: John Field for Edmund Paxton, 1650 [1649]), 5; Francis Freeman, *Light vanquishing darknesse. Or a vindication of some truths formerly declared* (London: [s.n.], 1650), 2.

77 Edwards, *The third part of Gangraena*, 93; [John Price or William Kiffin?], *Walwins wiles: or The manifestators manifested* (London: H[enry] C[ripps] and L[odowick] L[loyd], [1649]), 10.

78 Winstanley, *Truth lifting up its head*, 58–62.

79 Dominic Erdozain, 'Jesus and Augustine: The God of Terror and the Origins of European Doubt', *Journal of Religious History* 41.4 (2017), 476–504.

80 Richardson, *A discourse of the torments of hell*, sig. I10r.

81 Freeman, *Light vanquishing darknesse*, 8.

82 Milton, *De Doctrina Christiana*, 375.

83 Holland, *The Smoke of the Bottomlesse Pit*, sig. A3v.

84 Claxton, *The lost sheep found*, 25.

85 Edwards, *The first and second part of Gangraena*, part 2, 9.

86 Claxton, *The lost sheep found*, esp. 11, 16, 19, 21–3, 25–8.

87 Ibid. 32–3.

88 Howard, *Love and Truth in Plainness Manifested*, 13.

89 Bunyan, *The Pilgrim's Progress*, 129; and see above, pp. 1, 7.

90 Osborne, *Advice to a son*, 132.

6. The Abolition of God

1 Christian Kortholt the elder, *De tribus impostoribus magnis liber*
   Joachim Reumann, 1680). On the legend of *The three imposto*
   above, pp. 13–14. The 'four horsemen' label was applied to the
   minded atheists Richard Dawkins, Daniel Dennett, Sam Harris
   Christopher Hitchens in 2007 in the wake of a much-watched v
   discussion between them.

2 Edward Herbert of Cherbury, *Pagan Religion: A Translation of*
   religione gentilium, ed. John Anthony Butler (Binghampton, N
   Medieval and Renaissance Texts and Studies, 1996), 51–3; Edwa
   Herbert of Cherbury, *The Life of Edward, First Lord Herbert*
   Cherbury written by himself, ed. J. M. Shuttleworth (Oxford: Oxfo
   University Press, 1976), 25, 29.

3 Herbert of Cherbury, *Life*, 30–1.

4 Herbert of Cherbury, *Pagan Religion*, 52, 285, 339, 350.

5 Patricia Springborg, 'Hobbes on Religion', in Tom Sorell (ed.), *Th*
   Cambridge Companion to Hobbes (Cambridge: Cambridge University
   Press, 1999), 346–80; Alan Cromartie, 'The God of Thomas Hobbes',
   Historical Journal 51.4 (2008), 857–79.

6 The same goes for the slightly earlier denial of Moses' authorship in
   Isaac la Peyrère's *Pre-Adamitae*, written in 1641 but not published
   until 1655: la Peyrère 'wanted to raise a basic kind of religious scepticism about Scripture in order to justify his own religious views',
   namely a weird doctrine of human polygenesis. Popkin, *History of*
   Scepticism, 221–3.

7 Thomas Hobbes, *Leviathan*, ed. Michael Oakeshott (Oxford: Basil
   Blackwell, 1946), esp. 306, 327, 357.

8 Richard Hooker, *Of the Laws of Ecclesiastical Polity: Preface, Books I*

to IV, ed. Georges Edelen (Cambridge, MA: Belknap Press, 1977), esp. 32–3.

9   See above, p. 154.

10 Israel, *Radical Enlightenment*, 159–60, 230; cf. the similarly pivotal role Spinoza plays in Gray, *Seven Types of Atheism*, 147–52.

11 Fix, *Prophecy and Reason*, 151–5, 193, 200, 203; Richard H. Popkin, 'Spinoza's Relations with the Quakers in Amsterdam', *Quaker History* 73.1 (1984), 14–28; Karen Clausen-Brown, 'Spinoza's Translation of Margaret Fell and his Portrayal of Judaism in the Theological-Political Treatise', *The Seventeenth Century* 34.1 (2019), 89–106.

12 Richard H. Popkin, 'Spinoza and Bible Scholarship', in James E. Force and Richard H. Popkin (eds), *The Books of Nature and Scripture* (Dordrecht-Boston-London: Kluwer Academic Publishers, 1994), 15; Erdozain, *The Soul of Doubt*, 90, 97–9, 108, 112, 114; Baruch Spinoza, *The Chief Works of Benedict de Spinoza*, ed. R. H. M. Elwes (New York: Dover, 1951), vol. I, 83–4, 87.

13 [Pieter Balling], *The Light upon the Candlestick*, trans. Benjamin Furley (London: for Robert Wilson, 1663), 4–5, 10; Fix, *Prophecy and Reason*, 200–3.

14 As this makes clear, Balling may not have cited the Bible, but he was ready enough to quote it unattributed: [Balling], *The Light upon the Candlestick*, 13.

15 Pascal, *Pensées*, 28–9, 57, 135, 151, 182, 237; and see above, pp. 51–2, 64.

16 Shagan, *Birth of Modern Belief*, 190; cf. Sheppard, *Anti-Atheism in Early Modern England*, 74.

17 Pascal, *Pensées*, 122–3.

18 Ibid. 127.

19 Martin Mulsow, *Enlightenment Underground: Radical Germany, 1680–1720*, trans. H. C. Erik Midelfort (Charlottesville: University of Virginia Press, 2015), 79–82; Manfred P. Fleischer, '"Are Women Human?" The Debate of 1595 between Valens Acidalius and Simon

Gediccus', *Sixteenth Century Journal* 12.2 (1981), 107–20.

20 Fyodor Dostoevsky, *The Brothers Karamazov*, tr. Richard Pevear and Larissa Volokhonsky (London: Penguin, 2017), I.i.4.

21 Erdozain, *The Soul of Doubt*, 146; Thomas Paine, *The Age of Reason*, ed. Philip S. Foner (Secaucus, NJ: Citadel Press, 1974), 50.

22 Erdozain, *The Soul of Doubt*, 184–6.

23 Michael Bakunin, *God and the State*, ed. Paul Avrich (New York: Dover Publications, 1970), 17–18, 24–5.

24 Paine, *Age of Reason*, 60; Richard Dawkins, *The God Delusion* (London: Transworld, 2016), 51; Hugh McLeod, *Secularisation in Western Europe, 1848–1914* (Basingstoke: Macmillan, 2000), 162.

25 Bakunin, *God and the State*, 25, 28.

26 Dostoevsky, *The Brothers Karamazov*, I.ii.4.

27 Erdozain, *The Soul of Doubt*, esp. 130–1, 155; Paine, *Age of Reason*, 50.

28 Erdozain, *The Soul of Doubt*, esp. 120, 228.

29 Dostoevsky, *The Brothers Karamazov*, II.v.4.

30 Ibid. II.v.5.

31 Erdozain, *The Soul of Doubt*, 163; https://founders.archives.gov/documents/Jefferson/03-09-02-0216; Paine, *Age of Reason*, 54; John Stuart Mill, *Three Essays on Religion*, ed. Lou Matz (Peterborough, Ontario: Broadview Press, 2009), 123.

32 Gerald Parsons, 'Biblical Criticism in Victorian Britain: From Controversy to Acceptance?' in his *Religion in Victorian Britain vol. II: Controversies* (Manchester: Manchester University Press, 1988), 245–55.

33 *Hitler's Table Talk 1941–1944*, tr. Norman Cameron and R. H. Stevens (London: Weidenfeld and Nicolson, 1953), 76, 721.

34 For the tenor of this argument, Humphreys' website, http://www.jesusneverexisted.com/, is instructive.

35 Will Herberg, *Protestant – Catholic – Jew: An Essay in American Religious Sociology* (New York: Doubleday, 1956), 276; Michael Sherman, 'The Number of Americans with No Religious Affiliation Is Rising', *Scientific American* (2018): https://www.scientificamerican.

com/article/the-number-of-americans-with-no-religious-affiliation-is-rising/; and see above, pp. 1–2.

36 Hugh McLeod, *The Religious Crisis of the 1960s* (Oxford: Oxford University Press, 2007); Callum Brown, *The Death of Christian Britain* (London: Routledge, 2001).

37 Leigh Eric Schmidt, *Village Atheists: How America's Unbelievers Made their Way in a Godly Nation* (Princeton: Princeton University Press, 2016), esp. 249, 253.

38 Alec Ryrie, *Protestants: The Radicals who Made the Modern World* (London: William Collins, 2017), 264.

39 Callum Brown, *Becoming Atheist: Humanism and the Secular West* (London: Bloomsbury, 2017), 171–2.

40 Ibid. 162.

41 Ibid. 174.

42 Ibid. 162, 168.

43 *Letters of J. R. R. Tolkien*, ed. Humphrey Carpenter (London: Allen & Unwin, 1981), 78.

44 Gray, *Seven Types of Atheism*, esp. 72; Theo Hobson, *God Created Humanism: The Christian Basis of Secular Values* (London: SPCK, 2017).

45 Dmitra Fini, *Tolkien, Race and Cultural History: From Fairies to Hobbits* (Basingstoke: Palgrave, 2009), 131–59.

Index